GROWING UP GRAPHIC

STUDIES IN COMICS AND CARTOONS
Jared Gardner, Charles Hatfield, and Rebecca Wanzo, Series Editors

# GROWING UP GRAPHIC

The Comics of Children in Crisis

Alison Halsall

THE OHIO STATE UNIVERSITY PRESS
COLUMBUS

Copyright © 2023 by The Ohio State University.
All rights reserved.

The various characters, logos, and other trademarks appearing in this book are the property of their respective owners and are presented here strictly for scholarly analysis. No infringement is intended or should be implied.

Library of Congress Cataloging-in-Publication Data
Names: Halsall, Alison, author.
Title: Growing up graphic : the comics of children in crisis / Alison Halsall.
Other titles: Studies in comics and cartoons.
Description: Columbus : The Ohio State University Press, [2023] | Series: Studies in comics and cartoons | Includes bibliographical references and index. | Summary: "Considers graphic narratives for and about children to interrogate how these narratives contest images of childhood victimization and helplessness and present young people as social actors who attempt to make sense of the challenges that affect them"—Provided by publisher.
Identifiers: LCCN 2023023423 | ISBN 9780814215548 (hardback) | ISBN 0814215548 (hardback) | ISBN 9780814283097 (ebook) | ISBN 0814283098 (ebook)
Subjects: LCSH: Comic books, strips, etc.—History and criticism. | Comic books and children. | Children's literature—History and criticism. | Children in literature. | Literature and society.
Classification: LCC PN6714 .H354 2023 | DDC 741.5/9—dc23/eng/20230811
LC record available at https://lccn.loc.gov/2023023423
Other identifiers: ISBN 9780814258880 (paperback) | ISBN 0814258883 (paperback)

Cover design by Charles Brock
Text composition by Stuart Rodriguez
Type set in Palatino Linotype

CONTENTS

List of Illustrations                                                                                    vi

Acknowledgments                                                                                          ix

**INTRODUCTION**   Comics as Children's Literature                                                        1

**CHAPTER 1**      The Use of Childhood in War                                                           27

**CHAPTER 2**      Youthful Experiences of Immigration,
                   Migration, and Diaspora                                                               56

**CHAPTER 3**      Indigeneity and Resurgence in Canadian Comics                                         85

**CHAPTER 4**      Space and Orientation in LGBTQ+ Graphic
                   Narratives                                                                           125

**CHAPTER 5**      Young People and/in Graphic Medicine                                                 168

**CONCLUSION**     Comics and the COVID Crisis                                                          209

Works Cited                                                                                             221

Index                                                                                                   239

# ILLUSTRATIONS

| | | |
|---|---|---|
| **FIGURE 0.1** | Maurice Sendak and Art Spiegelman drawn in dialogue in "In the Dumps" | 19 |
| **FIGURE 0.2** | The second page of Maurice Sendak and Art Spiegelman's "In the Dumps" | 20 |
| **FIGURE 1.1** | Michel is commanded to shoot in Jessica Dee Humphreys and Michel Chikwanine's *Child Soldier* | 40 |
| **FIGURE 1.2** | Michel is forced to shoot in Jessica Dee Humphreys and Michel Chikwanine's *Child Soldier* | 41 |
| **FIGURE 1.3** | Tony is isolated from his fellow abductees in Sharon E. McKay and Daniel Lafrance's *War Brothers* | 46 |
| **FIGURE 1.4** | A displaced persons camp in Sharon E. McKay and Daniel Lafrance's *War Brothers* | 47 |
| **FIGURE 1.5** | The rehabilitation process as depicted in Sharon E. McKay and Daniel Lafrance's *War Brothers* | 48 |
| **FIGURE 1.6** | The opening close-up of Deogratias in Jean-Philippe Stassen's *Deogratias* | 51 |
| **FIGURE 2.1** | Samia at a displacement camp in Reinhard Kleist's *An Olympic Dream* | 60 |
| **FIGURE 2.2** | Portraits of new immigrants in Shaun Tan's *The Arrival* | 66 |
| **FIGURE 2.3** | The cover of Leila Abdelrazaq's *Baddawi* | 75 |

ILLUSTRATIONS • vii

| FIGURE 2.4 | War games as depicted in Leila Abdelrazaq's *Baddawi* | 78 |
| FIGURE 2.5 | Children play while threats loom in Leila Abdelrazaq's *Baddawi* | 79 |
| FIGURE 2.6 | The Takei family is taken to Camp Rohwer in George Takei et al.'s *They Called Us Enemy* | 82 |
| FIGURE 3.1 | Pete Carver's tattoo in Patti LaBoucane-Benson's *The Outside Circle* | 91 |
| FIGURE 3.2 | Indigenous Beothuk people encounter Europeans in David Alexander Robertson's *The Ballad of Nancy April* | 98 |
| FIGURE 3.3 | May encounters legacies of violence in David Alexander Robertson et al.'s *Will I See?* | 103 |
| FIGURE 3.4 | Edwin awakens in the hospital in David Alexander Robertson's *7 Generations* | 112 |
| FIGURE 3.5 | Bear's death in David Alexander Robertson's *7 Generations* | 113 |
| FIGURE 3.6 | Edwin confronts an image of his father in David Alexander Robertson's *7 Generations* | 115 |
| FIGURE 3.7 | Edwin and White Cloud are juxtaposed in David Alexander Robertson's *7 Generations* | 116 |
| FIGURE 3.8 | Captain Zaz and Ricky in Candy Land in Steven Keewatin Sanderson's *An Invited Threat* | 123 |
| FIGURE 4.1 | Barriers erected at Adrian's school in Hubert and Marie Caillou's *Adrian and the Tree of Secrets* | 142 |
| FIGURE 4.2 | Freddy breaks up with Laura in Mariko Tamaki's *Laura Dean Keeps Breaking Up with Me* | 146 |
| FIGURE 4.3 | Justin and Jesse meet Callie in Raina Telgemeier's *Drama* | 149 |
| FIGURE 4.4 | An ethnically and religiously diverse cast of characters in Carly Usdin's *The Avant-Guards* | 154 |
| FIGURE 4.5 | Maggie performs as Kevin in Maggie Thrash's *Honor Girl* | 160 |
| FIGURE 5.1 | Raina and her therapist discuss anxiety in Raina Telgemeier's *Guts* | 179 |
| FIGURE 5.2 | Cece searches for her mother in Cece Bell's *El Deafo* | 184 |
| FIGURE 5.3 | Cece's experience of speech using hearing aids in Cece Bell's *El Deafo* | 185 |

| | | |
|---|---|---|
| **FIGURE 5.4** | Ruth experiences a hallucinatory episode in Nate Powell's *Swallow Me Whole* | 199 |
| **FIGURE 5.5** | Ruth is swallowed by cicadas in Nate Powell's *Swallow Me Whole* | 201 |
| **FIGURE 5.6** | Tyranny loses its grip on Anna's story in Lesley Fairfield's *Tyranny* | 207 |

ACKNOWLEDGMENTS

Although much of this project was written during those long days of isolation and social distancing during the COVID-19 pandemic, the support of colleagues, scholars, family, and friends kept me writing. Even before the lockdowns, I discovered a group of scholars around the world at conferences and symposia who welcomed me into their various communities, often providing me with opportunities to present and share my work more widely. Thanks are due to: Jan Baetens, Natalie Coulter, Jodi Cressman, Lisa DeTora, Ramzi Fawaz, Hugo Frey, Angelo Piepoli, Umberto Rossi, and Myrna Santos.

Lesley Higgins and Marie-Christine Leps read drafts of this manuscript and offered invaluable advice. Not only are they my principal mentors, but their kind rigor always pushed me to think deeply about particular segments of the book. Knowing that I could trust them to give me sage advice is a continual comfort for me. Jonathan Warren is another principal mentor, whose friendship and collegiality I value deeply. His erudition, cosmopolitanism, and humor keep me laughing and thinking. My colleagues and friends Elicia Clements, Cheryl Cowdy, and Natalie Neill remind me to laugh and have offered advice and encouragement over many years.

Acquisitions editor Ana Maria Jimenez-Moreno at The Ohio State University Press has been a delight to work with since our first meeting in

Columbus, Ohio, in 2018. Since then, she has provided invaluable guidance throughout the writing and evaluation process. The editorial team at OSU Press has also been encouraging from the beginning. The opportunity to work with comics critics like Jared Gardner, Charles Hatfield, and Rebecca Wanzo was such a thrill. Significant thanks are also due to Siusan Moffat, for her excellent index.

I would like to thank the Faculty of Liberal Arts & Professional Studies, York University, Toronto, Canada, for the financial support it provided to this work. York University has always been extremely generous with its funding, for which I am very grateful, and has fostered a friendly and supportive environment in which I can think and teach.

Family, as I discuss in this book, can play such a crucial role in a person's life. Mary Lou and Colin, my mother and brother, are stalwart, loving presences; I value each and every conversation we have about the issues that this book discusses and so many more. Angela and Bob, Anne's parents, have always been so enthusiastic about my teaching and research.

My most significant and heartfelt thanks are reserved for my immediate family—Anne, Alex, and Claire. Those were long, challenging days during the lockdowns, and yet my three shining stars always had a smile and wonderful insights into the topics that I was thinking through. They showed me on a daily basis what resilience looks like, for adults and children. Their energy and belief in me keep me on track and excited about our next adventure.

Leuven University Press has kindly given me permission to reprint a modified version of an article that I published with them. "Graphic Experiences of Immigration, Migration, and Diaspora: Shaun Tan's *The Arrival* and Matt Huynh's Interactive Graphic Adaptation of Nam Le's 'The Boat'" was first published in *Graphic Embodiments: Graphic Perspectives on Health and Embodiment*, edited by Lisa DeTora and Jodi Cressman (U Leuven Press, 2021, pp. 61–73).

INTRODUCTION

# Comics as Children's Literature

> Images deliver us something words do not, however uncomfortable; that is part of their allure and danger.
>
> —Hillary Chute, *Disaster Drawn*

In recent years, publishers and children's book professionals have registered a new enthusiasm for comic and graphic narrative forms. In 2005 Scholastic Press launched its Graphix imprint with the reissue, in full color, of a child-friendly edition of Jeff Smith's *Bone*, an epic-length comic book series that is both light-hearted comedy and dark fantasy thriller. Although a text not originally created for a young audience, the popularity of *Bone* among young readers caught the attention of creators, publishers, and booksellers because it presented an opportunity to produce the comics for and about children that Michael Chabon had identified a need for the previous year.[1] Even more commercially successful than *Bone* was Jeff Kinney's "novel in cartoons" series, *The Diary of a Wimpy Kid* (2007–), which quickly became a publishing phenomenon, with print runs in the millions as well as a successful movie franchise. Since then, such publishing houses as Random House, HarperCollins, and Fantagraphics have created comics imprints that

---

1. When Pulitzer-winning author Michael Chabon delivered the keynote address at ComicCon International's annual Eisner Awards ceremony in San Diego in July 2004, he chided the comics industry for forgetting young readers. He ended his speech by calling for a new sort of graphic narrative for young people, "truly thrilling, honestly observed and remembered, richly imagined [. . . comics] *about children*" (Chabon, my emphasis).

specifically target the child and young adult (YA) demographic. First Second Books (an imprint of Macmillan Press) has established itself as one of the premier publishers of sharp, powerful graphic narratives for a variety of age groups. DC and Marvel Comics followed suit in 2006, founding Diamond Kids, a children's comics and books division. Such is their popularity, critic Heather Camlot affirms, that graphic novels and comics series for young readers in North America are now the fastest-growing category of the comics trade, bringing in over $1.095 billion (USD) in 2018, up from $805 million (USD) in 2012 (7).

As Michelle Ann Abate and Gwen Athene Tarbox explain in their insightful introduction to the collection *Graphic Novels for Children and Young Adults* (2017), in the late 1990s Japanese anime and manga imports, such as *Pokémon* and *Sailor Moon*, provided the initial impetus for North American publishers to recognize the potential for specifically youth-oriented comics and cartoons. Manga (Japanese comic books) has been a popular genre in Japan for decades, encompassing a wider variety of literary styles and themes than their American counterparts. School children in Japan are devoted to *shōnen* (boys' manga) and *shōjo* (girls' manga). Many of the more popular manga in Japan were adapted into anime (cartoon) series and movies, which were gradually exported to the West. During the 1980s and 1990s, the American manga and anime distribution and entertainment company VIZ Media, as well as some smaller publishers, began to translate manga serials into graphic novels for sale in the United States and Canada. By 1992 VIZ Media began distributing an entire line of original English language (OEL) manga ("Amerimanga" as it is more commonly called), an amalgamation of North American and Japanese cultural references, whose success in turn encouraged public libraries to expand their comics collections for young readers. Tokyopop, for example, a US-based producer of original English-language manga, began publishing numerous titles in the late 1990s, aggressively pursuing a child-age demographic (Abate and Tarbox 4).[2] Seeing a publishing and marketing opportunity, Dark Horse Comics began to collect manga serials into graphic novels and offer them for sale, relying on word of mouth

---

2. Angela Moreno Acosta provides a fascinating comparison of the particular strategies employed by Tokyopop and VIZ Media in marketing manga to North American readers. In 1997, to make manga more appealing to American fans, VIZ Media made manga fit traditional American comics formats by flipping the pages so that readers would read left to right and translating the sound effects into English. Tokyopop, however, promoted manga's "foreign" qualities, leaving the pages unflipped and the sound effects untranslated. "This not only satisfied readers' desire for 'authentic Japanese manga,' but also proved cost effective" (230). Manga sales skyrocketed, growing from $60 million in 2002 to $210 million by 2007 (229).

as well as manga and anime venues at comics and cosplay conventions to attract a preteen and teenage following (4). Thus, comics for and about young people began to make their move into the comics and children's literature industries.

Only recently, however, have comics been recognized by the publishing industry, as well as by readers and critics, as a dynamic genre that uses the power of the literary-visual medium to represent the lived realities of young people around the world and to engage with vivid and mature topics to transport readers, notably young readers between the ages of eight and eighteen, to settings past, present, and future.³ *Growing Up Graphic*, drawing on a resource base of more than fifty graphic narratives (originally written in English or translated into that language), considers graphic texts for and about children and youth from diverse cultural and ethnic backgrounds, varied regions of the world, and wide-ranging gender identities and levels of ability. This project has four primary objectives. First, it explores this visual and literary medium that is heavily invested in the representation of children and youth, especially in relation to the depiction of particular experiences (social, political, cultural, racial, sexual, ableist, etc.) that young people have undergone and through which they continue to live. These texts contest images of childhood victimization, passivity, and helplessness, presenting instead children as actors who attempt to make sense of the challenges that affect them. Second, it examines the many circuitous routes that comics for young people take in and out of discourses of nation, belonging, ableism, and identity, moving with and against currents of power. Third,

---

3. In this study I distinguish between short-form comics and long-form graphic novels. Banking on the important moniker "novel" as a "passport to recognition," the graphic novel notably "invigorated the critical discourse about comics" (Hatfield, *Alternative* x) in the mid-1980s and 1990s. Graphic novels can refer to anthologies of previously published comics that follow a consistent storyline, collections of comics art anthologized by theme/author, or to original, stand-alone narratives that became familiar to the public with the publication of Art Spiegelman's *Maus: A Survivor's Tale* (1986), Alan Moore and Dave Gibbons's bound version of *Watchmen* (1987), and the collected edition of Frank Miller's *Batman: The Dark Knight Returns* (1986). Although the first graphic novel is often attributed to Will Eisner, who published *A Contract with God, and Other Tenement Stories* in 1978, the term was used even earlier, in 1964, by American comics critic and magazine publisher Richard Kyle in an Amateur Press Association newsletter (Chute, *Why*; Beaty and Weiner; Gravett). In 1978, however, Eisner specifically deployed the term "graphic novel" to bring renewed legitimacy to this form, which opened up new storytelling possibilities. In this study I use the label graphic "narrative" as opposed to graphic "novel" because it is more inclusive, capable of encompassing different formats, genres, and storytelling traditions across cultures and from around the world. Most importantly, "narrative" suggests that the story that is being told in verbal-visual form is not fictional per se.

it participates in a crucial intersectional trend in children's publishing that looks to diversify the content and characters produced for young readers in the Global North. Specifically, it highlights visual representations of a range of young people, including child soldiers, migrants, Indigenous peoples in Canada, queers, and young people living with impairments and/or undergoing particular medical life events. In its investigation of such subjects, it also considers questions of age and audience. Finally, it considers the reader as a source of tension itself: the reader that is produced by the text and the empirical reader (who might be an adult, child, etc.). Ultimately, this project considers graphic narratives *for* children and *about* children to be an underexplored field in itself, one that provides surprising insight into the types of reading material that young readers gravitate toward and that complicate assumptions of readerly innocence.

Amulet Books, Annick Press, Candlewick Press, First Second, Graphic Universe, Graphix, Groundwood Books, HighWater Press, Kids Can Press, Papercutz, Scholastic, Square Fish Books, TOON Books, and the Indigenous Story Studio are just some of the new publishing houses and individual imprints that have been established to produce comics for young people. Many of their narratives are memoirs, biographies, and autobiographies of young people's lived experiences. All are stories about particular challenges that they endure. This study offers a new and unexplored approach to childhood in general and to children's literature more specifically.

## The Politics of Childhood: Reading Children

Reading can empower. Comics about predicaments and challenges that affect children can deepen young readers' sociopolitical understanding of the world and move them toward an awareness of social justice and perhaps even awaken a desire for activism. The inherent belief in the abilities of young people to cope with challenging reading material, which fuels this dynamic new genre, responds to the often-dismissive attitudes directed toward such readers by comics artists and critics alike. Critics Jan Baetens and Hugo Frey, for example, boldly claim that the content matter of the graphic novel is "adult" and "too sophisticated—or simply uninteresting—for a juvenile audience" (10). As such, their excellent analysis of this medium is limited to graphic novels directed at adults, with little to no acknowledgement of the graphic literature for young people that increases on an annual basis. In fact, the rapid growth in the comics industry for young readers easily discounts

Baetens and Frey's quick dismissal of comics for children. Like the texts they identify as being specifically "adult," graphic narratives for young people such as Mariko Tamaki's *Laura Dean Keeps Breaking Up with Me* (2019), Morten Dürr's *Zenobia* (2018), and David Small's *Stitches* (2009) gravitate just as frequently toward realism, autobiography, biography, documentary, reportage, and history as they do toward fantasy and superhero narratives. In the process, these texts tackle challenging, sometimes harrowing subject matter. *Child Soldier* (2015), *War Brothers, The Graphic Novel* (2013), and *Deogratias* (2006, in English), for instance, all explore child abduction and the enslavement of young people by rebel militias in verbal-visual form. *Adrian and the Tree of Secrets* (2013), *Drama* (2012), and *Skim* (2005) approach the complexity, ambiguity, and humanity of LGBTQ+ identity politics for young people. "Seeing ourselves reflected accurately in the world is crucial to a sense of well-being, to feeling whole and real," lesbian comics creator Alison Bechdel asserts in a 2012 foreword to Dylan Edwards's *Transposes*, six comics about transgender experiences. Bechdel's pronouncement applies equally to coming-of-age and coming-out narratives, comics about Indigenous experiences in Canada, forced migrations around the world, and ableist assumptions that govern the built environment through which young people (try to) navigate.

Many, if not all, of these comics rely on a desire to expose readers to some lived realities that young people living all over the world might tackle. They do this by means of the power of the visual and the hybrid possibilities of the graphic narrative, which target the multimodal capabilities that young readers already demonstrate. "The ability of cartoons to focus our attention on an idea is, I think, an important part of their special power, both in comics and in drawing generally" (31), Scott McCloud affirms in *Understanding Comics* (1993). Comics harness this power, provoking reader identification with a story's characters, which in turn helps to explain why cartoons have "historically held an advantage in breaking into world popular culture" (*Understanding* 42). Misguided dismissals of children's comics and their complexity betray an ignorance of the variety of visual narratives that currently dominate the comics and children's literature industries. Thus, Baetens and Frey's insistence that graphic narratives are "not just for kids" (74) is rooted in an assumption about the apolitical nature of children, about childhood innocence that critics from disciplines like children's literature, childhood studies, sociology, and visual art have been questioning for the past twenty years: "Their worlds [are] seen as social and cultural spaces, not political arenas," as Nicola Ansell states. "Children are understood to belong to the private sphere, whereas politics is confined to the public sphere" (205). The texts that *Growing Up Graphic* explores refute this assumption of the apolitical nature of young people; the acute personal and political challenges that youngsters face are vividly and deftly represented. Books and stories like *Honor Girl* (2017), "The Boat" (2015), and *El Deafo* (2014) contradict this association of childhood with innocence by focusing on topics as varied as deafness, forced migration, human trafficking, and human sexuality. The accessibility and adaptability of the comics form allow it to speak to diverse audiences about broadly ranging topics that affect the lives of children; the simplicity and childlike features of comics characters become the "blank slate" onto which readers can project themselves.

In general, I have selected graphic narratives that are grounded in a vision of the child that is empowered *in* and *by* the principles of the United Nations Convention on the Rights of the Child (UNCRC). This human rights treaty, adopted around the world in 1989, defines the rights of any child, anywhere, regardless of race, creed, or culture. The UNCRC is made up of fifty-four legally binding articles that aim to protect and promote children's rights in the fields of health, education, nationality, and the family. Arguably, its main importance lies in the breadth of its vision. It defines a set of rights that are intended to apply to all children, wherever they may be born and wherever they may live. This treaty considers children as active, independent persons with rights, interests, and most importantly, agency, that is, an ability to act and to make choices and decisions, albeit in a limited capacity given children's immersion in discourses as well as social and political structures that are not of their own making. This treaty is not without its limitations, however. Critics (Pupavac; Lewis) point to its universalizing vision. The UNCRC, they argue, is based on an idealized, Global Northern childhood that has little relevance to many children living in communities with vastly different understandings of adult-child relationships and where children are more economically and socially active within the family unit. Not surprisingly, regionally specific versions of the UNCRC—such as the African Charter on the Rights and Welfare of the Child (ACRWC)—were drafted to recognize specific cultural contexts and traditions not addressed by the UNCRC. The comics that I examine effectively highlight some contradictions between idea and practice by focusing on particular predicaments that young people endure in the Global North and Global South even though they are ostensibly protected by the principles of this document. In spite of the global endorsement of the UNCRC and the rights to provision, protection, and participation that the treaty guarantees for children around the world, implementation has been inconsistent, as so many of these graphic texts illustrate. Yet, in spite of the gap between principle and practice in the pursuance of these policies to protect and empower youngsters, these texts affirm an agentic vision of the child, one whose agency is demonstrated more through their ability to act than by their autonomy per se. Even though they are shaped by the countries and communities in which they live and affected by the political orientations of their governments, most of the young figures in these texts take an active role in relation to the events that affect them personally.

With great impact and immediacy, these comics frequently feature complex themes of war and its atrocities and provide a "counter story" or "counter history" to more official national histories. In the process, the narratives insert the forgotten or typically unexplored perspective of a young person. As it is the reader who brings the visual text to life in the very act of reading, the simple line-drawings in comics provoke reader- and viewer-identification, and the child witness-narrator in turn becomes a figure "through which to explore the relationship between historical public events and personal experience" (Gilmore 159). In volume 1 of *Persepolis* (2000), for example, titled "The Story of a Childhood," Marjane Satrapi employs the child witness-narrator to juxtapose young Marji's personal experiences of trauma within the political upheaval in Iran that she and her family endure in Tehran during the Islamic Revolution. The child witness solicits sympathetic readings of Satrapi's story, facilitating the author's desire to complicate Western readers' preconceptions and prejudices about Iranians and Middle Easterners in general and to resist a "facile sisterhood that often positions brown girls as subjects in need of rescue by the West" (Gilmore and Marshall, "Trauma" 29). Framed by Satrapi's adult perspective, *Persepolis* demonstrates the utility of a literary-visual narrative in telling a story compellingly, especially through its use of a child narrator. It mobilizes the visual to enhance the subjective and affective aspects of the content depicted, using the girl narrator to capture the "complexity of how controlling women is part of the Cultural Revolution that some women support" ("Trauma" 32). Private and public experiences are in this way blended by means of Marji as a character and a narrator—a technique that is employed by many of the texts that this study explores. Thus, comics about children present the opportunity to transmit the distant *there* to the immediate *here*, demanding that forgotten or ignored stories be recognized and, perhaps even more pertinently, demanding responses (emotional, intellectual) from their readers. As the epigraph to this chapter acknowledges, the "allure" and "danger" of the visual is the immediate "something" that comics communicate to readers: that is, images about diverse cultural locations; images of childhoods around the world; experiences of illness and disability; representations of identity, all of which have the potential to inspire a range of affective responses (both positive and negative) from their readers. These texts expand the cultural and literary boundaries of readers, reminding them of the "terrible things" (see figure 0.2) that children the world over experience, encouraging empathy and compassion in the process. Rebecca Scherr comments on the "haptic, visceral engagement with the pain of others" that comics allow (and encourage), an affective engagement that involves the reader in the world of representation, "experienced as bodily feeling" (20). Comics' tactile qualities, evoked in part by means of the artist's presence in the lines of the comic (especially in the case of graphic memoir), enhance their visceral capability and communicate the "subjective and affective dimensions of the content presented" (Scherr 24). The emotional charge of drawing draws readers into the narrative and is used, in many of these comics, to awaken readers to an affective dimension beyond the page itself.

Sidonie Smith coined the term "crisis comics" in a 2011 article to designate comics that draw attention to the misery that occurs around the globe, all in an effort to encourage transnational rights literacy and to encourage people to become activists. "Crisis comics are one of those modes of witness to radical injury and harm," she affirms (62). As she demonstrates, human rights advocates certainly make use of the alleged simplicity and accessibility of the comics' form to make human rights discourse available to diverse audiences (62). Campaigns that criticized the prison-industrial complex in the United States, for example, reached a substantial readership through The Real Cost of Prisons Project (63). These comic books were distributed to prisoners in every state prison system, every federal prison, and numerous jails across the United States to advocate for the end of the carceral state. Joel Andreas's comic *Addicted to War: Why the U.S. Can't Kick Militarism* (1991) chronicles the history of US foreign warfare, from the eighteenth-century Indian Wars to the wars in Iraq and Afghanistan. It was distributed to youth by the Office of the Americas for the Cause of Justice and Peace to expose American political and economic motives for entering into so many global conflicts. The World Health Organization (WHO) and the United Nations High Commissioner for Refugees (UNHCR) also used the comic books *HIV/AIDS: Stand Up for Human Rights* (2003) and *HIV and AIDS: Human Rights for Everyone* (2006) in their efforts to demystify the disease for marginalized youth in the Global South as well as to educate them about their human rights. In the Philippines, the Coalition against Trafficking in Women also produced comic books to illustrate stories of girls and women forced into the sex trade. The United Nations Children's Fund (UNICEF) continues to make use of cartoons to appeal to youth: It promotes children's rights in its series *Cartoons for Children's Rights,* animated shorts that focus on particular articles of the UNCRC. The Mexican intellectual, political cartoonist, and writer Rius used his nonfiction comics to bring awareness of Cuban history and revolution to the working class. For Sidonie Smith, crisis comics can be used variously and productively: to build awareness, to provide information, to raise consciousness, to solicit information, to teach an ethics of recognition, and to garner financial support (63). Generally, crisis comics represent and narrativize complex information about marginalization and suffering and encourage empathetic identification among their readers (62). As this study confirms, comics are especially persuasive tools for knowledge building for all ages of readers, narratives that can educate readers about their own rights and inspire those who want to become "individual agents of rights activism" (Smith 63).

Frequently used by governments as propagandist tools, however, crisis comics can also reproduce "colonialist, racist, and anti-Semitic tropes of difference through crude visual stereotypes" that depict their versions of political events or figures and demonize particular groups and/or demographics (Smith 62). Christine Hong concurs, acknowledging the potential for crisis comics to offer windows into distant settings and times distinguished by misery and terror, while at the same time affirming the centrality and agency of the intended viewer in the West. Such narratives adopt visual strategies of human rights campaigns that situate "the non-West as a portrait of strife, terror, and inhumanity" (Hong 194); the virtual viewer is comfortably remote from this violence.[4] While some critics have argued that bearing witness to individual suffering can encourage political activism, others have claimed that it simply promotes voyeurism and reinforces hegemonic politics (Goldberg; Dawes; Chouliaraki). Sidonie Smith strikes a cautionary note: She argues that in encouraging empathetic identification with personal situations, the "targeting [of] structural inequalities and formations of exploitation within and across nations" often falls to the wayside (65).

---

4. Human rights advocates and critics of children's literature acknowledge the dangerous commodification of disaster narratives by publishing houses. Kay Schaffer and Sidonie Smith argue that it is primarily the "Western-based publishing industry, media, and readership" that produce and consume such narratives (24). Elizabeth Anker writes about "human rights bestsellers" (frequently marked for women's book clubs) as contemporary texts that mobilize imperialist rhetoric and paternalistic observations about the "Third World" needing salvation. In such texts, the Western crusader archetype is deployed as "savior" of the postcolonial "victim" (Anker 36). Many of these bestsellers also gender the different characters along predictable lines: While women and children are frequently coded as victims, villains are predictably male (Anker 41). Some of the comics explored in this study could fall into this category, but most do not. Their critical importance, however, lies in their mobilizing of the child's perspective to uncover some lived realities of contemporary childhoods the world over.

Both building on and critiquing Sidonie Smith's theorization of crisis comics, this study explores comics that present various types of challenges and/or predicaments in the expectation of eliciting moral and ethical responsiveness among readers across cultures. These are graphic texts that theorize the productive tension between the desire to "know" something about the subject being represented and the limitations of that knowing. My project demonstrates that the study of personal and sociopolitical crises must always balance attention given to aesthetic questions of representation, reception, and artistic experimentation with a focus on sociopolitical issues relating to law, policy, and international agreements. Consideration of a text's determination to educate readers about experiences that young people endure is balanced with assessments of the information provided about the rights a person is due and the affective response from readers it solicits in the process. Human rights activist Barbara Bennett Woodhouse points to the particularly effective use of narrative (visual narrative, in our case) in the exploration of theoretical and legal issues for and about young people. "It brings the marginalized voice into the center of the conversation," she begins. "Narrative allows for complexity and ambiguity" (11). Most importantly, "narrative humanizes. It challenges at a very personal level the stereotypes we use to make those whom we marginalize seem less than fully human" (Woodhouse 12). I showcase how the multimodal affordances of the comic enhance the persuasiveness of these visual stories, offering insight into "society's soul through the way in which it treats its children," as Mandela discussed in his 1995 speech to launch the Mandela Children's Fund. "In an era of advanced global capitalism," Christine Hong asserts, "human rights-themed comics have been lauded as cause for hope for humanity in a mostly bleak world" (195). Indeed, a hope for humanity emerges in the figure of the young person—subject and reading-subject—whose personal (and sometimes political) agency is made concrete through the comics form. In issuing an ethical call to readers to recognize "the disjunction between the values espoused by the community and the actual practices that occur" (Schaffer and Smith 3), these comics—accessible, adaptable, compelling—are essential narratives that bear witness to and memorialize experiences of trauma, elicit empathy through the visceral engagement that they foster, and hopefully mobilize a reader's sense of social and political responsibility in the process.

I argue that most of the texts that *Growing Up Graphic* explores use the local to encourage readers to think more broadly about the discourses of nation and belonging that shape the experiences of young protagonists as they move with and against currents of power. More importantly, these comics narrativize the lived experiences of youngsters, and not necessarily in relation to a pattern of rescue or self-rescue. Indeed, the texts selected for this project are not rescue narratives per se or narratives that rely on rhetorical tropes of overcoming or victimization but rather narratives that seek to expand the boundaries of reading experiences, to think about individual experiences and how those experiences are *not* universal, and to encourage readers to reflect on and collaborate in the process of making and remembering alternative histories. I acknowledge, however, as in the example of *Persepolis* mentioned earlier, that in many cases these graphic narratives are shaped by a series of editorial interventions that inevitably frame the story and shape the subject and the scenario being depicted: Representative subjects witness their experiences; their narrated lives are remediated to "as-told-to" life writing that is then visualized by a third-person artist (Smith 64). Personal stories are heavily mediated events that have, in turn, become commodified by largely Western comics and children's literature publishers and can be seen to participate in a "global commodification of suffering" (71). This project is mindful of the impact of acts of collaboration between and among people and institutions that shape the final product and of creators' and editorial teams' remarkable determination to resist the narrative of victimhood. I am also conscious of my own particular positionality vis à vis this project that examines a number of distinct demographics (displaced peoples, victims of war, Indigenous peoples in Canada, LGBTQ+ youth, and people experiencing disability and/or bodily variation). I speak from the position of being a white, lesbian Canadian and a married mother of two young children who benefits from the distinct privileges accorded to a tenured professor in academe. As a member of white settler culture, I acknowledge and celebrate the current treaty holders, the Mississaugas of the Credit First Nation, of this beautiful area (Tkaronto) in which I live, think, work, and play. As a member of the LGBTQ+ community, I am ever mindful of the power relations that have shaped and continue to shape my life and of the power that I myself hold as a researcher and thinker. In my research and teaching, I am always conscious of the implications that my thoughts, ideas, and choices can have on the worlds around me.

Media commentary and public understandings of childhood have invoked a notion of "crisis" since the beginning of the twenty-first century—an idea that appears to be everywhere in the Western world. "A general assumption that childhood is not what it used to be and that this, in itself, signals catastrophe appears to saturate our social worlds," Mary Jane Kehily asserts (3). This "crisis" mentality has only been amplified by contemporary critics. Sue Palmer's 2006 text, *Toxic Childhood: How the Modern World Is*

*Damaging Our Children and What We Can Do about It*, for example, received significant coverage in the United Kingdom. Palmer identifies technological change, consumerism, a loss of places for young people to play, and the increased surveillance of children as the particular elements that fuel this current state.

The *Oxford English Dictionary* defines "crisis" as follows: "A vitally important or decisive stage in the progress of anything; a turning-point; also, a state of affairs in which a decisive change for better or worse is imminent; now applied esp. to times of difficulty, insecurity, and suspense in politics or commerce" (def. no. 3). *Growing Up Graphic* approaches "crisis" quite differently from Palmer; the crises it studies are particular predicaments that affect the lives of young people in the Global North, primarily, as well as in the Global South. The issues that these texts address are political, national, ideological, geographical, sexual, and personal, and oftentimes bridge many of these categories. Some comics might visualize the experiences of a Palestinian child coming of age while living in a refugee camp in Lebanon and his struggle to leave his homeland during the war (*Baddawi*), the particular challenges that reading and writing present for a young person who is struggling with dyslexia (*Mirror Mind*), or the racism in Canadian culture that shapes the daily lives of Indigenous girls and young women (*Will I See?*). Thus, "crisis" is a particularly resonant way to describe the manifold life experiences that people (ages eight to eighteen) experience, their vexing stages of development, and the point immediately before, during, and after a life change, emergency, or predicament that carries a significant impact. All of these graphic texts in turn figure "crisis" as a personal predicament—of both mind and body—on the parts of young people, as opposed to a crisis imposed by adults. This study does not examine the worlds of childhood and youth as somehow "polluted" or abused by adults; such an approach would reinscribe the victimization of young people. Instead, *Growing Up Graphic* analyzes the particular ontological and epistemological possibilities that such life events grant children and youth as well as the inventive visual and textual practices that such experiences inspire in the process. This study explores comics that depict war crimes or experiences in geopolitical "hot spots" (Rwanda and the Congo, the Middle East, and Vietnam) throughout the twentieth and twenty-first centuries. It explores the complexities of queer graphic memoirs, narratives of belonging, and the emerging trend of LGBTQ+ "camp" stories; it examines graphic pathographies—narratives about illness and disability conveyed in comics form—and it focuses on the crisis of Indigeneity in the Canadian context. The young people depicted are, in Marah Gubar's words, actors "who are simultaneously scripted and scripting" (295), a view that validates a child's agency while also acknowledging that they are shaped by discourses that preexist them (a condition that circumscribes adults as well).

"Stories transport us, and the younger we are the more absolute is our transportation," Desmond Manderson suggests. "The story has a power over the very young that it may never have again; but part of the power it has is the power to conjure that it permits children themselves to exercise" (91–92). The texts selected for this study remind readers that youngsters are always already political subjects. As Lara Saguisag and Matthew Prickett clarify, although young people make up approximately one quarter of the global population, they are a political minority that is often neglected and exploited. "Around the world, children are seen as too inexperienced and immature to be rights-bearing citizens and are thus often excluded from participating in civic, economic, and political spheres" (Saguisag and Prickett v). Saguisag and Prickett go on to explain that the majority of children lack access to the basic necessities of life (shelter, potable water, food, clothing, education, health care, and sanitation). Many young people are displaced, trafficked, enslaved, incarcerated, or forced to join rebel militias (v). With these sobering facts in mind, comics are especially powerful to "intervene against a culture of invisibility" (Chute, *Disaster* 5). In focusing on the experiences of children and youth, their challenges and hardships, comics remind readers, parents, librarians, and critics that young people are as deeply shaped by the political decisions made by the national governments, international organizations, corporations, and nongovernmental organizations (NGOs) that govern their existence and identities as are adults. And, increasingly, the political potentiality and agency of young people emerges in their advocacy, work that is in part inspired by narratives such as these.

## The Comics Industry and the Young Reader

Concurrent with these developments in the children's publishing industry is definite progress in ways of thinking about the role that graphic materials play in education. The belief, promoted by early picture book scholars like Perry Nodelman (1988, 2008) and Maria Nikolajeva and Carole Scott (2001), that illustrated narratives would encourage readers to turn to literary texts, has certainly been present in the marketing gambit of comics since the inception of the form in the early twentieth century. Early on, comics were aligned with literature, both in an attempt to deepen literacy among children and youth and also to legitimize comics culture itself. Contemporary comics continue these emphases, albeit with a different purpose. Significant critical attention has been given recently to reading comics as they enhance a reader's multimodal literacy skills (Burger; Kersulov et al.; Jacobs). With the omnipresence of the visual in contemporary culture—websites typically include text and image, advertisements, and links to related stories and embedded video or audio materials—readers (young and old) are "actively negotiating and choosing elements on which to focus rather than having a passive reading experience" (Burger 2). Increasingly, visual literacy and comprehension are crucial parts of communication. Negotiating graphic texts thus requires specific learning strategies for middle school and high school readers to hone their skills in reading and interpreting visuals, studying the interanimation of word and image, and addressing concepts that are applicable to them (hopefully serving as a bridge to other texts, both visual and literary).

In fact, the presence of graphic narratives in bookstores and on reading lists for children and youth, and even in middle school and high school curricula, gestures toward the need to provide and promote literature that appeals to the visual needs of youth and their propensity to select hybrid visual-literary narratives over strictly literary ones. In 2011 the Toronto District School Board hired the owners of The Beguiling comic book shop to serve as consultants for a report about integrating comics into the K–12 public school curriculum (Abate and Tarbox 8). In 2010 Diamond Kids "launched an annual list of over a hundred graphic novels that [met] specific guidelines in the Common Core State Standards Initiative" (8), an educational plan in the United States that details what K–12 students should know about English language arts and mathematics at the conclusion of each grade level. Researchers also acknowledge that the multimodalities of graphic texts speak to the diverse ethnic identities of students in the contemporary classroom. Some comics support a world culture in two ways, argues Michael Pagliaro: They are "deeply multicultural texts, and they have a visual focus that reflects the image-saturated Internet, the transmitter for global culture" (35). Graphic narratives can foster "students' critical literacies" and address the needs of the many English-language learners (ELLs) that are present in today's classrooms (Chun 144).

Quite recently, educators and community librarians have helped to increase the public presence, popularity, and critical esteem of children's and YA comics, even though skirmishes over appropriate topics for young readers remain common. The library market can be very supportive, especially for publishers of children's comics. According to publisher Mark Siegel, libraries purchase about one-third of American publisher First Second books (MacDonald 23). In a study of graphic novel circulation in US public libraries in 2013, Edward Schneider revealed that "98.1 percent of libraries now house a graphic novel collection, and that children under the age of eighteen represent over half of all graphic novel borrowing statistics" (Abate and Tarbox 8).[5]

Prize committees have also taken note of this genre, helping to solidify its respectability in the children's publishing industry. In 2007 the Young Adult Library Services Association introduced an annual award to honor the most outstanding graphic novels for teens. In 2006 *Publishers Weekly* named Gene Luen Yang's *American Born Chinese* the Best Comic of the Year; the *San Francisco Chronicle* named it Best Book of the Year. In 2007 it went on to win the Best Book Award from the Chinese American Librarians Association, the Michael L. Printz Award for Excellence in Young Adult Literature, and an Eisner Award for the Best New Graphic Novel. Literary awards enhance a text's respectability, which in turn increases its readership. In 2007 the Great Graphic Novels for Teens list from the Young Adult Library Services Association (YALSA), a new and vital tool for librarians and readers, was implemented. Not only does this list help librarians to find books that young audiences appreciate, but it also helps graphic narratives receive other American Library Association (ALA) awards (MacDonald 22), further expanding their cultural cachet and readership. TOON Books, whose titles have appeared on the YALSA list, for example, won several Geisel Awards honors. Raina Telgemeier's graphic narrative *Drama* was recognized as an honor book for the Stonewall Book Award in 2013, after being included on YALSA's list. By 2012 the Eisner Awards[6] had expanded their categories to offer three new prizes that recognize and celebrate child and YA comics in the industry: the Best Publication for Early Readers (up to age seven), the Best Publication for Kids (ages eight to twelve), and the Best Publication for Teens (ages thirteen to seventeen; Abate and Tarbox 5). By the 2010s comics and graphic narratives had finally achieved respectability and widespread industry recognition in the North American context.

These developments are remarkable for many reasons, not simply because comics have frequently had a tumultuous relationship with the

---

5. According to Schneider's 2014 survey of graphic novel collections and their use in American public libraries, the most frequent reader of comics and graphic novels was between the ages of twelve and fifteen (making up 23 percent of graphic novel circulation); readers aged ten to twelve made up 16 percent of the circulation; and readers fifteen to eighteen, 15 percent (74).

6. Named in honor of artist and writer Will Eisner, who was a regular participant in the ceremony until his death in 2005, the Eisner Comic Industry Awards are well-respected prizes given for creative achievements in American comic books.

public over issues of morality and the quality of literacy that such reading materials offer. In the 1940s and 1950s, for example, in response to the extreme popularity of comic books as children's texts in the United States, librarians, educators, religious leaders, and parents alike vocally railed against their unsavory commercialism and the perceived negative impact that this reading material was having on children's reading habits. Generally, these critical writings dismissed and even condemned comics, suggesting that they were a threat to literacy or "at best a crude primer for 'real' reading" (Hatfield, "Comic Art" 363).[7] Public outcry finally erupted when comic books were linked with immorality. In March 1948, American psychiatrist Fredric Wertham organized a symposium entitled "The Psychopathology of Comic Books," in which he claimed that comics encouraged juvenile delinquency and sexual deviance. Moral panic ensued among critics and the public: Towns and municipalities across the United States passed laws and ordnances to control the sale of comics. Comic book burnings took place in West Virginia, New York state, and Missouri. In 1954 Wertham went on to publish *Seduction of the Innocent,* in which he affirmed a connection between comic books, teen suicide, aggression, and even communism. This McCarthy-era hysteria brought about by his incendiary allegations led to hearings about the comic book industry by the Senate Subcommittee to Investigate Juvenile Delinquency. Wertham's anticomics crusade was fueled by a belief (first cultivated by Romantic philosophers and writers) in the inherent innocence of children and their vulnerability to the so-called "depravities" of mass media, an argumentative hobby horse that has been used more recently to describe the negative impact of video games on children's physical and mental health.[8] In response, comic book publishers formed a trade association, the Comics Magazine Association of America (CMAA), in an effort to minimize the bad publicity these hearings had generated and to stave off further legislative action. The coalition responded to Wertham's allegations by promising to self-regulate the contents of its members' publications, finally releasing on 27 October 1954 a list of forty-one guidelines that defined which storylines, words, and images were considered offensive content for readers (excessive violence, adultery, death, gore, sexual innuendo, etc.). The adoption of this regulatory code, with its

---

7. See Sterling North's editorial in the *Chicago Daily News,* 8 May 1940, for his invective against comics.

8. Carol Tilley's 2012 "Seducing the Innocent" gives numerous examples of how Wertham manipulated, overstated, and even fabricated research (especially evidence he attributed to personal clinical research he had conducted with young people) for rhetorical gain throughout his anticomics crusade.

accompanying "Seal of Approval," meant that only those comics bearing that seal could be sold to readers.

Wertham's anticomics crusade unleashed a firestorm that had ironic consequences. By demonizing them, Wertham granted comic books greater public significance and recognition that institutionalized the association of comics with children, for better or for worse. His argument still casts "a long shadow over the place of comics in society" (Tilley 405), a shadow that functions as subtext in censorship discussions about literature, debates that are, at heart, concerned with the discursive boundaries that separate "child" from "adult" and that are almost exclusively dependent on the adults who control the policing of these very categories.[9] That comics have inspired such hysteria Joe Sutliff Sanders attributes in part to the fact that comics appeal to a solitary reader who reads without adult supervision, "chaperoning" the words themselves to suit the visuals, whereas picture books involve an adult who, in the act of reading, monitors and fixes meaning in ways they deem "appropriate" for listeners, in the process interfering with the words in ways that have ideological implications (72). Comics do not provide the "potent cocktail of literacy, nostalgia, and acculturation" (75), Sanders continues, that picture books do; adults frequently select visual texts to read with their children that they themselves enjoyed as young people. In contrast, comics, by the disposable, nondurable, and ephemeral nature of their physical form and their subject matter, were considered to be antiliterary and, by default, dangerous. *Growing Up Graphic* demonstrates that comics are an important part of children's culture; the participatory involvement that young people have with this mass-produced, commercial, and seemingly ephemeral reading material frightened and continues to frighten adults and educators and fuels many of the anticomics arguments that still surface with frequency.

A 1993 comic printed in the *New Yorker*—cocreated by Pulitzer-Prize-winning comics artist Art Spiegelman and Caldecott-winning picture book creator Maurice Sendak—interrogates this myth of innocence that adults inscribe onto childhood and that often underlies many such moral panics about literature and popular culture, comics included. The cartoon visualizes an encounter between two artists as they discuss their craft. In 1993, at the pinnacle of the AIDS epidemic and a crisis of homelessness in the United States, Sendak had recently finished one of his most controversial picture

---

9. Challenges to comics are so common that the Comic Book Legal Defense Fund (CBLDF) has created a resource page for librarians and educators that includes numerous handbooks for frequently challenged comic books and graphic novels. The CBLDF has also drafted detailed discussion guides for shelving comics by age categories and for speaking to parents, educators, and librarians about the genre as a whole.

books, *We Are All in the Dumps with Jack and Guy*. In the comics dialogue that takes place (literally and visually), Spiegelman articulates his astonishment that Sendak is "doing a book for grownups," referring to illustrations that Sendak was then producing for Herman Melville's novel *Pierre*. Sendak's response to his colleague is emblematic of his resistance to the discursive categories that separate "child" from "adult" when it comes to reading material: "Kid books . . . grownup books . . . that's just marketing. Books are books!" Sendak insists (see figure 0.1). Spiegelman responds with a defense about the need to protect children from harsh realities, calling it "child abuse" when parents present their kids with *Maus*, his Holocaust memoir, to read. In fact, Spiegelman is very content with his then six-year-old daughter Nadja thinking that "Daddy draws mice!" Spiegelman's mice in concentration camp uniforms hover in the not-so-distant background, bearing witness to this powerful conversation about the abilities of youngsters to cope with challenging reading material.

Reacting to Spiegelman's determination to protect his daughter from threatening topics, Sendak launches into a passionate diatribe against protectionism, against sugar-coating the world for readers, young and old. "Art—you *can't* protect kids . . . they know *everything*!" he insists. Sendak argues against the idealized vision of childhood innocence that stems as far back as Romantic thinkers and poets like William Wordsworth and William Blake and their visions of a childhood that is "all quaint and succulent, like Peter Pan," as Sendak ironically and dismissively characterizes it. According to Jacqueline Rose's widely respected study *The Case of Peter Pan, or, The Impossibility of Children's Fiction* (1984), the child within children's literature is an impossibility, always already an adult construction. At stake in literature for children is "the adult's desire for the child," Rose affirms (3), the desire of an adult for a vision of sheltered and pure childhood that reinforces the ideological stability of the adult as opposed to the existence of the "real" child (see figure 0.2). Sendak's view of children and the act of reading is shaped by this radical revisioning of the very assumptions about what it means to be a child. Children have "desperate day-to-day needs that [have] to be met no matter what," Sendak insists—and this study concurs. The panel of the comic that draws the reader's gaze, located in the very middle of the second page, visualizes Sendak's radical response to this unpalatable vision of childhood. "Childhood is cannibals and psychotics vomiting in your mouth!" a crazed Sendak shouts at the reader (and at Spiegelman). His angry face strains the very frames of the panel itself, which seem barely able to contain the threat of his passion and anger about such overly reductive ways of interpreting the capabilities of youngsters. Turning to his colleague,

FIGURE 0.1. Maurice Sendak and Art Spiegelman drawn in dialogue. "In the Dumps," *New Yorker*, 27 September 1993.

Sendak delivers "truths" about childhood (as he sees it) that destroy this myth of innocence that adults crave. "In reality, childhood is deep and rich. It's vital, mysterious, and profound," Sendak muses, against a backdrop of his own whimsical illustrated scenes. "I remember my *own* childhood vividly . . . I knew terrible things . . . But I knew I mustn't let adults *know* I knew . . . It would scare them." In this comics dialogue, Sendak addresses a concept that has preoccupied comics and children's literature readers and critics for many years: the discursive boundaries that separate "child" from "adult" and the conceptions and misconceptions that adults have about the inherent nature of young people and about the topics with which they can cope.

As Charles Hatfield has argued, children's literature specialists "have treated comics for and about children in a sweeping manner without a sustained interest; this lapse has sorely impoverished the field" ("Comic Art" 361). *Growing Up Graphic* seeks to address this oversight, linking internationalism and interdisciplinarity in the synergies it hopes to affect and inspire between comics and children's literature, linkages that have gone unrecognized for too long now. This study brings together these still disparate fields to engage in a multidisciplinary analysis of how crises that affect children and youth are depicted in comics. As I argue, graphic narratives for and about young readers offer important insights into the interests and capabilities of these youngsters as readers and as potential agents of change. Comics *as* children's literature offers an exciting new type of text for children and youth, employing words and images to remind them of their complex responses to crises and the particular resilience they display as they try to survive conflict and trauma.

FIGURE 0.2. The second page of Maurice Sendak and Art Spiegelman's "In the Dumps." *New Yorker*, 27 September 1993.

Even though the audience of early comics and "funnies," as they were more commonly called, were young readers, and although many of the characters in these strips were youngsters (Richard F. Outcault's The Yellow Kid, Winsor McCay's Little Nemo, Harold Gray's Little Orphan Annie, Hergé's Tintin, José Escobar's Zipi and Zape, Wilhelm Busch's Max and Moritz, etc.), analyses of the origins and sociohistorical context of comics are predominantly preferred[10] over the examination of comics' varied representations of childhood and youth and, even more pertinently, the lived realities of contemporary children around the world. Similarly, literary criticism of children's literature has tended to ignore or, at best, marginalize comics for

---

10. Preferred by such critics as Paul Williams and James Lyons, Douglas Wolk, and Roger Sabin.

young people. This "blind spot" in children's literature and comics criticism, as Hatfield called it on a number of occasions ("Charles"; "Introduction"), is only now being addressed. Most recently, Gwen Athene Tarbox's exploration of *Children's and Young Adult Comics* (2020) provides a revised history of North American children's literature that moves "comics from the periphery to the center of the discussion" (3), describing the shifts that have occurred throughout the twentieth and early twenty-first centuries in terms of children's reading material and reading patterns, as well as contextualizing the social and cultural impacts that comics have had on young readers. Lara Saguisag's *Incorrigibles and Innocents* (2019) examines the omnipresence of child characters in American newspaper comics supplements in the late nineteenth and early twentieth centuries. Her fascinating analysis argues that "comics and childhood were tightly braided with contemporary discourses of citizenship and nationhood" (1). Turn-of-the-century American newspaper comics featuring children used "notions of race, ethnicity, gender, and class" to sort children into the "categories of 'future citizen' or 'noncitizen'" (Saguisag 5). Mark Heimermann and Brittany Tullis's collection of essays, *Picturing Childhood: Youth in Transnational Comics* (2017), is the first anthology that examines predominantly twentieth-century representations of children and childhood in comics. Yet, no book-length work has been done on this rapidly expanding genre of graphic narratives for young people about the sociopolitical experiences they endure in their respective environments. Such comics provide complex human interest stories (told from the perspectives of the frequently marginalized) and as such represent powerful examples of a new type of children's literature, whose reliance on the visual affords it a level of persuasiveness for its young audiences.

## Chapter Overview

*Growing Up Graphic* answers the need for a scholarly yet accessible study of this compelling field. The corpus of primary source texts for this project consists of approximately fifty comics selected from a range of cultural contexts, predominantly North American but with some noteworthy exceptions. These texts of varying length, all of which were originally published in English or have been translated into the language, have been written with a young reader in mind. I am focusing on texts that have been published or translated into English to narrow the parameters of my large topic and to focus on commonalities between and among the disparate texts that I have selected. In terms of this preference I give to texts published or translated into English, the project pointedly attempts to probe the remediations that shape the story being considered. What, for example, are some of the epistemological considerations involved in the mediation of a text written by an adolescent from the Democratic Republic of the Congo versus by a North American comics creator? How do such considerations shape *Child Soldier* and *War Brothers,* among other texts? What assumptions do these texts make about the reader? Do these assumptions challenge dominant notions of children, rights, culture, identity, ability, and so forth?

The first two chapters, "The Use of Childhood in War" and "Youthful Experiences of Immigration, Migration, and Diaspora," explore how this medium both shapes and interrogates our perceptions of childhood and youth in the contemporary world. Departing aesthetically and thematically from early representations of childhood and youth in comics culture (specifically the innocent child myth, which in turn continues in Harold Gray's *Little Orphan Annie,* Winsor McKay's *Little Nemo,* and Bil and Jeff Keane's *The Family Circus*), the texts that I analyze deliberately shatter the myth of innocence by means of innovative visual approaches to the representation of traumas and experiences pertinent to contemporary readers. These chapters focus on texts that visualize war crimes or particular challenges that children and youth endure in conflict zones, such as Africa, Vietnam, and the Middle East. Leila Abdelrazaq's visualization of her father's youth spent in a Palestinian refugee camp in Lebanon (*Baddawi*), Michel Chikwanine's depiction of his training as a child soldier in the Democratic Republic of Congo (*Child Soldier*), and Morten Dürr and Lars Horneman's tale of a harrowing refugee crossing across the Mediterranean (*Zenobia*) all help to move beyond North American and Eurocentric perspectives of children and youth to develop a more nuanced vision of global childhoods under threat of war, persecution, and indoctrination. In turn, as most of these comics speak from the perspective of the child or adolescent in question, these texts mobilize the local crisis of a young person to speak to large-scale world concerns, such as armed conflict, forced migration, exile, and political oppression. The primary texts showcase three crucial cultural and artistic factors: the potency of this medium as a mode of communication for readers, the ability of comics to tell tales that inspire affective engagement and action, and the inventive visual and textual ways with which these comics encourage readers to reflect on the power relations generated in the process.

Chapter 3, "Indigeneity and Resurgence in Canadian Comics," examines texts that visualize the intergenerational traumas experienced by Indigenous peoples in Canada because of European and Canadian colonialism. Although the practices of child removal and forced assimilation were classified as cultural genocide by the United Nations in 1948, residential schools for Indigenous children were not fully abandoned as a practice in Canada until 1996. Recognition by Canadians of the profoundly devastating impact of the schools on Indigenous peoples, and of the effect that these stolen generations continue to have on Indigenous cultures, is ongoing. As recently as February 2023, Indigenous investigations across Canada continued to uncover hundreds of unmarked graves at sites of former schools, bearing terrible witness to the violence committed against young Indigenous people by the Canadian government. As the bourgeoning Indigenous comics industry testifies, Indigenous experiences and resistance have become "narratable" as a valid and valuable testimonial discourse. As more narratives about child removal emerge, these visual stories are powerful resources with which to educate readers in Canada (and throughout the world) about the crises that Indigenous peoples continue to endure. In addition to the growth of comics that visualize the intergenerational traumas that Canada's Indigenous peoples suffer (*The Outside Circle* and *Betty: The Helen Betty Osborne Story*), there is another trend that is equally powerful: comics that are written by Indigenous peoples in Canada and that are circulated in particular to Indigenous youth by the nonprofit press the Indigenous Story Studio (formerly known as the Healthy Aboriginal Network), located in Courtenay, British Columbia. Funded by various governmental bodies and agencies, comics published by this press (*An Invited Threat, Lighting Up the Darkness, Kiss Me Deadly*, etc.) explore issues that are particularly topical for Indigenous youth and that attempt to enable them to respond to the cultural crises that affect them. These two trends in Indigenous comics visualize the legacy of colonialism and theorize about the stakes involved in offering textual and visual interpretations of past and present human rights violations. They also provide compelling examples for those committed to issues of Indigeneity in other countries and circle back to the issues of settlement, nationhood, and cultural genocide first explored in chapters 1 and 2.

Chapters 4 and 5 explore uniquely personal and medical crises that young people experience across country, nation, or creed. Queer comics are the "fastest-growing area in comics now" (*Why* 349), Hillary Chute affirms. LGBTQ+ stories are especially common in graphic narratives for young readers. The fourth chapter, "Space and Orientation in LGBTQ+ Graphic Narratives," explores queer stories that seek to explore and empower lesbian, gay, bisexual, transgender, and queer youth. Childhood and adolescence are complicated by issues of identity, cultural belonging, sexuality, and race in texts as diverse as Tee Franklin's *Bingo Love* (2018), Mariko Tamaki's *Laura Dean Keeps Breaking Up with Me* (2019), and Melanie Gillman's *As the*

*Crow Flies* (2017). In terms of children's literature, the YA genre has been very receptive to lesbian and gay themes, first because "coming out" is often described in adolescence and captures that timeframe "as an intense period of sexual attraction, social rebellion, and personal growth" (Kidd, "Introduction" 114). In 1998, when Kenneth Kidd noted that there were no picture books about lesbian and gay children, he explained this as due to a "lingering belief that homosexuality in particular is incompatible with, or even antithetical to, childhood and its culture" (114). Increasingly, however, homophobia has replaced homosexuality as a "problem" to be addressed, especially in these queer comics, and sexual orientation has begun to intersect with issues of class, race, and geography. LGBTQ+ comics, however, like Raina Telgemeier's text *Drama* and Jul Maroh's *Blue Is the Warmest Color* (2013), still face controversy and are the subject of numerous book bans in libraries and schools because of a still prevalent desire to presume that children are innocent of sexuality.

Chapter 5, "Young People and/in Graphic Medicine," focuses on an important topic that is still gaining prominence in comics studies and children's literature, more generally: Physical impairments, learning challenges, mental disorders, visual and hearing impairments, and neurological disabilities are increasingly represented in comics. So omnipresent have graphic texts become about health and illness that they sparked the Graphic Medicine movement. Its 2015 manifesto advocates for a "more inclusive perspective of medicine, illness, disability, [and] caregiving." The six "pioneers" of graphic medicine who drafted the *Manifesto* resist the notion of the "universal patient" by encouraging multiple approaches to the representation of health and disease in graphic form (Czerwiec et al.). Questions of health and ability affect many, if not most, areas of life for a young person (for any person, actually), as *Guts* (2019), *Stitches* (2009), and *Swallow Me Whole* (2008) visualize: Poor health inevitably influences a child's performance at school and their ability to enjoy leisure time. Ill health in childhood and youth can have effects that last throughout life. Chapter 5 provides an informative overview and compelling case studies of comics that examine how illness and disability impact the health and development of a still underrepresented demographic. Yet many of these graphic texts about illness and health focus primarily on the Global North. An area for growth in this industry, then, would be to diversify representations of health and disability across the globe.

Following up on the work of chapter 5, the conclusion draws on the COVID-19 comics that emerged in response to the recent global pandemic in their explorations of the subject positions of children and young adults, not to mention the role that they played (and continue to play) in visualizing the sociopolitical and emotional implications of this global crisis.

As Jonathan Todres and Sarah Higinbotham's groundbreaking study *Human Rights in Children's Literature* (2016) attests, children's literature has always been political in its depiction of conflict, trauma, and darkness, from early picture books like Dr. Seuss's *Horton Hears a Who!* and fairy tales like *Cinderella*, to memoirs like *The Diary of Anne Frank*. As some of the first artifacts with which infants and toddlers come into contact, books have always presented opportunities to learn about and engage with rights discourse. Comics are no exception, especially given their new omnipresence in the publishing industry. In their explorations of the subject positions of children and young adults, and their awareness of the child as active agent empowered in and by the principles of the UNCRC, comics can provide the groundwork for a more empathetic and affirmed childhood. Human rights education research shows that just a few of the positive outcomes of teaching children about their own rights include "increased self-esteem, heightened respect for other's rights, [and] a reduction in bullying" (Todres and Higinbotham xvi). Although materials and methodologies to teach people about their human rights have a limited distribution (child-friendly versions of the Universal Declaration of Human Rights do circulate, for example), children's books already exist as "a rich source of core human rights principles" (Todres and Higinbotham 6). To that list of resources I would add comics, literary-visual texts that enshrine a vision of young people as rights-bearing individuals with the capacity to express their own views.

"Children did not abandon comics; comics, in their drive to attain respect and artistic accomplishment, abandoned children," Michael Chabon asserted in his impassioned call for the need to create comics for and about children. Visual and literary critics have been slow to address the figures of the child and adolescent (reader and subject and reading-subject) that feature so ubiquitously in this medium. Although the graphic narrative form was originally created to distinguish adult-readership comic books from more child- and youth-oriented comics, graphic narratives now constitute a major focus in the children's publishing industry. Such texts have a powerful ability both to address and construct their readers, to keep children and youth reading, and to use their innovative abilities to address complicated issues for people the world over.

In particular, comics about individual predicaments and young people's lived experiences have the potential to accomplish many things. They can clarify and dispute historical narratives, protest current social and political practices around the globe, inspire resistance, and promote reconciliation, among other positive outcomes. Furthermore, the literary-visual story becomes the medium through which a young person can think about the "disrupting emotions" that often accompany growth, as picture book creator Maurice Sendak alluded to in his acceptance speech for the Caldecott Medal in 1964: "What is just as obvious—and what is too often overlooked—is the fact that from their earliest years children live on familiar terms with disrupting emotions, that fear and anxiety are an intrinsic part of their everyday lives, that they continually cope with frustration as best they can" (151). In response to critics' insistence that graphic narratives are "too sophisticated" for a juvenile audience, these comics prove them wrong—and provide the literature *about children* that Michael Chabon called for in 2004 as well as childhood in all its wondrous complexities.

CHAPTER 1

# The Use of Childhood in War

> Complex and sensitive national and sociocultural issues can also be expressed and explored in comics through the use of child characters.
>
> —Mark Heimermann and Brittany Tullis, *Picturing Childhood*

In an April 2018 special issue of the *Times Literary Supplement*, Eric Bulson announced that "the comics age is upon us" (7), thanks to the plethora of graphic novels, anthologies, collections, reprints, and critical works about comics that are already in circulation and that continue to emerge on a regular basis. "But the medium is and always has been global" (7), Bulson goes on to declare, a bold statement that counters a still-prevalent assumption that the most significant output of comics comes from the United States.

This global aspect of comics is increasingly apparent on the shelves of connoisseur and amateur alike. As early as 2006, Gillian Whitlock alluded to "a global network of sequential art" ("Autographics" 969) by means of which different formats, genres, and storytelling traditions across cultures and from around the world come into contact. In this global network of comics, "varieties of storytelling engage with one another transculturally and transnationally, thanks to the accessibility and adaptability of comics art" (Halsall and Warren 107). In many respects, comics and graphic narratives are a part of the "global literature" about which Adam Kirsch writes: texts that engage in a complex exchange of ideas and strategies of representation across borders, languages, cultures, even generations, texts in which the local and the global are interconnected (25). It is in comics' capacity to

27

reveal humanity to itself that the hope of the global comics text—and, more specifically, the graphic narratives about sociopolitical predicaments that shape the lives of young people—lies. These texts visualize challenges and changes that have a palpable impact on the lives of people (children and adults), both at the local level and frequently at the global level. These two levels are not separate; they are connected by the processes of globalization.

Comics and graphic narratives are predisposed to border crossings because their unique verbal/visual interface seems to translate more easily across nations and cultures, as critics have begun to analyze with increasing frequency.[1] An Iranian exile who works with the French comics collective *L'Association* in Paris, Marjane Satrapi is an ideal example of a comics artist who makes use of these "global transits of sequential artwork" (Whitlock, "Autographics" 971) to challenge Western preconceptions of Iran, Iranian women, and the veil in *Persepolis* (2007) and *Embroideries* (2005). Satrapi's works have been translated and distributed across Europe and North America and have been taken back to the Middle and Far East in English translation as well.[2] Increasing attention to international politics, reportage, and autobiographical modes in comics suggests that they are useful tools for meditating about the particularly traumatic aspects of personal and global histories. For Jan Baetens and Hugo Frey, these global graphic narratives have the potential to transform political predicaments and catastrophes "into a more manageable and human form" (96), one that allows readers to explore different ways of being in the world. Troublingly, Baetens and Frey identify graphic novels that gravitate more toward the realist mode (thus, auto/biography, documentary, reportage, and history) as being more "adult" in contrast to the more "traditional" and, by implication, escapist fare reserved for children (13). Many of the comics that these next two chapters explore, however, represent children's particular experiences of hardship and disaster, in spite of this claim that global experiences are the unique purview of more "mature" graphic narratives.

This chapter and the next focus on the increasingly transnational and transcultural dynamics that shape the field of contemporary graphic storytelling by focusing on comics for young people in geopolitical conflict zones around the world (e.g., Africa, Vietnam, Palestine), comics that visualize war

---

1. See, for example, Halsall and Warren; Davies, "Dreamlands"; Davies and Rifkind; Rifkind, "Migrant," "Spotlight," "Refugee"; Mickwitz, "Comics"; Aldama "Putting," "Multicultural"; Denson et al.; Parker Royal, "Foreword," "Coloring."

2. Because of the political situation in Iran, however, *Persepolis* cannot be officially translated into Farsi or even published there. In an interview, Satrapi mentioned that there is a Persian version (which she has not authorized) that is in circulation on the black market (Chute, "Retracing" 94).

crimes or particular traumas that children and youth endure. Frequently, these texts mobilize the local experience of a young person to speak to large-scale world concerns, such as armed conflict, forced migration, exile, and political oppression. The comics that I have selected specifically remind readers that the often-desperate experiences children endure in these texts are a far cry from the escapist content offered by some fantasy comics or comics considered to be "appropriate" for young readers. As these texts visualize, young people's identities and their socialization are shaped by the politics of the countries and communities in which they live. They are deeply affected by the political orientations of national governments, international organizations, corporations, and NGOs that govern their everyday lives. The youthful protagonists of these graphic texts frequently take an active role in political events. "As agents with voice, children construct their own worlds of meaning and shape their surrounding social relations," John Wall writes. "They form responses to poverty, make uses of mass media, give meaning to families, direct their experiences in classrooms, and engage in philosophical and religious thinking—and with as much complexity and diversity as adults" (37). As the epigraph to this chapter suggests, comics for young readers use the personal and the local to encourage readers to think more broadly about the narratives of nation and belonging that shape the experiences of these protagonists as they move with and against currents of power. By examining comics that represent and narrativize complex information about marginalization and suffering, chapters 1 and 2 demonstrate how these texts also encourage and rely on empathetic identification among their readers, raising important questions about acts of witnessing and representation, especially when dealing with trauma and scenes of atrocity. As persuasive tools for knowledge-building, these graphic texts have the potential to educate readers about their own rights and global humanitarian issues and can inspire those who want to become individual agents of rights activism.

*Barefoot Gen, Baddawi, Palestine, Safe Area Goražde, The Unwanted, A Game for Swallows, Persepolis, The Arab of the Future,* and *Deogratias,* among others, point to the omnipresence of the genres of auto/biography, testimony, documentary, and slow journalism in the comics industry (Rifkind, "Spotlight"). A 2018 *INKS & the Comics Studies Society* blog entry affirms that comics creators are "working across" these genres to explore diverse experiences of war, trauma, migration, exile, and diaspora, while attempting to encourage the possibility for shared ethics and political solidarities between the Global South and the Global North. This chapter in particular features visual narratives about young people's experiences of war, abduction, and child soldiery on the African continent, interrogating the shared roles of perpetrator and victim with which they themselves struggle. *Child Soldier: When Boys and Girls Are Used in War* (2015), written for the youngest reading audience (ages ten to fourteen), looks to educate Global Northern reading audiences about child soldiers. It reminds readers that young people are "agents with voice," as John Wall describes them, and yet insists that this agency does not preclude their vulnerability to threatening militia groups as much as to their own communities if they are lucky enough to return. Sharon E. McKay and Daniel Lafrance's *War Brothers, The Graphic Novel* (2013) addresses an older audience (ages fourteen and up) and attempts to visualize contrasting experiences of child soldiers, using a collective protagonist. In contrast to *Child Soldier*, *War Brothers* visualizes the violence and trauma of abduction, emphasizing the deep emotional scars that these experiences leave for young people to process, alone, after their escape. Finally, Jean-Philippe Stassen's *Deogratias, A Tale of Rwanda* (2006) is a study of the psychological torment with which the protagonist is condemned to live after taking part in the ethnic cleansing of the Tutsi and the Twa. The text specifically manipulates readers into feeling compassion for Deogratias, the Hutu protagonist, only to destroy this sympathy at the end, refusing the comfort offered by narrative closure so distinctive in overcoming or transformation narratives. Importantly, these three texts resist the rhetorical conversion of child perpetrator to victim, so typical of literary representations of child soldiers consumed by Global Northern audiences (Hesford, *Exceptions* 129). Likewise, in interrogating the particular agency of the young people involved and in seeking to understand the ethical complexities of this subject position, these texts forgo the tendency to argue that young people need to be protected or have their innocence cherished as well as the tendency to position these young people as objects of pity or compassion (Martins 437).

## Active and Activist Reading

In *Understanding Comics* (1993), McCloud argues that comics is one of the few forms of communication "in which individual voices still have a chance to be heard" (197). He goes on to suggest in *Reinventing Comics* (2000) that comics can be used to diversify readers' perceptions of the world (19). Undoubtedly, the auto/biographical, reportage, and documentary modes in comics appear on the "activist end of comic book culture" (*Alternative* 111), as Charles Hatfield characterizes it, offering an alternative to escapist trends prevalent in other areas of the comic industry. In particular, comics are effective at enlightening readers about children and youth as a group of people who have been "hidden in plain sight," as Barbara Woodhouse suggests, belonging to a political minority that is often neglected, exploited, and disenfranchised. In the process, comics employ the child witness-narrator to visualize for readers experiences of political upheaval or personal and collective trauma. The comics studied in these two chapters renounce this perception of young people as marginal, neglected, and exploited. Instead, texts that visualize experiences young people endure in particular conflict zones collect a chorus of engaged voices that demand to be heard and that in turn invite responses from readers, promoting social justice through the visual and narrative exposure of abuses of power.

"It is precisely in its insistent, affective, urgent visualizing of historical circumstance that comics aspires to ethical engagement," Hillary Chute observes about politically oriented graphic narratives such as *Palestine* and *Persepolis* ("Literature" 457). Her assertion could apply equally to comics that document children who are displaced, trafficked, enslaved, abused, and forced to join militias. In bearing witness to authors' own traumas or the traumas of others, comics materially eschew erasure and effacement: "They repeat and reconstruct in order to counteract" (Chute, *Disaster* 4). Intervening against a "culture of invisibility," such comics figure that "trauma does not always have to be disappearance; it can be plenitude, an excess of signification" (5). In turn, these comics are frequently structured as narratives of growth, "of hybrid identities and developing selves," and as such are particularly powerful at evoking the disparate experiences of childhood (Chute, *Why* 280). Such graphic texts expand the generic parameters of children's literature by providing opportunities for readers to gain insights into the diverse experiences of children and youth around the world, using the particular affordances of comics to depict characters and situations that speak to larger national and international concerns. Some of the visions of childhood that these graphic texts feature are active and agentic, even though the young people might still be constrained by adult structures of power and control, and are thus reminiscent of the vision of childhood that is endorsed and institutionalized by the United Nations Convention on the Rights of the Child (UNCRC). Shaped by the rights-based movements that emerged in the 1960s and 1970s, the 1989 UNCRC articulates rights for children in terms that shift the idea of children and their rights from "protection to *autonomy*, from nurturance to *self-determination*, from welfare to *justice*" (Cregan and Cuthbert 66). Comics—such as *War Brothers*, *Zenobia*, and *An Olympic Dream*—evoke an agentic vision of childhood and youth, even in the midst of catastrophe.

Many of these graphic texts visualize how people around the world are directly affected by oppression, political instability, military conflict, and terrorism. Although Riad Sattouf's *The Arab of the Future: A Childhood in the Middle East* (2015–) was not written specifically for young readers, it bears mentioning as an important childhood memoir of tyranny that depicts Sattouf's experiences of growing up in Libya and Syria between 1978 and 1987. Sattouf captures the immediacy of his childhood and the fervor of political idealism, focusing on his nomadic childhood in rural France, Muammar Qaddafi's Libya, and Hafez al-Assad's Syria, always under the roof of his father, a Syrian pan-Arabist who clings to grandiose dreams for the Arab nation. As Sattouf's graphic memoir catalogues, young people are directly affected by conflicts, catastrophes, and emergencies because of their presence in conflict zones or their explicit participation as armed combatants. They are also directly affected by genocide, displacement, and migration; authoritarian and totalitarian regimes as a result of adults' reduced capacities for protecting and parenting them; experiences of social dislocation; a loss of education and other supports that contribute to their development; and deprivation of all kinds (Williams and Drury 58–59). Current statistics about the lived experiences people have with global crises are staggering. Children continue to be disproportionately affected by armed conflicts around the world. According to a report issued by the UN Secretary General about "Children and Armed Conflict" in 2019, verified cases of the recruitment and use of children as combatants, informants, servants, and sex slaves quadrupled in the Central African Republic and doubled in the Democratic Republic of the Congo (DRC), when compared with a report produced just two years before (United Nations, "Armed"). The number of verified cases of recruitment, violence, and abuse of young people in Somalia, South Sudan, the Syrian Arab Republic, and Yemen persists at alarming levels. Increases in the exploitation of children also coincide with increasing levels of killing or maiming them. For example, according to this 2019 report, spikes in armed clashes and violence led to a substantial increase in the number of child casualties in Iraq and Myanmar. Afghanistan, the Syrian Arab Republic, and Yemen saw the highest number of human casualties. In Nigeria, Boko Haram continues to force civilians (many of whom are young people) to perpetrate suicide attacks, which in turn have led to more than half of all verified child casualties in the country (United Nations, "Armed"). Young people are indeed at the epicenter of violent conflicts.

Increasingly, comics visualize such social and political predicaments, narrated from the perspectives of "at risk" subjects. In all instances, however, these texts renounce the ontology of victimhood, sometimes through inventive visual and textual practice and always through the narrating perspective of the child or youth, eager to recenter such peoples from the margins to the center of public discourse. The protagonist at the center of the story is often the driver of personal change, modeling this agentic behavior for young readers. In dramatizing lived experiences of trauma, injustice, and exploitation, texts such as these ask readers to reflect on power, control, and change and intensify readers' abilities to empathize with people who are caught up in wars that are not of their own making.

Implicit in the creation of these comics is a responsibility to tell stories. Too often, predicaments, catastrophes, and emergencies become invisible or unspeakable, and narrative art appears seemingly inadequate in the face of suffering. Recently, Kenneth Kidd has argued that children's literature has become "the most rather than the least appropriate forum for trauma work" (*Oz* 181). He explains that this trauma literature is part of the "complex history of childhood's revaluation, of its merger with the idea of interiority and the position of vulnerability" (183). There is an urgent need for these difficult and traumatic stories to be told. Katharine Capshaw Smith insists in a 2005 issue of *Children's Literature*: "These are not stories to *pass on*, to pass up, because ignorance about historical trauma is an enormous risk" (115). Instead, narratives about young people who have experienced trauma invite readers to live through this experience as well, in the process privileging "evidence of the child reader's survival ability as well as identification with a suffering protagonist" (118), thus moving past the "innocent child" paradigm that requires adult protection and guidance toward a more active model of readerly involvement and participation. Kidd suggests that picture books about the Holocaust offer the "most dramatic and/or ironic testimony to trauma" because the presumed innocence of the format carries "greater power to shock and presumably to educate" ("Auschwitz" 137). To that argument I would add graphic narratives because the substantial length of the text and the time spent navigating word and image allow readers to immerse themselves in the story. Comics can defamiliarize standard representations of history by capturing and textualizing the particularly youthful bearing witness to trauma, visualizing complex histories of violence that are both personal and public. Especially powerful as visual tools that "intervene against a culture of invisibility" (Chute, *Disaster* 5), comics are suited for the representation of nonfiction because of the iconic nature of the traumatic image, fragments and memories over which a reader can mull for as long as they want, thanks to the literary-visual format (Chute and DeKoven 193). These particular graphic texts unsettle commonplace frames of difference and thematize issues of witnessing, remembering, and producing art in a time of the global commodification of suffering. Motivated by an impulse to remember, to reveal, to remind, and (sometimes) to resolve, these texts visualize historical catastrophes in an attempt to expose abuse or to ensure that it is not repeated.

But how do we account for the means by which these graphic narratives arrive at closure regarding a story and an experience that for many readers and survivors of genocide, or personal and political trauma, cannot be safely tied up or fully explained? This is a question that many of these texts indirectly (and at times directly) address. Adrienne Kertzer explores this conundrum in relation to Holocaust literature directed at children by suggesting that such literature often allows readers to close the book and leave with a message of hope, something that is entirely inconsistent with the lived experiences of genocide ("Words" 23–24, 29). Indeed, this final message of hope is often a convention that points to its intended youth readership. Expectations of a happy ending are something that Kertzer struggles with as a critic, asserting that North American children's historical fiction is "desperate to find some optimism, some way of writing about the Holocaust as an adventure; the result is a literature that focuses on the exceptional: the survivor story, the rescuer story" (*Voice* 38). Noting tendencies in children's Holocaust literature to modify truths about the genocide, she suggests that such developments point to a longing for a new and different story, for "memoirs that impress us, not because they are historically accurate, but because they resemble the patterns of fiction" ("Words" 24). Children's picture books about the Holocaust provide consolations of a shaping narrative order, focusing on survivor and rescuer narratives and especially on hopeful resolutions, conventions that in turn signify that the narrative is "suitable" for young readers.

Kenneth Kidd's assertion that Holocaust picture books are the "primal scene" of kids' trauma literature, one that addresses the tension between invisibility and representation, gets to the heart of the matter about reading and representing trauma for young readers. Balancing this need for traumatic stories to be told is an implicit worry about protecting children from difficult subject matter or overly simplifying subjects by imposing an optimistic ending. This is a challenge that directly affects the telling and the packaging of these texts in general. As graphic "narratives" per se, comics point to the process involved in shaping life stories into a literary and visual whole and invite readers to reflect not simply on the crises that these comics describe but also *how* and *why* the text tells its story in the manner that it does. Nina Mickwitz invites readers to reflect on the limitations involved in comics about migrants and refugees, especially, since "all strategies and representational schemes are partial and imperfect" ("Telling" 286). In the case of these three comics about child soldiers, the particularly inventive visual approaches to narrating historical catastrophes disallow a mask of invisibility and unspeakability, promoting social justice by exposing abuses of power.

Childhood is a predominantly Western concept and is a lived reality that transforms in relation to war, a social and political crisis. "Violence, conflict, and war challenge received, normative understandings about the 'nature' of children and boundaries of childhood," Daniel Cook and John

Wall assert at the beginning of their collection about children and armed conflict (1). In such instances, children live through the traumas of war and often become actively involved in the conflict. They are not the visions of perfect innocence and purity (clichés that childhood studies and children's literature specialists have been dismantling for the past twenty years).[3] More children's literature foregrounds this new conception of childhood as active and agentic, endowed with personal and political rights not just on a local but also on a global scale. This is the fundamental purpose of children's literature, as Kim Reynolds defines it in *Radical Children's Literature*: literature that contributes to the social and aesthetic transformations of culture by encouraging young readers to think about ideas from new perspectives in the interests of producing change (1). Reynolds points out that much of the "symbolic potential of childhood" stems from the fact that youngsters have most of their choices still in front of them (2). Although writing for children has often been the focus for those looking to disseminate new world views, values, or social models (Puritan values, for example, in the eighteenth century), children's literature has often provided a space for writers, illustrators, and publishers to play with and contest cultural norms, introducing radical and innovative ideas (Reynolds 2–3). Crisis comics are part of this practice.

Graphic narratives about particular challenges, predicaments, and crises thus provide a radical platform from which to empower readers about their own human rights and responsibilities and to educate them about attitudes and values that are necessary for the promotion and protection of the rights

---

3. From the 1980s onward, groups of children at risk have sounded an alarm on a global scale, complicating Western conceptions of childhood. The prominence of "child victims"—street children in Jakarta, child soldiers in the DRC, children involved in the commercial sex trade, and AIDS orphans—in media and human rights campaigns have come to symbolize, for many, the Global South. Because in the primarily Western public imagination these at-risk children have come to represent *all* children in the Global South, such assumptions help "to construct an image of the majority world as uncaring, incompetent and in need of intervention by the minority world" (Ansell 155). Even more worryingly, images of these at-risk young people "solicit our gaze in order to engage us in an immediate and paternalistic relationship with the famine victim (almost always a child) that displaces not only the [Global South] parent as a figure of competence and efficacy, but also the very possibility of a future for the [Global South]" (Batty 18). In the process, the "child victim" as a recipient of Western empathy and assistance reinforces colonialist ideas about hierarchical divisions between developed and developing countries and peoples (Batty 24). Wendy Hesford concurs and notes the irony inherent in the US's ratification of the two Optional Protocols of the UNCRC—the one about involvement of children in armed conflict, and the other about the sale of children, child prostitution, and child pornography—but its refusal to ratify the UNCRC document as a whole and thereby to acknowledge the violence against children that is being committed on American soil (*Exceptions* 124). Most, if not all, of the comics that this study examines refute this narrative of victimhood that has too often marginalized young people in sociopolitical and literary discourse.

of others. Frequently, in earlier picture books for children, narrative and visual structures communicated ideas about participation rights to young people—rights to be seen *and* heard—and engaged children in participatory reading and learning experiences (Todres and Higinbotham 42). Contemporary picture books like *Click, Clack, Moo* and *Harold and the Purple Crayon* feature settings and stories for the child reader to observe and experience characters voicing their need and right to be heard. As in the case of *Harold*, some picture books "place the child *into* the story as creator of the story itself," foregrounding a figure through whom the author can investigate the relationship between personal and aesthetic experience (Todres and Higinbotham 43). Similarly, graphic texts ably communicate difficult ideas, paving the way for new and complex concepts to be called into language.

## Children in/at War:
### *Child Soldier* and *War Brothers*

The publishing industry and internet are full of images, autobiographical testimonies, journalistic reports, novels, and films (fictional and documentary) of children directly involved in armed conflict. As Nicola Ansell reminds us, "Child soldiers have attracted intense attention for two key reasons: the changing character of war and changing understandings of childhood" (165).[4] The very juxtaposition of the terms "child" and "soldier" is unsettling

---

4. The concept of child soldiers is not a recent one. David Rosen (2005) traces this phenomenon back to the Middle Ages, when boys were routinely recruited by the military. In the late nineteenth century, various institutions systematized the recruitment of young men for war: In Great Britain, the Royal Hibernium Military School was founded in 1765, and the Royal Military Asylum was established in 1803 by the Duke of York. Among the Royal Hibernium Military School's earliest recruits were twelve- and thirteen-year-old boys, who were placed in regiments and served under General Thomas Gage in 1774 to suppress the growing American Revolution (D. Rosen 4). The American Civil War was "a war of boy soldiers" (5), as Rosen characterizes it: Boys were sometimes recruited at school and in other instances were brought to recruitment centers by their parents. Supporting roles that they held at first quickly transformed into combat roles. Rosen estimates that between 250,000 and 420,000 boy soldiers served in the Union and Confederate armies alone (5). He employs these statistics to suggest that the concept of child soldiers as victims of war is a modern one. This new concept, he continues, is part of a tendency to criminalize war and to identify the military and associated cultural and social links with criminality and/or deviancy (9).

In 2000 the UN Optional Protocol on the Involvement of Children in Armed Conflict was added to the UNCRC document, designating child soldiers as those who "directly" participated in armed conflict, with minimal recognition of those who were "indirectly" involved (particularly girls, recruited as sex slaves, subjected to rape and forced marriage, serving as unwilling domestic aids and cooks; Hesford, *Exceptions* 128).

because the terms evoke conflicting—ostensibly incompatible—images: "Child" refers to "a number of varied realities" that are dependent on age, sex, geography, and culture; "soldier" refers to everything from armies, rebel groups, conscripted minors, and/or voluntary recruits, "with distinct motivations and subjectivities" (Martins 434). Wendy Hesford describes the "crisis temporality" of the child soldier, positioned between child as victim and as lethal danger, all in relation to the lived experience of genocide ("Vulnerabilities" 73). In all respects, the child soldier calls into question Western expectations about the constitution of the child and the condition of childhood itself. "Clearly, what is at stake here is the political agenda that is created by interlinking both terms: one that underlines vulnerability and the need for protection with another that connotes extreme violence" (Martins 435). In fact, as Wendy Hesford, Nicola Ansell, and Daniel Cook and John Wall suggest, representations of child soldiers as victims, vulnerable and exploited, may in fact be silencing children through dominant models of persuasion and according to the political agendas of the minority world that construct the majority world as "uncivilized." For Catarina Martins, Western rhetoric about child soldiers is based on a hierarchy of values between the Global North and South: "When the North 'globalizes childhood,' imposing criteria of legality concerning the child that can hardly be applied to other cultural and social realities, the South is necessarily produced as an outlaw territory—a territory of child abuse, which carries more emotional weight than other situations of illegality" (436). This epistemological position leads to a "neocolonial civilizing mission," lending it the moral weight of redemption. "The moral and affective value[s] invested in a portrait of the child-soldier built upon a western notion of childhood as fragility and innocence," Martins continues, "are instrumental in reinforcing this discourse and, in turn, legitimizing imperial domination by the North over the South" (444).

Not all child soldiers are victims, Nicola Ansell reminds readers. Some volunteer for a number of reasons: out of intimidation and fear, as a chance to escape poverty, as a result of unemployment or domestic violence, out of a desire to seek adventure, or out of a sense of political cause (166–67). Other pressures for children to become soldiers include the loss of families and caregivers, the loss of access to food and money, a desire for revenge, ideological and religious commitments, and a desire to save one's self. Thus, the occurrence of children involved in armed conflict, as a lived phenomenon and as a humanitarian crisis, is anything but simple and transparent and often features the dichotomous experiences of young people around the world as "victimized and agentive, traumatized and resilient, vulnerable and empowered" (Wall and Cook 209). Wall and Cook in fact suggest that children in armed conflict are not either at risk victims or agents, but can be both (211). Comics about young people involved in armed conflict thus have a particular responsibility to bear in representing this humanitarian crisis from a nuanced perspective.

"My name is Michel Chikwanine. The story you are about to read is true. It is my story, and it is just one of thousands like it. But I want you to know that these events did not occur out of the blue and won't suddenly happen to you. Many years of war, poverty and desperation passed before people in my country resorted to the use of child soldiers" (Humphreys and Chikwanine 3). So begins *Child Soldier: When Boys and Girls Are Used in War* (2015), a first-person graphic narrative told from the perspective of Michel Chikwanine and mediated by Canadian writer and researcher Jessica Dee Humphreys, who specializes in international humanitarian, military, and children's issues.[5] *Child Soldier* is part of Citizen Kid, a collection of books published by Kids Can Press that "inform[s] children about the world and inspire[s] them to be better global citizens," as its website proclaims. The press classifies *Child Soldier* as being appropriate for readers in grades 5 to 9 (for ages ten to fourteen), which is confirmed by the book's accessible approach to the topic (it does not delve too extensively into historical and political context).

The opening words of Chikwanine's text accomplish a number of rhetorical functions in the spirit of informing and educating readers about child soldiers: They affirm the "truth" of the narrative, they point to the similarity of this particular story to many others like it, and they assure (predominantly Western) young readers that this story would not likely happen to them. This text, then, signals a divide between East and West, Global South and Global North, a dichotomy that is in turn played out visually on the first page: The retrospective narration is framed by Michel's arrival in Canada in the middle of the winter and his ensuing sense of cultural displacement. Looking off into the distance through the snowy windows in an airport, finally safe from the trauma he experienced in the DRC, Michel is in a space in which he can reflect on past experiences and share them with his readers and listeners in the present. "Then I looked up at the snow softly falling," he muses. "There were no bullets. There were no bombs" (3). Notably, *Child Soldier* repudiates the ontology of victimhood in its visualization of Chikwanine's story: He narrates while Humphreys brackets his story of enslavement by a rebel army with historical context about the lead-up to the

---

5. Humphreys coauthored two books with Roméo Dallaire: *Waiting for First Light: My Ongoing Battle with PTSD* (2016) and *They Fight Like Soldiers, They Die Like Children* (2010). Dallaire served as Force Commander on the ill-fated United Nations peacekeeping force for Rwanda between 1993 and 1994.

conflict in the DRC. Illustrator Claudia Dávila visualizes Michel's narrative, adjusting her color palette and images to suit a younger reading audience. A paratext that follows the text further attests to Chikwanine's authenticity as a soldier and as a writer.

> Michel has worked long and hard to heal from his experience as a child soldier. It is a label that was forced on him, but it is only a very small part of who he is. Michel is a student, an activist and an athlete. Today, along with researching root causes of poverty and conflict, Michel continues to share his powerful and inspiring message of hope with people all over the world. (Humphreys and Chikwanine 42)

Humphreys's affirmation emphasizes Michel's self-empowerment in spite of his horrific experiences in the DRC. She also includes a definition of child soldiers, contextual information about children involved in armed conflict, and a description of work that is currently being accomplished to address this problem at the regional, national, and international levels. Thus, *Child Soldier* positions itself as a teaching and learning tool that communicates ideas about human rights violations and engages readers in learning experiences that stretch past the practice of reading the comic itself, outreach work that is similar to the public lectures Michel himself delivers about his past.

Abruptly, the narrative switches from Michel's eventual arrival in Canada to Michel's brief personal summary of the historical and political context that shaped his country, beginning with his depiction of how local and national interests began to intersect with his own experiences of war and deprivation. The story proper begins in 1993, when Michel was living in Beni with his family: "I was five years old. There were rumblings of chaos growing in the distance, but I didn't hear them. I played soccer, I watched TV, I went to school, and I daydreamed" (Humphreys and Chikwanine 6). Growing political instability in his country quickly bleeds into Michel's everyday life; after school one Friday, he and his friend Kevin are abducted by rebel militants (see figure 1.1). Illustrator Claudia Dávila's visualization of Michel's forced initiation into the rebel militia through drugs ("Brown Brown," a mixture of gunpowder and cocaine) and the moment when he is compelled to shoot his best friend Kevin is rendered as an impressionistic swirl of confusion and chaos, perhaps a more accessible visual and narratological choice given the text's target audience of middle school readers. Pointedly, Humphreys and Dávila temporarily shift the perspective away from Michel at this crucial moment: Michel's eyes (and, in effect, those of

FIGURE 1.1. Michel is commanded to shoot. Jessica Dee Humphreys and Michel Chikwanine, *Child Soldier: When Boys and Girls Are Used in War*. Illustrated by Claudia Dávila. Citizen Kid, 2015, p. 18.

the text's readers) are blindfolded before the act of violence, the horror of Michel's murderous act implied rather than depicted explicitly. Kevin's bare foot and misaligned flip-flops imply his death, the horror enhanced by Michel's matter-of-fact statement: "Kevin was lying in front of me in a pool of blood. I had been forced to kill my best friend" (19; see figure 1.2). Humphreys and Dávila's stylistic choices speak to the remediations that writer and artist in the Global North make to the lived experience of a young

FIGURE 1.2. Michel is forced to shoot. Jessica Dee Humphreys and Michel Chikwanine, *Child Soldier: When Boys and Girls Are Used in War*. Illustrated by Claudia Dávila. Citizen Kid, 2015, p. 19.

person in the Global South, shaping it to suit the expectations of their particular age group of readers, readers who (arguably) have little prior knowledge about child combatants.

The cover illustration of *Child Soldier* suggests this tension concerning the depiction of graphic violence for middle school readers. Five silhouettes of boy soldiers who walk against a backdrop of a jungle at sunset jar against the traumas that these youngsters endure after their abduction, traumas that define them, for the time being. This stark contrast reflects the textual and visual collaboration that Chikwanine, Humphreys, and Dávila perform in delicately representing the unspeakable horrors that these youngsters endure. "Each day was hard and terrible," Michel explains, "filled with fear, torture and death. From the moment the sun came up, we were forced to carry heavy packs and weapons, to run, to fight, to kill" (21). References to violence and killing occur in Michel's narrative proper, as opposed to on the visual plane, refusing to reference the horror through grisly visuals. Michel's description of the "threats, drugs, amputations, killing" (23) that they endured for two weeks, and then the suggestive words "and worse," evoke trauma through understatement. The text also avoids addressing the sexual exploitation of young girls. Perhaps also because of its target audience of middle school readers, Chikwanine's narrative does not address the rape and enslavement of girls and women that frequently occurs by these rebel militants.

*Child Soldier* briefly addresses the challenging process of reintegrating child soldiers into their communities because of the suspicion and fear that people around them feel. Nicola Ansell's research confirms that the demobilization of child soldiers is especially difficult because of the "stigma and rejection" they face due to the active role they played in armed conflict. "In parts of West Africa, youths are feared and believed to be out of control, fuelled by frustration, lack of education and easy access to both drugs and weapons" (Ansell 168). In Angola and Mozambique, they are understood to be contaminated by the spirits of the dead and are thus perceived as a threat to society (168). Many undergo rehabilitation programs to help them reintegrate into their communities, both to assist with their own psychosocial healing and also to make members of their communities become more aware of the stigma and rejection that they often direct at these survivors. After escaping from the rebels, Michel tells his readers: "But nothing could erase what had happened. I didn't know who I was anymore. I didn't want to play with other children. I didn't want to play at all" (30). Michel also acknowledges that his father wanted to "give [him] back [his] childhood. But he couldn't" (30). One of the many difficulties occasioned by the recruitment of child soldiers concerns the question of responsibility, since many are forcibly recruited and made to commit horrific acts of violence. Michel's experiences of brutality, bloodshed, and personal trauma shatter Western associations of childhood with innocence, especially because of the personal role he plays in Kevin's murder. Humphreys's text visualizes the dichotomy of child soldier as both victim and agent. Not surprisingly, given its place in the Citizen Kid collection, Chikwanine's narrative is eventually framed as a success story, refusing the narrative of victimhood by emphasizing its protagonist's important activist work spent educating people in the Global North on the traumas that afflict children and youth back home.

Chikwanine's retrospective narration emphasizes his development as an empowered person in spite of his traumatic experiences. By exposing the enslavement and abuse he suffered, Michel encourages readers to empathize with a victim-perpetrator, using personal experience to convey the diverse experiences that people endure elsewhere and also to inspire them to realize that they can take an active role in events (traumatic and not) that shape them personally. Chikwanine and Humphreys frame this narrative as a story of social responsibility. Michel's final message to the reader is the advice his father gave him: "Remember, Michel, a great person is not described by their money or success . . . But rather by their heart and what they do for others" (39). Chikwanine reveals that most of his family sought out shelter in Canada, except his older sister Viviane, who never made it out of the DRC, and his father, who was poisoned by enemies in Uganda. Michel's final words speak to his need to communicate his story and encourage activism among young people: "So I share my story, as painful as it is for me to tell and as sad as it is for you to hear. In doing so, I have discovered that people do care! I am part of a movement of young people who want to help, who are passionate and who will take action so that what happened to me will not happen to the children of the future" (40). Michel's experiences make him a model of agentic subjectivity for readers because of his experiences as a child soldier.

Chikwanine's testimony uses narrative interiority to evoke sympathetic identification for child soldiers. It focuses the reader on a single case rather than on general reportage in an effort to humanize this crisis, while resisting specifics to make the narrative accessible to a broad range of middle school readers. Sharon E. McKay and Daniel Lafrance's *War Brothers, The Graphic Novel* (2013) addresses an older audience (ages fourteen and up), provides more social and historical detail, and attempts to visualize several contrasting experiences of child soldiers using a collective protagonist (Jacob, Tony, Paul, and Norman). Based on interviews in Gulu, Uganda, *War Brothers* is the fictionalized life narrative of Jacob, a member of the Acholi tribe. Paratextual elements situate the reader geographically and offer testimony of the abuse and violence that Joseph Kony, leader of the Lord's Resistance Army (LRA), and his forces routinely direct at young people. A map of Africa and of Uganda in particular as well as a letter that Jacob wrote to his young readers introduce them to Kony and his army of abducted children, who seek to fight the Ugandan government and create a country of Christians called

"Acholiland."[6] "My story is not an easy one to tell, and it is not an easy one to read," Jacob observes, anticipating his reader's reactions. "The life of a child soldier is full of unthinkable violence and brutal death. But this is also a story of hope, courage, friendship, and family. We Ugandans believe that family is most important. I thought you should be prepared for both the bad and the good. There is no shame in closing this book now" (McKay and Lafrance 2). Jacob's personal testimony provides a sense of immediacy, making reference to particular acts of violence that he has committed, thus deepening the narrative's authenticity for a reader. As with *Child Soldier*, *War Brothers* refutes the ontology of victimhood by affirming the importance of family, friendship, courage, and smart choices that eventually saved Jacob. His handwritten letter and the sentiment with which it concludes—that a reader could close the book if they are not ready to absorb its lessons—also invites a reader into the reading experience while warning about the violence that the story will describe.

In contrast to Chikwanine and Humphreys's *Child Soldier*, which communicates through suggestion rather than specifics, *War Brothers* visualizes the violence and trauma of abduction, the deep hues of color capturing its intensity. This graphic text vividly communicates the anxiety that the Acholi tribe feels about the festering political unrest in their country of Uganda and about Kony, the terrorist who is attacking members of his own tribe and abducting children to be used in his violent cause. (Elder Musa Henry Torac has lost his grandson to Kony, whom Jacob and his friends eventually meet and come to know as "Lizard"). The power of McKay and Lafrance's text lies arguably in its visualizations of the abduction and horrors the boys experience, although the text finally concludes with a faint message of hope. The comic begins, conventionally, in medias res; the reader is immediately disoriented by the image of a terrified young boy, Jacob, hiding in the grass, machete in hand, waiting for a convoy of soldiers to arrive. First-person narration encourages the reader to sympathize (if not identify) with Jacob. The black gutters that separate the panels and the somber palette "braid" (Groensteen) together to create a sense of ominous anxiety as the convoy arrives and another young boy opens fire on the truck with his AK-47 rifle, forcing it to overturn, and then mercilessly murders the driver. Jacob realizes in horror that the convoy is full of women and schoolchildren, not government soldiers as they had been told. The rebel militia separates the children from their mothers, murdering the women without provocation. Gutters and

---

6. Joseph Kony has been accused of abducting children to become child soldiers and sex slaves. Approximately 66,000 children became soldiers, servants, and wives to LRA commanders. In 2005 Kony was indicted by the International Criminal Court for war crimes and crimes against humanity. He has never been captured.

panels quickly become less regular and stable as McKay and Lafrance capture the sense of horror and despair that Jacob quickly comes to feel when ordered by the rebel leader to "kill the mother" (9). Panel after panel feature close-ups of Jacob's face as he wrestles with this order, the increasing violence of the leader pushing him to terrible actions. Bearing in mind Groensteen's discussion of the "expressive" margin—"in playing with diverse parameters, [the margin can] inform the contents of the page and inflect its perception" (33)—Jacob's deep disgust and horror at his actions, which bleed across his whole psyche, are communicated by the black margins that are pushed to the side. The image becomes all-encompassing for the reader.

Also striking in its visualization of violence is the sequence in which the children are abducted. Twenty-seven arresting panels slow down the reader's experience of the story, in the process enhancing the horror and encouraging the reader to identify with the Ugandan boys. Close-ups of an axe hacking through a locked dormitory door and the terror in the boys' faces deepen their sense of vulnerability. Each child appears in separate panels to enhance his personal sense of horror and the physical abuse that he suffers from the rebel leader. Jacob's loss of consciousness after being hit by a rifle butt is conveyed by the predominantly black page, which features two speech bubbles that seem to materialize out of the darkness. The page's special configuration calls attention to the effects of the physical assault on Jacob himself. The boys are still buoyed by hope that their parents will come looking for them, but the darkening sky on two full-panel pages suggests otherwise. Over the course of thirty-three successive panels, McKay and Lafrance's graphic narrative visualizes the brutalities to which the children are exposed: endless walks, starvation, physical and emotional abuse—the severity of this abuse captured in a visual assault of violent images. In contrast to *Child Soldier*, *War Brothers* also acknowledges the wives of the soldiers, who are off-limits to the boys, and presents Hannah, a young woman whose ears have been cut off after trying to escape and who now cooks and attends to the leaders of the LRA, as the embodiment and emblem of the violence committed against women by these rebel militias. Similarly, although *Child Soldier* tries to provide minimal visualizations of violence and trauma, McKay and Lafrance's text refrains from tempering the personal responsibility that a young person bears in the murders of his friends, focusing instead on the psychological trauma that such forced activities in turn produce. One of the friends from school, Tony, is deeply damaged emotionally after he is forced to murder another boy, Adam. Temporality is effectively manipulated: In the visual equivalent of slow motion, panel after panel multiply to extend the reading experience of Tony's act of murder. The panic and terror that accompany this act, which leave him a shadow of his former self, are

FIGURE 1.3. Tony is isolated from his fellow abductees. Sharon E. McKay and Daniel Lafrance, *War Brothers: The Graphic Novel*. Annick Press, 2013, p. 59.

starkly expressed (see figure 1.3). The horror of Tony's actions is enhanced by the knowledge that readers had gained previously: Tony was hoping to become a priest after finishing his studies at the George Jones Seminary (the boys had been abducted from the school). To communicate Tony's profound psychological distress, McKay and Lafrance separate Tony visually and spatially on the page to signal his difference from the other boys and to contrast his tormented isolation with the brotherhood, friendship, and loyalty that the other abducted youngsters demonstrate for one another.

Part of the narrative strength of *War Brothers* is the diversity of perspectives that governs the narrative, showing multiple psychological responses to the armed conflict that the young people witness and thereby avoiding the transformation of perpetrator to victim so typical of literary

FIGURE 1.4. Depictions of a displaced persons camp. Sharon E. McKay and Daniel Lafrance, *War Brothers: The Graphic Novel.* Annick Press, 2013, p. 68–69.

representations of child soldiers consumed by Western audiences (see figure 1.4). Jacob eventually makes friends with Hannah, who tells him about the deaths of her family and her life spent living in a displaced persons camp in Gulu. Impressionistic images wind around the pages, representing Hannah's arduous journey to the camp, her frequent attempts to rebuff men's sexual harassment, and her eventual abduction by the LRA. Silhouettes of displaced peoples imply the vast number of people who have been relocated by governmental policies or fear. Hannah's refusal of Jacob's sympathy over her lost ears reminds readers (and Jacob) about her refusal of victimhood: "I am lucky and I am strong," she insists. "As long as I do not get sick, I will live and I will escape, one day!" (70). Tellingly, Hannah agrees to help Jacob and his friends escape the camp: She distracts the commanders, giving the boys time to rescue Norman, who is being kept in another section of the camp.

Like Michel Chikwanine's *Child Soldier*, *War Brothers* visualizes the process of rehabilitation the boys endure while they are interrogated and receive medical treatment and psychological support. In a striking sequence that

FIGURE 1.5. The rehabilitation process. Sharon E. McKay and Daniel Lafrance, *War Brothers: The Graphic Novel*. Annick Press, 2013, p. 144.

braids together different expectations that are projected onto the "returnees," the boys are rendered as shadows, husks of their former selves. They are tended to by military officials, police, and social workers but struggle to cope with the traumas they have endured and, more specifically, with the doctors' advice to "forgive [them]selves" (144; see figure 1.5). The boys in this text are regarded with suspicion and fear by all, separated in word and image from the people around them, overwhelmed by their fear, shame, and anger. James Kelley observes that child soldiers suffer from high levels of guilt, which in turn lead them to be at risk of developing PTSD and other mental and emotional disorders (97). Even upon their return, abductees (like the fictionalized characters in *War Brothers*) remain "fighters," only this time they fight against the memories they retain, the guilt of inaction or fear, and they fight for survival and even the guilt of surviving (Kelley 102). The ending of *War Brothers* is similar to that of *Child Soldier* in its cautious optimism: Both narrators speak from positions of relative empowerment, eventually using their traumatic experiences to educate listeners and readers from the Global North. Michel does so through speaking engagements; the character of Jacob, through his writing. *War Brothers* concludes with family, both biological and chosen, suggesting that this is a central healing factor: Hannah returns to visit Jacob, years later, and he reminds her that even though she lacks a biological family, he is her family now. Their shared experiences of trauma have ended in a strong connection, like the one that he shares with his "war brothers." McKay and Lafrance's graphic text, like *Child Soldier*, visualizes for young Western readers a humanitarian crisis that targets young people in Uganda yet also educates them about different experiences that children have the world over. And all the while, the books negotiate the slippery distinction between victim and perpetrator.

## Representing Unimaginable Violence: *Deogratias* and Ethical Ambiguity

Jean-Philippe Stassen's *Deogratias, A Tale of Rwanda* (2000 in French; 2006 in English) is uncompromising in its visualization of war crimes in Africa, using the comics form to address an audience of even older readers (ages fourteen to eighteen and up). The text, a twist on the coming-of-age story, presents fictional protagonist Deogratias (whose name means "Thanks be to God") in 1994, leading up to the Rwandan genocide. The author is a Belgian comics creator who currently lives and works in Rwanda. *Deogratias* is a graphic narrative that relies less on personal testimony than on the protest mode, wearing "its cause on its sleeve, reading as a manifesto or prophetic indictment" (Galchinsky 71). Unflinchingly, it exposes the Rwandan genocide, relying on visual representations of extreme forms of suffering (e.g., mass graves, executions, rapes) to make its arguments—its outrage at ethnic cleansing—seen and heard. In 2000 the text won the René Goscinny award; it was also included on the 2007 Young Adult Library Services Association (YALSA) Great Graphic Novels for Teens list. The text's older reading audience is signaled by the opening paratext: A lengthy introduction written by translator Alexis Siegel provides both a summary of Rwanda's colonial history leading up to the genocide of 1994; the extermination of the Tutsi minority by the country's majority ethnic group, the Hutu; and a general introduction to Stassen's comic. Deogratias survives the genocide but remains shattered by it psychologically; Stassen's empathetic narrative encourages the reader to view the acts of violence that Deogratias commits more sympathetically. "This is the tale of Deogratias, one young man caught up in events that no human being should ever have had to experience," Siegel suggests.

> Stassen's compassionate narration and his beautifully expressive artwork enable us to imagine the unimaginable, in a way that few will forget. We come through the fire of that experience a better person, I feel, because it is only through deep, heartfelt understanding that we have a chance to overcome—within ourselves, first—the false divisions that have brought such horrors into the world. And find reasons to hope.

This final message of hope that Siegel claims readers will take away with them is debatable and is perhaps more emblematic of Global Northern readers' cravings for satisfying narrative closure. In truth, the ambiguous ending to Stassen's graphic narrative is particularly haunting, leaving unanswered and deeply troubling questions about colonialism and its legacy of ethnic violence in Africa.

Stassen's *Deogratias, A Tale of Rwanda* is a more immediately challenging text than *War Brothers* and *Child Soldier*, leaving the reader unclear for much of the narrative about how to view the troubled protagonist (see figure 1.6). Ambiguity is generated by the very first panel of the text: It features a close-up of Deogratias, with torn T-shirt and wide, feral eyes. This close-up of a traumatized older boy suggests that Deogratias has lived through the genocide in Rwanda, but the extent of his experiences remains a terrible secret that Stassen's graphic text withholds until the very end. Periods both pre- and postgenocide are juxtaposed by means of black frames that distinguish

FIGURE 1.6. The opening close-up of Deogratias. Jean-Philippe Stassen, *Deogratias: A Tale of Rwanda*. Translated by Alexis Siegel. First Second, 2006, p. 1.

the panels and entire sequences that take place after the killings. In this way, Stassen visualizes and dramatizes traumatic memory through the coexistence and tension between present and past on the same page. Deogratias's haunted face in the present opens the narrative; his terror-filled, staring eyes engage the eyes of the reader, even inviting them to sympathize with and possibly identify with him, though they are left wondering what happened in the past to occasion this state. Deogratias's muteness in the present, his inability to speak about his experiences, produces a profoundly terrible silence, leaving the reader to their own thoughts and fears. His silence also avoids spectacularization: Rather than meditating freely about the genocide, Deogratias prevents a reader from too easily consuming this narrative of trauma, torture, execution, and war while also leaving one at the mercy of one's own imagination and fears. As the text progresses, "retroactive resignification" occurs (Postema, *Narrative* 113): Stassen weaves back and forth between past and present to create plot out of the gaps, eventually positioning the protagonist as perpetrator. Unlike *Child Soldier* and *War Brothers*, Stassen's comic avoids providing readers with the comfort that a survivor narrative typically offers because, although present-day Deogratias is undeniably alive, his psyche has been irrevocably damaged due to his complicity in horrific acts of violence.

At first, in the present, the cockroaches on the wall of the bar behind a French army sergeant allude to the derogatory slurs that Hutus used to address Tutsis, slurs that devalued the humanity of an entire population and helped to rationalize genocidal violence.[7] In his traumatized state, Deogratias receives conflicting responses from the people who interact with him, anticipating the personal role he played in the killing. Although the manager of the restaurant beats him away with a stick, the French army sergeant, Bosco, greets Deogratias as a long-lost friend, though he quickly shows himself to be racist and misogynistic in the degrading language that he uses to describe two Tutsi women who pass by the bar. Deogratias's stunned silence amplifies the French sergeant's inhumanity, which reminds the boy of the past and fuels his decision to begin to poison the sergeant. At the outset, Stassen's graphic text undoubtedly employs "strategic narrative empathy" to establish Deogratias as a victim caught up in a war that was not of his own making (Keen 145). At first the text appears to focus on the horrors of the Rwandan genocide; as it progresses, the uniqueness of Stassen's book lies in its attempt to visualize the ambiguous role that the youthful perpetrator plays. Stassen's graphic and fictional representation of historical atrocity allows previously marginalized voices to come to the foreground in the representation of this particular historical moment.

Every character's position is as conflicted and confused in relation to the ethnic violence as that of Deogratias. Stassen's text thus avoids simplifying a deeply complex world event. Ultimately, local and global intersect; the adolescent characters (Deogratias and his two female friends, sisters Apollinaria and Benina) find themselves caught up in the conflict. Deogratias's youthful desperation for his first sexual encounter prompts him to proposition his two Tutsi female friends (first Apollinaria and then Benina) until one expresses interest in him. The increasing flashbacks to these young women and to Deogratias's present state of trauma intimate the terrible story that is waiting to be told as Deogratias wanders the countryside looking for Urwagwa (banana beer) to deaden his paralyzing sense of guilt. The panels of the comic narrow noticeably when depicting Deogratias as he experiences his posttraumatic stress. Sounds of dogs barking provoke a fugue in which he finds himself reliving the horrors of the ethnic cleansing: "My head is spilling out. Dogs! The dogs are eating the bellies," he moans frantically as memories of Apollinaria and Benina's shocking deaths return to him (Stassen 26). These sounds in turn initiate his shrinking in physical stature so

---

7. Before the killings, Radio Télévision Libre des Mille Collines broadcasted anti-Tutsi propaganda, referring to the Tutsis (and others considered to be enemies of Hutu nationalism) as "Inyenzi" (cockroaches; Arseneault 128). This derogatory term not only served to justify the genocide of the Tutsis as pests that must be eliminated; it also enforced the sovereignty of the Hutu nation state.

that he comes to resemble a dog, eventually dropping to the ground and crawling on all fours. For one significant panel, Stassen allows readers to look from Deogratias's terrified perspective, approximating the psychological trauma that he lives with daily. By separating Deogratias's thoughts from the panel visuals, Stassen conveys the fracturing of his young protagonist's psyche (a large rectangular panel depicting a seemingly beautiful night sky also implies the terror that the sky provokes in him). Deogratias loses consciousness, suggested by the whiteness of the rest of the page.

A key moment in Stassen's text occurs when the plane carrying Rwandan president Habyarimana (as well as the president of Burundi) is shot down on 6 April 1994, apparently by the Rwandan Patriotic Front. This event propels the genocide forward. Carefully orchestrated plans for the mass killings of Tutsis are launched by incendiary radio broadcasts. This event occurs the night that Deogratias and Benina consummate their relationship. Deogratias, fearing for his lover's life, shelters her in his home to protect her from the violence that she will surely encounter outside. Eventually, however, Benina insists on finding her mother, Venetia, and sister, Apollinaria, and Deogratias, in a fit of anger, tries to use force to control Benina: "Since you don't want to be reasonable, I'll save you in spite of you: every morning, I'll lock you up!" he yells at her (64). Soon after, Deogratias finds himself circulating among other ordinary Hutus who become caught up in the ethnic violence. Crucially, Stassen's comic presents few graphic and bloody images; thus, the three small panels that visualize the rape and murder that all three women later suffer at the hands of a group of Hutus produce an immediate impact of horror in readers. As Michelle Bumatay and Hannah Warman argue, "The understatement of acts of violence serves to avoid desensitization" (335). Increasing flashbacks represent Deogratias's role in Benina and Apollinaria's degradation. We see his grief and descent into madness following their deaths—to the point that he believes that he is a dog. Stassen's coming-of-age story transforms into a confession narrative in the closing pages of the comic, when Deogratias happens upon Brother Philip, a European missionary once affiliated with his church. In conversation with his friend, Stassen's protagonist relates the final days of the girls' lives: their terrified escape, the weeks they spent sheltering in latrines as they struggled to survive. Deogratias even confesses to his own acts of revenge: poisoning everyone around him who bore some responsibility in their deaths (the French army sergeant and Julius, a leader in the Hutu militia). Through suggestion, Stassen links Benina and Apollinaria to Deogratias's psychological transformation into a dog, because he bore witness to the stray dogs scavenging their bodies after their rape and murder, acts of degradation that he himself watched passively without intervening to prevent. By representing Deogratias's canine metamorphosis, Stassen visualizes the dichotomy of beast versus "civilized" person. Collapsing the categories of human and dog are in this way similar to the categories of victim and perpetrator that the narrative also collapses. The responsibility that Deogratias bears in the young women's horrific murders is at the root of his present traumatized state; Stassen's depiction of his protagonist as an unhappy, cringing dog evokes narrative empathy (to a certain extent). Yet, affect is complicated by the fact that a collaborator has been placed at the center of the moral world of the text.

Stassen's visual and narrative representation of Deogratias's experience during the Rwandan genocide rests on a tension between responsibility and victimhood (common among young people involved in armed conflict). In this regard, Stassen refrains from ending with a message of hope, in spite of what translator Alexis Seigel asserts at the beginning of the text. Indeed, the comic ends with an "ethical anticatharsis," as Kate Polak describes it (41). Rather than tell a conventional survivor's story, Stassen tells the story of a perpetrator that leaves no room for hope, redemption, or even the reclamation of innocence. The final page of Stassen's text resists imposing closure on this profoundly disturbing narrative; instead, it leaves the narrative unresolved, with Brother Philip's sad (and deeply ambiguous) description of Deogratias after his arrest as "a creature of God" (78). Philip's unsatisfying declaration reminds readers of the position of privilege he occupies as a white man who has the ability to escape ethnic tension and who mobilizes this position of privilege to pass judgment on a youth who made unbearable choices during an unbearable time. After Brother Philip's ambiguous pronouncement, the final panel of Stassen's graphic narrative features the beautiful night sky that hovers over Rwanda (and its horrific history), the same starry sky that continues to weigh heavily on Deogratias, reminding him of his complicity in the deaths of his friends and lover. The reader is thus left to process the inventive visual and narrative approach that Stassen has taken to the Rwandan genocide, one that relies in large part on the reader's difficult and disturbing identification with the main character, walking the line between perpetrator and victim and yet never finding a way to sit comfortably with either role.

As *Child Soldier, War Brothers,* and *Deogratias* demonstrate, one of the many problems raised by the phenomenon of child soldiers concerns the question of responsibility, because many youngsters are forcibly recruited or volunteer willingly. Thus, in committing or in being forced to commit atrocious acts of violence, many armed combatants are both victimized and also directly involved in acts of violence. Ultimately, child soldiers find themselves in the midst of particular crises, assuming a harrowing agency and a particular vulnerability in the face of intolerable conflicts. These comics about child soldiers seek to approximate the complexities of this subject position without positioning these young people as objects of pity or compassion, an approach that the comics about migrants, refugees, and detainees in camps explored in chapter 2 also address.

CHAPTER 2

# Youthful Experiences of Immigration, Migration, and Diaspora

> Where writing does join cause with righting is in its creativity—its art.
>
> —Lyndsey Stonebridge, *Writing and Righting*

Increasingly, firsthand experiences of people from the Global South who seek asylum and/or legal immigrant or refugee status in North America, southwestern Europe, and Australia are a particular focus of comics (*The Unwanted: Stories of the Syrian Refugees*, *Illegal*, *The Arrival*, and *Azzi in Between*, to name a few). Migrant literature—novels, short stories, comics, and poems that feature people moving across borders, anxious to trade poverty and exploitation for the education and political freedom available elsewhere—are a part of global literature texts that remind readers how arbitrary those boundaries in fact are. As this chapter argues, graphic texts can humanize experiences of migration from the perspectives of young people and affirm their experiences of displacement and diaspora in the process. The "laboured etchings of comics journalism" help to counteract the proliferation of photographic images of violence and suffering that circulate endlessly on the internet (Davies, "Borders" 182). In a "Spotlight on Migrant and Refugee Comics," Candida Rifkind notes that key plot moments shared by these comics are typical of the migrant experience, moments that in turn enhance the precarity of this experience: "the destruction of home; the planning and negotiating escape; risky and frightening journeys" by boat, car, or on foot; "border stops and controls; the incomprehensibility of bureaucracy in general and language barriers specifically; and, the dual boredom and ingenuity of life in detention camps and prisons" (Rifkind, "Spotlight"). Comics about displaced persons and their experiences of immigration, migration, and exile often feature moments of deep trauma, distinguished by the separation of family, disappearance, and death. But these comics also "find hope in people's resilience, generosity, solidarity, efforts to build new lives" (Rifkind "Spotlight"). Comics for young readers that foreground such experiences of displacement have the potential to recover the humanity of refugees by emphasizing their individual experiences, to encourage readers to make connections between themselves and the lived experiences of other people around the world, to raise consciousness about episodes of traumatic history, and to resist considering displacement and migration through the lens of invisibility, misinformation, or bigotry. Inventive textual and visual practices are central to the comics' success. Philip Nel suggests that such tales can also serve as a mirror for displaced children's deep anxieties as they struggle with the realization that they might never find a new home: "Stories like these help, even though they are no substitute for home itself" (359).

Chapter 2 of *Growing Up Graphic* explores this new trend in comics for young readers, that is, visual texts "that document the undocumented" (Whitlock, "Implicated" 495), stories about immigration, migration, and diaspora told specifically from the perspectives of young people. Many critics address the tension in comics between a demand to document and the recognition of the ethical limits of representation; a worry about reproducing victim tropes and, in the process, depoliticizing aspects of advocacy work; and an anxiety about participating in the contemporary fascination with shocking images known as "wound culture."[1] In all instances, storytelling must be aware of its own limitations and motivations. And yet, even though "all strategies and representational schemes are partial and imperfect, [they are] nevertheless vital for communicating the refugee experience" (Mickwitz, "Telling" 286). This chapter offers a survey of comics about immigration, migration, and diaspora that are about the lives of children and that are directed at young readers. Morten Dürr and Lars Horneman's comic *Zenobia* provides insight into the current Syrian refugee crisis from the perspective of a young girl named Amina who, along with countless other migrants, flees the instability of her homeland on a precarious dingy. *Zenobia* performs a kind of "wake" work, as critical race scholar Christina Sharpe theorizes it, as it visualizes the abjection that generations of Black and diasporic peoples

---

1. See, for example, Bigelow and Singer; Davies, "Dreamlands"; Mickwitz, "Telling"; Naghibi et al.; Rifkind, "Migrant"; Chute, *Disaster*; Sontag, *Pain*; Seltzer.

have endured as their basic humanity has been (and continues to be) devalued. Likewise, Shaun Tan's *The Arrival* and Matt Huynh's digital adaptation of Nam Le's short story "The Boat" provide two other case studies of particular experiences of migration as depicted in graphic literature for young readers. Huynh's digital adaptation emphasizes many of the harrowing elements of migration but, as with *Zenobia*, leaves readers with a sense of dynamism and life in direct response to the death and dissolution that too frequently await displaced peoples. *Baddawi* and *They Called Us Enemy* offer two distinct visual approaches to experiences that young people had in displacement camps in the Global South and North, respectively. Both reject representing refugees as passive victims waiting to be "saved," insisting instead on refugees as bearers of human rights, as individuals who are shaped by historical and political circumstances. In all of these texts about immigration, migration, and diaspora, the undocumented become "visible actors," and readers are summoned to account, as Gillian Whitlock puts it, "as implicated subjects, as beneficiaries, as activists" ("Implicated" 499).

## On the Move:
## Migration in *Zenobia*, *The Arrival*, and "The Boat"

Development organizations are very concerned about what they refer to as "children on the move" and the wider impacts that migration has on young people (Ansell 444). Since 2015, according to the International Rescue Committee, the world has been in the middle of the largest social and spatial displacement of people in over twenty-five years. In April 2018, for example, an estimated 13.1 million Syrian nationals were made homeless by civil war; 5.6 million sought refuge outside Syria. In fact, the most recent United Nations High Commissioner for Refugees (UNHCR) statistics place the total of forcibly displaced persons worldwide at 89.3 million (2021). Of the 27.1 million refugees within this number, around half are under the age of eighteen. The stakes of this problem are high. According to Europol, the law-enforcement agency of the European Union, more than 10,000 migrant and refugee children have gone missing in Europe since 2014 (Collins), prey to people smugglers and human-trafficking groups that exploit them for money, sex, and/or slavery. This situation is not limited to Europe, however. The United States Department of Health and Human Services "admitted that it had lost track of 1,475 children who had crossed the US–Mexico border [seeking asylum and that] some of those children are now believed to be in the hands of human traffickers" (Nel 358). Western assumptions about stable, protected childhoods therefore conflict with the lived experiences of migrating and refugee children (Ansell 444).

Humanizing these statistics often requires visual as well as textual information, and comics attempt to accomplish this. Written for readers between the ages of six and twelve and endorsed by Amnesty International UK, *Azzi in Between* (2012), Sarah Garland's comic, tells the story of Azzi and her parents, who, displaced by war, are forced to relocate to an unnamed country by boat, leaving Azzi's grandmother behind. Garland's text relies on a number of moments that are typical of refugee experiences—a sudden and harrowing boat trip across the ocean, an overwhelming sense of cultural dislocation upon arrival in a foreign land, anxieties about acceptance, and worries about those left behind. Thanks to her school environment, Azzi learns the language and begins to acclimatize to the new country, making friends and sharing her cultural traditions with her classmates at school. The overwhelming message that this text leaves with a young reader is hope, as the entire family eventually reunites in the new country.

Not all migrant comics end so optimistically, however. In *An Olympic Dream: The Story of Samia Yusuf Omar* (2016), Reinhard Kleist relates the tragic story of an Olympian who represented Somalia in the 200-meter sprint in the 2008 Beijing Olympic games and who made the difficult decision to leave Mogadishu afterward because she could not train properly there as a female athlete. Mogadishu was controlled by the Al-Shabaab militia, who threatened to kill her (as they had killed her father previously) because the family did not adhere to Sharia law, a body of law that forms part of the Islamic tradition and that does not value the human rights of women and girls. Determined to find a way for Samia to travel first to Addis Ababa, Ethiopia, and then to Italy to train with the track team in the hopes of competing in the 2012 London Olympic games as a way to support her family back in Somalia, Samia and her Aunt Mariam consider alternative options to get to Europe. Relying on people smugglers, Samia boards a rickety boat, which was turned around midway through the voyage by Italian officials, and she (and the rest of the passengers) are taken to a displaced persons camp. Thirty-two panels on two adjoining pages convey the different stages of incarceration that she endures in this camp: line-ups for processing, numerous interrogation sessions, incarceration in a cell, and, finally, arrival at a camp where her wait to get to Europe continues (see figure 2.1). Throughout this ordeal, Samia wears a T-shirt that bears the slogan "run," an ironic commentary on her motivation for this trip and her need to flee the oppressive conditions that she and her family endure in Somalia. Samia's eventual boarding of another rubber dingy destined for Italy with a group of

FIGURE 2.1. Samia at a displacement camp. Reinhard Kleist, *An Olympic Dream: The Story of Samia Yusuf Omar*. SelfMadeHero, 2016, p. 109.

migrants does not end positively. Although the graphic text arrives at closure with a splash page that depicts Samia in mid-sprint—reminding readers of the hope that she associates with athleticism—she joins the legions of other migrants whose attempts at escape were unsuccessful. Similar to some of the graphic texts about child soldiers, *An Olympic Dream* avoids embodying the expectations of *"resilience humanitarianism,"* as defined by Dorothea

Hilhorst, a narrative trope that places "emphasis on individual overcoming and/or adapting to perpetual states of emergency" (Hesford, *Exceptions* 6). Many of these comics about migrants and displaced persons specifically eschew casting the young protagonists as heroes and/or victims whose stories are intended to inspire. Instead, texts such as these attempt to humanize the refugee crisis, moving it away from an abstract experience by grounding it in the individual lived experience of a young person.

Too frequently, the terms that are used to describe people who leave one country to seek another—"refugee," "asylum seeker," "economic migrant"—carry a number of connotations, more negative than positive. "Immigrant," for example, is often associated with illegality (Arizpe et al. 12). Former US president Donald Trump's three executive orders on immigration not only barred refugees but targeted asylum seekers, many of whom were children. In September 2015, images of three-year-old Alan Kurdi, who drowned with his mother and older brother while attempting to escape from the war in Syria, prompted international responses to this specific refugee crisis, helping to humanize statistics about the many people who experience migration, exile, and diaspora around the world. Media articles proliferate about migration crises, the deportation of undocumented migrants, limiting public services for the undocumented, the separation of asylum-seeking children from their families at national borders, and the construction of physical barriers. As Nina Mickwitz reminds readers, the term "crisis" conveys a sense of impermanence to the refugee experience that is simply not accurate ("Telling" 278). Lyndsey Stonebridge's *Placeless People* (2018) argues that the mass movement of people has in fact become normalized over the past century: "Refugees were—and are—the overlooked victims of modern politics. [. . .] They are the flotsam and jetsam of conflict, the unfortunate victims of history, who only constitute a 'crisis' if they get too close to home" (vii). Comics certainly encourage empathy for people on the move, but perhaps more importantly, they encourage readers to think "about rights, citizenship, and sovereignty [. . .] when the question of what it mean[s] to belong to a nation [is] at its most vexed" (Stonebridge, *Placeless* 19).

Morten Dürr and Lars Horneman's graphic narrative *Zenobia* (2018 in English; 2016 in Danish) depicts the horrors of Syrian displacement, only this time from the perspective of a young girl, Amina, whose uncle helps her to flee once the war reaches her small village and her parents are killed in the conflict. Visualized primarily by full-page panels that feature very little dialogue, *Zenobia* allows the intolerable experiences of a young refugee to stand for themselves. That the title refers to the great warrior queen of Syria, whose territory stretched from Iraq to Egypt to Turkey (267 to 272 AD) and who declared her independence from Rome, mirrors the young refugee Amina's bravery and strength in boarding the rickety fishing boat that takes her away from her homeland. Several splash pages present Zenobia in military and regal poses to convey her importance to Amina, who thinks of the ancient queen as a representation of the strength, talent, and ability of Syrian women. This figurehead, also suggestive of a more peaceful time for Syria, contrasts ironically with the present ruined state of Syria that Dürr and Horneman visualize in their comic: shelled and abandoned homes, airplanes and bombed-out tanks that litter the streets, armed officers from whom Amina and her uncle hide as they escape, dead bodies abandoned in streets that are now only inhabited by roaming dogs. Zenobia offers a very fragile and ultimately empty promise of hope in a story that, for many refugees, ends (as Amina's life does) drowned in the ocean.

The text opens with an image of a rickety boat crammed full of refugees, only a fraction of whom are wearing lifejackets (and all of those are male). Three panels on the page convey the vastness of sea and sky and the corresponding vulnerability of the boat. The boat's size spells its doom. Sure enough, as soon as they encounter turbulent seas, Amina (along with all of the other passengers) is thrown helplessly into the ocean.[2] Dürr and Horneman slow down this moment, depicting Amina as she flies out of the boat over the course of seven separate panels and then another four panels that visualize her sinking below the waves. A simple, declarative assertion—"No one can find me here" (18)—speaks to Amina's quiet acceptance of her abject fate. Her terrifying fall into the sea provokes a series of flashbacks to her past with her parents in Syria—the comfort of her mother and the games of hide and seek they played and memories of cooking dolmas—moments of connection and comfort that stand in sharp contrast with current images of Amina floating underwater. The relative safety of the domestic space and a mother who cherishes her contrast greatly with the vastness of the ocean into which she sinks. It is Amina's mother who teaches her about Zenobia, about resilience, strength, and perseverance. Zenobia offers her hope and inspiration: "If Zenobia could so can you!" (43),

---

2. Christina Sharpe's incisive analysis of anti-Black racism, *In the Wake: On Blackness and Being* (2016), invites a comparison of the abjection that migrants and diasporic peoples experience with that of Black people living "in the wake" of slavery. In the imagery of the migrant boat, Sharpe draws a parallel with the "semiotics of the slave ship" (21), ships full of people who were and are understood as nonbeings condemned to death. In the presence-absence of Amina's mother (her disappearance motivates Amina's choice to board this ship), we are reminded of generations of humans whose humanity was and is devalued and whose lives are "produced and determined, though not absolutely, by the afterlives of slavery" (Sharpe 8).

Amina reminds herself. Full pages picturing Zenobia's strength emphasize her centrality to Amina's thought process while floating in the ocean but also stand in dramatic irony when compared with Amina's young body as it sinks below the waves. By the end of the text, Zenobia has been emptied of all hope, like the wrecked vessel that rests at the bottom. In Dürr and Horneman's uncompromising text, Amina and the hundreds packed onto the fishing boat represent the millions of refugees fleeing from their homelands in search of something better, forced to rely on people smugglers who do not value their lives. Closure comes with the implied loss of Amina's life; the creators in this way do not sanitize this story of forced relocation. Readers are left to contemplate Amina's humanity rather than its denial. Thus, Dürr and Horneman humanize the brutal experiences of children on the move to acknowledge the suffering of the powerless. The comic's refusal to visualize Amina's safe arrival leaves a young reader with a sense of discomfort that can perhaps inspire them to political action.

Shaun Tan's wordless graphic narrative *The Arrival* (2006) was one of the first visual texts for young readers that explored experiences of immigration and diaspora in detail, though not from the perspective of a child. Originally conceptualized as a thirty-two-page picture book, this form quickly became insufficient for Tan's story of immigration, providing too little room for narrative continuity and detail: "The real-life immigrant stories I had been researching, full of hardship, vulnerability, and complex humanity, made my own picture book illustrations seem clumsy, simplistic, and emotionally vapid by comparison" ("Accidental" 3). For this reason, he settled on the form of the graphic narrative and enjoyed its affordances. The "experimentation, playfulness, even irreverence, when it comes to rules of form and style" that typify the graphic narrative, facilitated Tan's particularly multimodal approach to migration ("Accidental" 5). Thanks to the remarkable creative transformations that it underwent, Tan's transnational text shows in image rather than word how it crosses borders among artistic genres and cultures to tell its story of displacement and new beginnings.

The design of Tan's immigrant story undoubtedly contributes to the way in which the story makes meaning: The book is printed in the format of an old photograph album, possibly an album brought from the home country, complete with pages with worn, frayed edges; sepia photographs; and watermarks, wrinkles, and stains that decorate the individual pages. The title page resembles the inside of a passport; the "inspection card" at the bottom of the page is one of the only documents that English-speaking readers can understand. In his "Artist's Note," Tan describes how much of the book was inspired by "anecdotal stories told by migrants of many different countries and historical periods, including my father who came to Western Australia from Malaysia in 1960."

In acknowledging that some of these renderings of immigrant processing, passport pictures, and the arrival hall are based on photographs of European immigration to the US via Ellis Island, New York, from 1892 to 1954, Tan unfortunately enshrines his immigration narrative within the American experience, his visuals suggesting that this particular story of immigration is the definitive narrative of displacement. More recent graphic texts about immigration, such as Thi Bui's *The Best We Could Do* (2018), depict the arrival in America much more ambiguously, identifying the racism and economic deprivation that newcomers experience and implicitly critiquing Tan's representation of an America as a fantastical land of opportunity. Certainly, a reader's awareness of recent stories in the media about immigration into the United States also call into question Tan's implicit focus on arrival in America as "the" narrative of immigration. Tan's protagonist bypasses stereotypical tendencies to represent the migrant or immigrant as either "victim" or "threat." Rather, Tan's "arrival" is the embodiment of the American Dream, a self-made man who arrives at economic stability through his own hard work and perseverance. This idealized immigrant forms a community in his new country, finding friends who show him hospitality, warmth, and happiness. Closure comes with the arrival of the man's family from back home. The final image features his daughter in turn providing direction to another girl who has recently arrived. Thus, Tan's immigrant story balances the frightening and traumatic side of such experiences with the solidarity and hope offered by strangers and other immigrants to the "great country" of America, reinscribing a narrative that is more fiction than fact.

Wordless graphic narratives like *The Arrival* often feature narratives of misunderstanding, isolation, and displacement typical of the immigrant or displaced person's experience, specifically by means of their wordlessness. Shaun Tan addresses the particular advantages offered by wordlessness in his visual narrative: The absence of language "leaves it open to all," he affirms in reference to *The Arrival*, "not just by avoiding English (my own language) but also by ignoring levels of literacy education too, depending entirely upon pictures for meaning. I was interested in returning to an original state of observation" (Arizpe et al., xiv). In large part thanks to its wordlessness, Tan's story is accessible to many through its images and thus infinitely useful as a medium to tell a story about immigration. Barbara Postema argues that "wordless comics can be seen as a challenge to written literature while at the same time foregrounding processes of literacy that go beyond recognising letters and words" ("Following" 312). The "literacy" that wordless comics teach, then, is one in which people separated by language and culture practice "reading" one another's body language (317). As such, wordless picture books and graphic narratives like *The Arrival* require a reader's active participation in making meaning. Young readers consuming *The Arrival* can appreciate the linguistic and cultural displacement experienced by an immigrant because of the absence of contextual narrative information. Like the principal character of Tan's visual text, readers empathize with the cultural dislocation that a person would feel upon arrival in a strange, Western country because they cannot speak, read, or understand the language (spoken or written), they know no one, and they are oftentimes isolated and alone.

Little moments of alienation and isolation multiply in Tan's text. This alienation begins as soon as a reader opens the book. Tan's wordless text is actually about a variety of arrival experiences at the turn of the twentieth century: that of the principal "arrival" himself; a young woman who escaped to the city after being forcibly enslaved in her home country; a couple who fled from a totalitarian regime in Europe; and an older man who left to join the army, experienced the devastation of war (and permanent injury), and also found a home in the book's phantasmagoric city, so visually reminiscent of early twentieth-century New York City. Their particular stories, shared through "the recurring use of impromptu sign language" (Postema, "Following" 317), are bracketed by the paratexts (the document fragments on the title pages, publishing information, and blurbs) and the many passport pictures of people—men and women, young and old, from all different countries and ethnicities—that decorate the flyleaves of Tan's graphic narrative and suggest that their experiences of "arrival" share similar emotional and narrative elements (see figure 2.2). The sheer number of faces forces readers to acknowledge the diverse experiences of arrivals throughout history, gleaned from a text that does "not get hung up on words and spellings" but rather draws attention to "the active processes involved in reading and interpret[ing]" body language (Postema, "Following" 320). In the text's visual evocation of New York City, it implies that the United States of America embodies ideals of freedom and possibility. Tan's title is especially interesting, read in this context, in that it acknowledges the dehumanizing process of immigration. The principal character is defined by his "arrival" rather than by his actual name. Even more optimistically, the title enshrines the importance of the act of arriving and the moment of arrival itself. In this regard, Tan's characters are defined by the "immigrant" identity assigned to them upon arrival, a tendency that is still very much consistent with contemporary American immigration rhetoric.

FIGURE 2.2. Portraits of new immigrants. Shaun Tan, *The Arrival*. Arthur A. Levine Books, 2007.

If wordlessness is particularly well-suited to capture the spatial displacement and cultural dislocation that immigrants can experience the world over, multimodal platforms are effective also at providing an immersive experience of diaspora for readers to explore. For Jennifer Phillips, interactive graphic literature (such as Nam Le's short story "The Boat" and its online adaptation by Matt Huynh) can create empathy about the global migration crisis that is necessary to break through some of the inertia encouraged by media saturation in the age of information overload and the statistical numbing that results (150). Joseph Stalin's now infamous statement that "the death of one man is a tragedy, the death of millions is a statistic" outlines the inability of statistics to evoke empathy and feeling as well as their converse tendency to dehumanize refugees and migrants so that they become projections of fear and sometimes even loathing. Vietnamese-born Australian writer Nam Le's collection of short stories, *The Boat,* was the first in a trend-setting series of Australian transnational writing. The seven narratives in *The Boat* speak to a global literature, taking the reader to such places as Columbia, New York City, Iowa, Tehran, Hiroshima, and small-town Australia. The titular short story is informed by Le's own experiences of migration when he and his parents sailed to Australia after fleeing Vietnam. Even more importantly, because the story is told from the perspective of a young girl, Le challenges the adult-centrism of migration research and in so doing queries dominant views of migrant children as vulnerable and powerless.

The online graphic adaptation—combining brushwork, animation, text, sound, and archival images—was created by Matt Huynh, an Australian-born, New York–based visual artist and storyteller whose animation, paintings, and comics frequently interrogate war and diaspora. Refugees, asylum seekers, and migrant communities dominate his oeuvre. In combination with producer Kylie Boltin and designer Matt Smith, Huynh's animated adaptation of Le's short story "The Boat" was launched in recognition of the fortieth anniversary of the fall of Saigon and forty years of Vietnamese resettlement in Australia. It is particularly well suited for multimodal readers: Huynh's brush-and-ink paintings are informed by Eastern Sumi-e ink traditions and popular contemporary Western comic books; his hybrid aesthetic is a reflection of his global identity. Both short story and interactive comic gesture toward derogatory rhetoric about Australian "boat people" (including Australian prime minister Tony Abbott's "stop the boats" mantra during his 2013–15 leadership) but emphatically humanize the experiences of these displaced peoples, transforming and reclaiming "the term 'boat people' as a badge of honor, rather than a term of political disdain" (Phillips 155). The horrifying realities of a refugee boat on the South China Sea break through the abstract political rhetoric used about these "boat people" that debases them further.

Le and Huynh humanize the migrants by focusing on three principal characters—Mai, Truong, and Quyen. Readers grow to identify with these people, specifically through the immersive and interactive graphic mode. Mai, Truong, and Quyen are the only ones among the two hundred migrants populating the tiny boat who are given names (the lack of proper names further dehumanizing this abject human cargo). By means of the interactive graphic mode, Huynh does not provide an abstract narration of the Vietnam War and the difficult decision these characters made to flee. Instead, a representation and a performance of how these events were experienced and remembered from the perspectives of these three characters are stressed—and in turn how they are experienced by readers in the multimodal format.

Winner of a number of interactive media awards, Matt Huynh's adaptation of Le's short story is immersive, drawing a reader immediately into its harrowing tale of migration. A boat carrying hundreds of people travels from Vietnam to Australia on the South China Sea. With the click of a mouse, a reader is immediately plunged into the middle of a turbulent ocean: thunder, howling wind, and driving rain seeming to drive out of the computer screen to strike the reader. The first thing one sees is a tilted boat that barely remains afloat in the terrible storm; the reader then scrolls down to begin navigating through the story. Huynh divides Le's short story into various chapters, reproducing segments of prose exactly while superimposing them over dynamic visuals. The horrors and desperation of her situation assault young protagonist Mai (and the viewer) immediately. The character in the titular story is a transnational subject, trapped between two states, fleeing from "home" but not yet having arrived in a "host" nation, "caught between larger global movements initiated by French colonialism and American and Chinese imperialism" (Goellnicht 211). Huynh vividly captures the chaos below deck during the storm: As the reader scrolls through the text, panels that depict abstract masses of bodies tilt abruptly to and fro, colliding with one another according to the rocking and tossing of the rickety boat. The shock of bodies as they slam together through the constantly shifting visuals is captured, contributing to the reader's own feeling of disorientation. The abstract, Picasso-esque visualization of bodies jumbled together because of the storm renders explicit the desperation of these migrant people, expressed by the synecdoches by which they come to be defined. These are migrants without names, recognized only by thighs, ribs, arms, and heads that stand out temporarily from the crowd. Yet, amid all of this visual chaos, emotional and physical upheaval, and the stench of human misery stands the static image of six-year-old Truong, another migrant: "There he was, knees drawn up to his chin, face as smooth and impassive as that of a ceramic toy soldier." In stark contrast to the degradation around him, Truong's portrait is stable, beautiful, and carefully rendered. The peace that imbues his face provides Mai with a moment of relief amid the turbulence of the physical and emotional storm. In both texts, Nam Le and Matt Huynh build empathy for the two principal characters, but not by situating them as victims. Instead, Le and Huynh capture their horrifying lived experiences on the dilapidated junk (and, in the process, allow a reader to live through this event too), experiences that facilitate personal growth, both positive and negative.

Matt Huynh's immersive adaptation of "The Boat" balances past and present by means of the diegetic singing of an old Vietnamese folk song that Mai (and the reader) become aware of as soon as they continue to scroll downward throughout the online graphic text. Diegetic sound, ink painting, watercolor, and handwriting contribute to the revenants of tradition and heritage that offer Mai small comfort while trapped for days on the boat as it crosses the sea to Australia. Sound and color work together to clarify the deep need that motivates Mai's migration. The song reminds Mai of her family: Her mother had sung it to her in the past to comfort them both when Mai's father had gone out to sea on his fishing boat and when he had left to fight the Communists during the war. Her mother's story of raising a daughter by herself and her father's return from the reeducation camp and then his long hospital stay at Vinh Long because he went blind are the painful traumas that Mai carries with her on her journey. Both parents recognized the very limited opportunities left for their daughter in Vietnam and made the difficult decision to help her escape. Huynh's online text captures the chilling exchange between Mai and her father, Ba, when she visits him for the last time in the hospital. Huynh divides this sequence into eleven panels, slowing down Mai's departure from her sick father and emphasizing the long-term pain that remains with them both. This is followed by the abrupt departure that Mai takes from her mother, who finds a human smuggler who will help Mai escape. Huynh visualizes this painful departure over the course of seven panels, all silent, a harrowing experience upon which Mai is left to reflect over the long thirteen days she is trapped on the boat. This emotional wound is one that Mai carries with her in her migration. Remembering and retelling these final "home" moments offer Mai both pain and comfort and capture the torment that she suffers in her journey toward something better. Le's story denies the reassurance promised by the United States, suggested by Tan's *The Arrival*: Instead, as with *Zenobia, Illegal*, and *An Olympic Dream*, the derelict junk is full of bewildered migrants who are trying to escape a homeland that is no longer safe and survive as their unstable world changes around them. In all cases, the texts focus on the humanity of the migrants, attempting to address and alleviate their state of abjection. Thanks to the immersion offered by the online platform, a reader can invest emotionally in the story, compelled to scroll down to see how the narrative plays out.

It is during the escape from Vietnam that Mai meets Quyen, a young mother, and they form a bond. Mai's first impression of the boat that she hopes will transport them to Australia offers her anything but relief. Embodiment shifts in response to experience: Huynh represents the chaos of intertwined bodies impressionistically rather than realistically to emphasize the mass of displaced people whose desperation to escape their country motivates them to pay significant sums of money and submit themselves to degrading conditions. "Inside the hold, the stench was incredible, almost eye-watering. The smell of urine and human waste, sweat and vomit. The black space full of people. Bodies upon bodies. Eyes and eyes and eyes." Two hundred people are packed into an area that is equipped to hold no more than fifteen. The precarity of their experience is emphasized visually in the commingling of words, images of people packed in tightly, and speech bubbles warning about the Viet Cong and guns, all compressed visually into a very small space. The reader is asked to toggle right with the mouse to learn more about Truong's father (Quyen's husband), who is waiting for them in Pulau Bidong, one of the larger Malaysian refugee camps. Archival photographs of a refugee camp form the backdrop for this part of the story, locations of transition frequented by millions of people on the move. Throughout the adaptation, such photographs curb the tendency to sanitize experiences of displacement and enhance the verisimilitude of the story to counteract reader apathy.

Protagonist Mai is not rendered as a victim but rather as a young person of remarkable strength, even and especially in relation to the conditions she experiences on the boat. Bodies litter the ship's deck after the boat is crippled during the storm. Bodies become increasingly angular as day after day passes without food or fresh water. The diegetic sound of the infrequent waves and the blinding sunlight evoke for a reader the blistering heat. Huyhn employs abstract suggestion to represent the first dead body being thrown overboard. Breaking up the sequence into six square panels, Huyhn uses the visual equivalent of a slow-motion camera so that a reader must consider the process by which the shrouded body becomes an abstract heap discarded into the sea, in turn helping the reader to fully appreciate the aftereffects of abjection. The splash as the corpse hits the water disturbs the monotony on the broken-down junk (and the relative silence of the reading experience), demonstrating how quickly the migrants grow accustomed to this degradation. Mai's terrible thirst and then her feverish hallucinations about her father make her realize two things: that her parents sacrificed everything for her so that she could escape and that she has gravitated toward Truong because he reminds her so much of her father. Through abstraction, Huynh suggests the parallels shared by these two figures, both so central to Mai's life: world-weariness and despair. Their victimhood fuels Mai's own remarkable determination to survive, even in the middle of this intolerable experience.

Huynh's aesthetic grows more and more abstract as the online text progresses, reflecting how the migrants' grasp on reality begins to fail. The horror of a young girl casually toppling over the side of the boat or allowing herself to fall into the water is conveyed ironically by six panels that feature almost stick-person sketches, conveying minimal details, but breaking that desperate moment down into smaller vignettes (the sound of a splash communicating the terrible finality of that event). The perspective of each moment grows narrower, as the use of close-ups bears witness: a flask of water; Truong's distressed and semiconscious face as Mai nurses him back from the brink of death; a close-up of Mai's face as she is assaulted for giving Truong someone else's portion of water; and the sound of water leaking out of the flask when she drops it accidentally, emphasizing the hopelessness of their situation. The despair that they come to embody is so all-encompassing that it even calls into question traditional family bonds: Quyen suggests that Mai take Truong, that she look after him during the boat ride and afterward until Quyen can tell her husband the truth about the boy's very existence. Quyen has shut down emotionally in this desperate situation, recognizing that Mai acts more maternally than she. The interactive graphic format specifically allows Huynh to demonstrate how personal and historical events become catalysts for change—for better or for worse—and for the different ways that a character evolves.

Huynh deepens a young reader's empathy for the migrants through the terrible contrast upon which the multimodal text depends: the hope that sight of land evokes and Truong's particularly awful death. Gone is the optimism of Shaun Tan's *Arrival*. Mai, Truong, and Quyen never actually arrive at their point of destination; they are only ever known in relation to this dehumanizing journey. On the thirteenth day, Truong succumbs to death, the slow pounding of a drum conveying a sense of ominousness as they prepare to throw his body overboard. There is no hope associated with Truong's death (or the end of Nam Le's short story or Matt Huynh's graphic adaptation, for that matter), only the indignity of the dead migrant body being torn apart by sharks. Sharks, both literal and figurative, convey the precarity of migrant experiences, the traumas that accompany forced relocation, migration, and diaspora. Yet, part of the power of Nam Le's short story "The Boat" and Matt Huynh's interactive graphic adaptation relies on their embodiment of Mai's quiet resilience in the midst of this personal crisis, the fortitude that she maintains under duress, and the larger meditation about human rights upon which her harrowing experiences encourage a young reader to reflect.

Comics about particular geopolitical crises, including the current global migration phenomenon, have become a potent vehicle for advancing human rights claims and campaigns. The texts about migration that this chapter explores link the local with the global, evoking embodied experiences of crisis and arrival and relying on memories, family stories, and sources like letters, journals, archival photographs, and conversations to make abstract statistics come alive. Humanizing a crisis that too often gets caught up in the political crosshairs of particular regions of the world, these comics do so from the perspectives of young people, who too rarely are featured in migrant and refugee stories. All of these texts foreground experiences of deep trauma but more importantly focus on the personal experience of a young person on the move who is in a state of profound transition. Rather than reiterating the victimization of these people, their focus is almost uniformly given to the child's resilience.

## Childhoods in Refugee and Displacement Camps: *Baddawi* and *They Called Us Enemy*

As the comics in the previous section remind us, mass displacement is frequently the product of violence and political oppression. For Lyndsey Stonebridge, the history of the modern refugee is also the "history of the changing meanings of political and national citizenship," with the "spectre of rightlessness" hovering in plain sight (*Placeless* 2). Writing in the 1940s, Hannah Arendt suggested that statelessness was a political as well as an existential experience: As people were denied political sovereignty, their experiences of dehumanization required "new forms of thinking and imagination" (qtd. in *Placeless* 4). It is all too easy to oversimplify the relationship between poverty and refugee movements, culminating with the misconception that refugees and migrants are a problem unique to the Global South. If we accept that poverty, political oppression, and the mass displacement of people are all global or world-systemic phenomena, then it becomes difficult to localize them in the developing world. Indeed, as Stonebridge reminds readers, "the history of placelessness is everybody's history" as opposed to being an occurrence that affects the "poor unfortunates of the world" (*Placeless* 3).

There is no real beginning to the phenomenon of the refugee. The term has "analytical usefulness," according to critic Liisa Malkki, not as a label for a special, generalizable "type" of person but as a "broad legal and descriptive rubric that includes within it a world of different socioeconomic statuses, personal histories, and psychological or spiritual situations" (496). In the genealogy of "the refugee" as concept, the period during and immediately following World War II witnessed the deployment of this term on an international scale. During the same period in Europe, certain key techniques for managing mass displacements of people first became standardized and eventually globalized (497). The prisoner-of-war or internment camp, for example, became a vital "technology of power" for the spatial ordering of people in cases of mass displacement: the segregation and organization of nationalities, the creation of medical and hygiene programs, the accumulation of documentation about the camps' inhabitants, law enforcement and public discipline, and schooling and rehabilitation (498). Arendt describes displaced persons camps as a "political and juridical hinterland," frequently built on borders for symbolic and practical reasons: "The people in them are deemed to exist beyond the nation state, its laws, and protections" (Stonebridge, *Placeless* 47). Giorgio Agamben agrees, describing such camps as "pure space[s] of exception," ones that demand that the "concept of the refugee be resolutely separated from the concept of the rights of man" (134). But even Arendt, observing conditions in the later 1940s, could not imagine the scale on which some of the refugee camps would operate in the twenty-first century.

In large part due to the existence of these displacement camps, the "modern, postwar refugee emerged as a knowable, nameable figure and as an object of social-scientific knowledge" (Malkki 498). Thus, the existence of refugees was *not* originally approached "institutionally or discursively as an international humanitarian problem" (499). In the final years of World War II and the immediate postwar years, displaced peoples in Europe were classified as a military problem instead, falling under the jurisdiction of the Displaced Persons Branch of the Supreme Headquarters Allied Expeditionary Force (499). It is thus a tragic irony that many of the hundreds of labor and concentration camps in Eastern Europe were transformed into so-called "Assembly Centres" for refugees after the war ended; such camps were military in design and especially suited for the mass control of people (499–500). This unpleasant association of the refugee or displacement camp with human rights violations stemming from mid-twentieth-century cultural genocides is one that continues in the current day and is a focus of the graphic texts *Baddawi* (2015) and *They Called Us Enemy* (2019).

In 1951, once the UNHCR was established, refugees began to appear more clearly as an international social and humanitarian challenge rather than a distinctly military concern. International refugee law and related legal instruments grew out of the aftermath of the war (with its attendant postwar shame). The Universal Declaration of Human Rights was first adopted in 1948, as was the Genocide Convention. The declaration helped to establish the basic legal definition of refugee status, which in turn represents a critical moment in the institutionalization of the post–World War II system for handling refugees (Malkki 501). According to the 1951 definition provided in the "Convention Related to the Status of Refugees," a refugee is a person who

> owing to a well-founded fear of being persecuted for reasons of race, religion, nationality, membership of a particular social group or political opinion, is outside the country of [their] nationality or is unable or, owing to such fear, is unwilling to avail [them]self of the protection of that country; or who, not having a nationality and being outside the country of [their] former habitual residence as a result of such events, is unable or, owing to such fear, is unwilling to return to it. (Stonebridge, *Placeless* 17)

This definition certainly affirms an individual's feelings and experiences of persecution that are the implied result of the horrors of totalitarian persecution, but it does not adequately account for the anxiety about statelessness that Japanese Americans facing internment during and after World War II in the United States and Canada experienced or the daily deprivations of living in Palestinian or Syrian refugee camps today.

Erasing the humanity of displaced peoples and migrants is a strategy employed by politicians and mass media the world over so that such individuals become projections of fear and sometimes even loathing. Although in no way a graphic narrative written for young readers, Joe Sacco's masterwork *Palestine* (2015) is an undeniable example of the important critical work that a comic can perform by humanizing refugees ghettoized into camps. Sacco resists the refugee camp heterotopia—spaces that are created "to accommodate groups considered deviant, as an expression of their relation to dominant accounts of normality" (Adams 138)—by humanizing Palestinians who have been forced out of their homeland and into camps for decades that have spanned entire generations. Challenging "the representation of refugee camps as ahistorical spaces of timeless—and agentless—suffering" (Stonebridge, *Writing and Righting* 116), Sacco depicts the domestic and interior lives of Palestinians, in part by focusing on their tea ritual of hospitality, to refute anti-Palestinian propaganda that circulates widely in the media and to make personal their daily experiences of statelessness. For Lyndsey Stonebridge, stories about refugees do not "just" open up a spot for pathos; instead, as *Palestine*, *Baddawi*, and *They Called Us Enemy* prove,

FIGURE 2.3. Leila Abdelrazaq, *Baddawi*. Just World Books, 2015, cover.

comics about refugees visualize experiences of displacement to address how issues of rights and citizenship link the personal and the political. For Leila Abdelrazaq and George Takei, creating "was a means of excavating the mind in transit between different modes of political and historical belonging, as well as exploring the suffering of powerlessness" (Stonebridge, *Placeless* 20). In their inventive visual approaches, *Baddawi* and *They Called Us Enemy* function as responses to refugee histories, resisting the depiction of refugees as passive victims waiting to be "saved," "assisted," or "protected" by nonrefugee others and instead insisting on refugees as bearers of human rights, as individuals who have been shaped by historical and political circumstances.

*Baddawi* (2015), Leila Abdelrazaq's text about her father's youth spent in a Palestinian refugee camp in Lebanon, educates readers about the Palestinian-

Israeli conflict and the Lebanese civil war from the perspective of a child. This one child is also representative of one of the largest refugee populations in the world, numbering more than five million. The cover imagery signals immediately Abdelrazaq's determination to visualize her father's experiences in camps throughout the Palestinian territories by focusing on his remarkable resilience while living in this conflict zone (see figure 2.3). A ten-year-old boy faces away from readers, his hands clasped contemplatively behind him. An elaborate frame surrounds this young boy—sheltering rather than enclosing or imprisoning him—a frame that evokes the geometric, pixelated patterns of traditional Palestinian embroidery (*tatreez*). Throughout her comic, Abdelrazaq visually invokes elements of Palestinian culture to ornament the pages. The experiences of Palestinian refugees are often overlooked in general discussions about displaced peoples, even though Palestinians have long existed as a stateless people.

Palestinian *tatreez* and child are intimately connected. The ten-year-old boy on the cover evokes the iconic character Handala, created by Palestinian artist and political cartoonist Naji al-Ali in 1975. Naji al-Ali promised that once the Palestinian people were free and allowed to return to their homeland, Handala would grow up and turn around so that the world could finally see his face. Naji al-Ali was assassinated in London in 1987 because of his criticism of the Arab regimes and his political opinions; Handala still has not turned around. Abdelrazaq explains in the preface to her comic, "Today, he is one of the most prominent symbols of Palestinian resistance, and the definitive symbol of the Palestinian refugee child" (11). By visually conflating her father and Handala, she links the experiences of the Palestinian refugee child and the traumatic Palestinian past. Both embody the figure of the seeing child who bears witness to the atrocities of war, an active agent in the political unrest through the power of observation (Cheurfa 366–67). Throughout the comic, Abdelrazaq draws attention to the historical and political conditions that shape her father's life and his autonomy as a Palestinian subject, in the process challenging a "depoliticized humanitarian reading that discards material histories and events in favour of eliciting an emotional response" (Alfarhan 155). A sequence titled "Cluster Bombs," for example, visually juxtaposes Ahmad's youthful experience of the everyday with the comforting routine of baking bread practiced by his cousin Zuheir's wife. A sequence that juxtaposes close-up panels of Ahmad's eyes with two fighter jets flying low over Baddawi propel the violent impact of personal and political, as the explosion of the cluster bombs that the Israeli army released over the camp "sent [Zuheir's wife] headfirst into the oven as she was baking" (Abdelrazaq 64). The Palestinian *tatreez* that surrounds their perspectives and the panels configured as a house literalize the impact of these bombs on Ahmad and his community, in turn emphasizing their continuous state of precarity. Unlike Handala, whose acts of seeing are acts of witnessing, Abdelrazaq emphasizes Ahmad's agency through his political awareness, which emerges through the atrocities that he witnesses and speaks about (Cheurfa 372).

The story begins in 1948 with her grandparents' escape from Safsaf in Palestine during Israel's War of Independence to a northern Lebanese refugee camp. The map that Abdelrazaq includes emphasizes the remarkable odyssey her family endured. Her grandparents always expected that they would return to Safsaf eventually, especially given UN Resolution 194, the Right of Return, which states that Palestinian refugees and their descendants have the right to return to their homes in Palestine. This did not happen. Baddawi, the refugee camp outside of Tripoli in Lebanon, where thousands of Palestinians fled after the Nakba (the mass exodus of Palestinians following the 1948 war that established the state of Israel), became their home away from home for generations. The name of the camp derives from the term "Bedouin," meaning "nomad." The forced nature of their migration is captured by an early image that shows they must transplant their Palestinian culture and traditions to a completely new country. Abdelrazaq's depiction of her family's displacement through the denial of their history and past visualizes Stonebridge's claim that "if the refugee is the opposite of the citizen, the stateless person is her absolute negative: a person-zero" (*Placeless* 169). Beginning as the text does with the historical and political circumstances that shape her father's life—events such as the Nakba, al-Naksa ("the Setback") of 1967, the Cairo Agreement of 1969, the Lebanese Civil War of 1975, and the 1973 operation "Spring of Youth"—*Baddawi* "seeks to emphasize the ways in which history collides with the individual and shapes their autonomy as a subject" (Alfaran 158). One particular full-page spread guides a reader's eyes down the page, prompting them to take note of how the seemingly abstract choices that Hafez Al-Assad and Ariel Sharon make about military spending and war maneuvers impact the fighting soldiers (rendered as abstract silhouettes shooting at one another) and in turn the war games that the children wage among themselves in the streets of Beirut. The joy that they find in their agentic play stands as a tonic to the acts of violence that are committed around them (see figure 2.4).

One of the particular strengths of Abdelrazaq's comic is its use of the child protagonist to convey the resilience of a person living in a refugee camp via the humdrum routines of life that are frequently interrupted by terrible and violent experiences. The first section of the text, set in Baddawi

FIGURE 2.4. War games. Leila Abdelrazaq, *Baddawi*. Just World Books, 2015, p. 84.

between 1959 and 1969, begins with a verbal and visual summary of the first grade and the emotions created when Ahmad (and, presumably, many others) encounters the random rules created by organizations like the United Nations Refugee and Works Agency, which prescribes the daily routines of young Palestinians throughout the Middle East: anxiety over school supplies and footwear, the segregation of girls and boys in the classroom, the microcosmic war between factions at school that mirror the ethnic tensions in the refugee camp itself. Ahmad's almost visceral need for a pair of soccer cleats (to play with his peers but also to fit in with them socially) prompts him to devise a scheme to use a game of marbles to make money from the kids living around him. Embarrassed by Ahmad's swindle, his mother uses this experience to remind him about his Palestinian traditions, sending him out into the mountains to gather thyme to make za'atar. The meditation that Ahmad performs while picking thyme and then laboriously preparing the

FIGURE 2.5. Children play while threats loom. Leila Abdelrazaq, *Baddawi*. Just World Books, 2015, p. 40.

herbs is transformative; Abdelrazaq communicates the importance of this experience in her page that refutes the strict regularization of panels.

Ahmad and his family live in perpetual longing to return to Palestine, confident that the Arab armies are going to defeat the Israeli army, but their condition of statelessness does not recognize their extreme vulnerability so much as it confirms their powerlessness. Al-Naksa, "the Setback," occurs in 1967, however, when the Arab armies lose to the Israelis. Ahmad's youthful experiences of Ramadan and Eid in Baddawi, as well as taking taxis to visit his mother's parents in the neighboring refugee camp, Nahr al-Bared, again emphasize the surreal "normalcy" of their cultural traditions and routines while living in this indefinite period of statelessness. Amid all of the supposedly regular childhood experiences, like bird hunting and swimming at the seaside, the Palestinian children living in Baddawi are also aware of the torture and imprisonment that people could experience if they said or did the wrong thing. (Children talk in subdued voices about a man who raised the Palestinian flag outside his house and was arrested and beaten by the Lebanese army.) Night raids in Baddawi, during which the Israeli and Lebanese armies invade the camp to eliminate any members of the Palestinian Resistance movements, prevent the children from going to school (see figure 2.5). This image juxtaposes the palpable threat that overshadows the refugee camp with the children who play on the beach. Abdelrazaq's shift between Ahmad's personal story and the larger political and historical narrative creates "a claustrophobic sense of history," Haya Saud Alfarhan argues (162). As such, it is difficult for a Western reader to read passively and to empathize without "feeling historically implicated in the violence" (Alfarhan 154).

*Baddawi* also visualizes the extreme choices that Palestinians must make simply to subsist, get the medical treatment that they need, or have access to the education that they require to set them up for adulthood. Ahmad's father relocates to Beirut, leaving behind his family in Baddawi, to find a means to sustain them; Ahmad's mother also leaves for Beirut to seek medical treatment. As school is still in session, Ahmad is left behind with his one sister and three brothers to finish off the year in the refugee camp. Abdelrazaq captures the frustration Ahmad feels, having to parent his siblings in the absence of his own parents. His shrewdness, however, equips him with a survival instinct that stands him in good stead. Once they all move to Beirut, Ahmad successfully navigates the mounting tensions between political factions. He takes the brevet, the national tenth-grade entrance exams in Lebanon, on the very day when a bus full of Palestinians is attacked and the passengers are massacred by Phalangists, initiating Lebanon's fifteen-year civil war. Games of chess are played while they take refuge in the basement during air strikes. And the realization that school continues in Baddawi while it is cancelled in Beirut propels Ahmad to return to the refugee camp to seek opportunity. This passage is ironically entitled "The Return," referring not to the return of Palestinians to their homeland but to the camp that has become their home for a number of generations. Abdelrazaq's text in this way reminds readers of the paradoxical permanence of life in refugee camps, "the legal and socio-cultural impacts that span generations" (Mickwitz, "Telling" 278), and the extent to which power structures create situations of violence and marginalization.

George Takei's comic specifically refutes the assumption that refugees and detainees are a problem unique to the Global South, visualizing the incarceration of Japanese Americans by the United States government in the days following the bombing of Pearl Harbor. *They Called Us Enemy* (2019) is an important graphic memoir in the present moment because of the connections it makes between current policies toward racialized "others" in the United States and those from the past. Takei's narrative outlines his childhood spent in American displacement camps as one of the 120,000 Japanese Americans who were interned by the US government during World War II. "I know what concentration camps are [. . .] I was inside two of them, in America. And, yes, we are operating such camps again" (Cavna), he states in an interview with the *Washington Post*. Takei is referring to the immigration detention facilities along the US–Mexico border established by Donald Trump during his presidency and to a recent period in American history (June 2018) when nearly 2,000 immigrant children (mostly Mexican) were separated from their parents or caregivers and detained in cages along the US–Mexico border.³ Written for older grade-schoolers, *They Called Us Enemy* employs its accessibility to educate readers about a chapter of US history that many people still only vaguely understand, reminding readers that power structures (even at home) can create situations of violence and marginalization. Takei (like many people living in the US) had to come to terms with the imposed identity of racial outsider even though he was born in America.

Takei's memoir describes how his father, who had lived in the US for twenty-five years without being allowed to become a citizen, and his Sacramento-born, American-citizen mother were declared "enemy aliens" by a presidential proclamation in 1942. Franklin Delano Roosevelt's Executive Order No. 9066 sent more than 110,000 people of Japanese descent to "relocation centers" after the seizure of their financial assets, property, and businesses. Curfews and restrictions of their movements became a daily reality. Panel after panel of *They Called Us Enemy* depict the gradual erasure of the humanity of Japanese Americans by the American government, which culminated with the condition of statelessness they endured in these internment camps. In spring 1942, Takei and his family were brought by train to the Santa Anita racetrack and herded into stables, each family assigned a horse stall "still pungent with the stink of manure" (Takei et al. 32) and forced to shower outside in the horse paddocks. Takei visualizes the general racism among Americans that this proclamation encouraged, further justified by governmental agencies whose treatment of its own citizens was all too reminiscent of some of the degradations practiced in the worst concentration camps in Europe (tagging, violence, food shortages, barbed wire fences, guard towers, etc.). In this regard, Takei makes use of the slower time frame of the visual narrative to provide a structural understanding of the underlying causes of this humanitarian disaster by means of the individual human experience and its distinctive knowledge of powerlessness (Davies, "Borders" 188).

In a similar fashion to Abdelrazaq's use of the child protagonist to convey the resilience of a young person living in a refugee camp, Takei's memoir balances the visualization of these torturous experiences with the freshness of its child protagonist, who, in retrospect, acknowledges the extreme efforts

---

3. Detention facilities in the United States are not a new phenomenon, nor is the separation of child from parent, unfortunately. Testimonies of children of color being separated from their families reach as far back as the history of slavery, the 1830 Indian Removal Act, the 1850 Fugitive Slave Act, and the 1882 Chinese Exclusion Act (Hesford, *Exceptions* ix–x). Indian Residential Schools in Canada also separated child from parent, as chapter 3 will explore.

FIGURE 2.6. The Takei family is taken to Camp Rohwer. George Takei et al., *They Called Us Enemy*. Art by Harmony Becker. Top Shelf, 2019, p. 51.

made by his parents to protect their children from realizing the severity of their situation (see figure 2.6). George's memory of the lengthy train ride to Camp Rohwer, the displacement camp in Arkansas and their future home for four years, was quite positive given that his father described their trip as a "vacation" (38) that they were taking; he also reflected fondly on the "wonderful bag of goodies" (49) his mother brought along to distract them during the traumatic relocation. "This made for two starkly different journeys," he observes. "One, an adventure of discovery . . . the other, an anxiety-ridden voyage into a fearful unknown" (49). This relocation—experienced differently by parent and child—is emphasized visually by the panels themselves, which depict the children's limited understanding of the situation and distinguish it from their parents' experience of worry. Counterpointing caption and image, Takei notes how his memories "are especially slippery" (51), rendering the trauma of the experience less potent somehow, in spite of the soldier's threatening presence in a number of panels, the soldier's hand that grabs George, and his parents' subdued behavior suggesting otherwise. He acknowledges, "I know that I will always be haunted by the larger, vaguely remembered reality of the circumstances surrounding my childhood" (51). The position of privilege that his childhood accorded him because of his parents' desire to protect him shields George from an early awareness of the degradation that his country forced his family to endure, in turn highlighting "the critical contradictions of the history of internment" (Davis 362) by means of these contrasting positions. The text juxtaposes young George's perception of himself as an American child "with that of America's classification of [his family] as foreigners" (Davis 359).

The third of February 1943 brought with it a major change in military policy that would allow Japanese Americans to enlist in the war effort as long as they completed a questionnaire correctly. The questionnaire, however, had two now-infamous questions that highlighted the racism that governmental policy still endorsed. Question 27 asked individuals whether they were willing to serve in the Armed Forces to defend America (a country that had imprisoned them in displacement camps). Question 28 asked individuals if they were willing to swear unqualified allegiance to the United States and to forswear any form of allegiance to the Japanese emperor, thus implying that *all* Japanese people had a racial allegiance to the emperor of Japan. This impossible choice resulted in his parents being labeled "No-Nos," answering "no" to each question in an act of principled protest. By way of punishment, the family was once again displaced, this time to a camp for "disloyals," people who, in answering "no," were supposedly declaring their allegiance to Japan. As a chronicler of refugee history, Takei writes about displacement to imagine citizenship and sovereignty in America at a time when these concepts are especially fraught. Takei narrates primarily from his remembered childhood self, sanitizing the degradations that his family and thousands of Japanese endured but also emphasizing their vulnerability when subjected to racist governmental policies. This comic—as well as the crucial activist work that Takei performs advocating for Japanese American affairs—confirms that the act of creation "was a means of excavating the mind in transit between different modes of political and historical belonging, as well as exploring the suffering of powerlessness" (Stonebridge, *Placeless* 20). In the closing pages, Takei invites readers to see parallels between then and now. And, in spite of Trump's separation of adults and children at the US–Mexico border and his ban on immigration from Muslim countries, Takei's graphic memoir celebrates the "shining ideals of democracy" (178) that in principle can be protective but that can also be misapplied to target particular racial and ethnic groups. Interestingly, both George Takei and Shaun Tan maintain a strong faith in the principles of democracy upon which America is built, in spite of the racism and oppression that both experienced in their own journeys to find belonging.

Comics about particular geopolitical conflict zones around the world offer the potential of transmitting the distant *there* to the *here* for readers. Rather than situating the Global South as a portrait of strife, terror, and inhumanity, and the predominantly Western viewer as comfortably remote from this violence, visual accounts of crises (such as forced migration, exile, and political oppression) and the particular traumas that individuals endure implicate the reader, even in the act of reading and talking about the text. The texts that this chapter explores clarify and dispute historical narratives, express solidarity, mourn, and, ultimately, remind readers that young people are already political and that their subject positions are shaped by the politics of the countries and communities in which they live. As the Indigenous graphic texts of the next chapter will visualize, comics about immigration, migration, and diaspora also confirm Stonebridge's claim that prefaced this chapter: "Where writing does join cause with righting is in its creativity—its art" (*Writing and Righting* 14).

CHAPTER 3

# Indigeneity and Resurgence in Canadian Comics

> Much of the current state of troubled relations between Aboriginal and non-Aboriginal Canadians is attributable to education institutions and what they have taught, or failed to teach, over many generations. Despite that history, or perhaps more correctly, because of its potential, the Commission believes education is also the key to reconciliation.
>
> —Chelsea Vowel, *Indigenous Writes*

Nelvana of the Northern Lights debuted in Hillborough Studios' *Triumph-Adventure Comics* #1 in August 1941. The "first Canadian national superhero" (J. Bell 47), Adrian Dingle's Nelvana was a sexy and adept superheroine who predated Wonder Woman by several months. Franz Johnston, a member of the Group of Seven school of art, contributed to Dingle's initial conception of Nelvana. After a trip to the Arctic, Johnston told Dingle about a powerful Inuit mythological figure, an elderly woman and old crone, called Nelvana. Captivated by the prospect of a Canadian superheroine, Dingle reinvented her to suit the requirements of the genre: "I changed her a bit. Did what I could with long hair and mini skirts. And tried to make her attractive. [. . .] Then we had to bring her up to date and put her into the war effort. And, of course, everything had to be very patriotic" (J. Bell 60–62). Daughter of Koliak the Mighty, King of the Northern Lights, and a mortal, Nelvana flew at incredibly fast speeds and had the power of invisibility. In comics between August 1941 and May 1947, Nelvana protected the Arctic North and her Arctic brothers from enemies as diverse as Nazi invaders, the Japanese, dubious fur traders, subterranean Mammoth-Men, and interdimensional ether people.[1]

---

1. Nelvana lives on in the name and logo of Nelvana Limited of Toronto, one of Canada's leading producers and distributors of children's animated and live-action content.

In 2006 historian and archivist John Bell insisted that although Nelvana was meant to personify the North, she was *not* in fact Inuit. Rather, he maintained, she belonged to a tradition of white goddesses and queens from popular culture, a combination of H. Rider Haggard's *She* (1886–87) and Sheena, the white jungle queen who made her debut in American *Jumbo Comics* in 1938 (J. Bell 62). Adrian Dingle's initial description of his Nelvana is thus very telling of visual and literary representations of Indigenous figures in American and Canadian comics in the twentieth century. Expanding on the stereotypical, formulaic roles generally available to male Indigenous characters (the "Native" as racial threat, childlike dupe, and/or faithful sidekick), Nelvana exemplifies the "Indian princess-as-sexpot ideal" that is in turn supported by the Hollywood film industry (Sheyahshe 169). To slot this new Canadian figure into the growing superhero tradition, Dingle had "to make her attractive," as he put it, play down her Inuit heritage, sexualize her, and bring her out of her "primitive" past to deploy her for the Canadian and European war efforts.[2] The modifications Dingle made to this mythological figure speak to essentialist associations of Indigenous peoples as unmodern and ahistorical, stereotypes that in turn complicate Dingle's already ironic reassignment of an Inuit demigoddess to the protection of Canada's national boundaries. Sixty years later, little change had occurred to these stereotypes: John Bell distances Nelvana from her Inuit foremother, resituating her between the imperialist literature of nineteenth-century England and American examples of the "Mohican Syndrome," whereby a non-Native character absorbs all things seemingly positive about Native culture by osmotic metamorphosis (Sheyahshe 13). In the process, Dingle and later Bell significantly claim Nelvana as Canadian—and, specifically, *not* Indigenous—and in so doing silently erase her original associations with Inuit mythology in the service of Canadian patriotism. Essentialist depictions like

---

2. This tendency to sexualize Indigenous peoples is certainly not a practice relegated to the annals of history (or to comics). In "Playing Indian and Other Settler Stories" (2015), Sandrina de Finney explores the contemporary commodification of Indigenous peoples as disposable consumer goods. Indigenous bodies and imagery are gaining "pop culture currency," she argues, stereotyped as inherently mystical, natural, and spiritual beings. Contemporary musicians Gwen Stefani, Lana del Rey, Madonna, and Kesha have performed wearing Native American headdresses and feathers. Popular American lingerie chain Victoria's Secret draped its runway models in headdresses and princess wear. Urban Outfitters and H&M were boycotted for their "Navajo" merchandise. In fact, after producing a "Navajo hipster panty," Urban Outfitters was sued under a US federal law that protected the intellectual property of Indigenous nations (de Finney 175–76).

these of North American Indigenous peoples continue in such superhero comics as DC Comics' *Tomahawk* (1998) and *Manitou Raven* (2002).[3]

In the twenty-first century, Canada's dynamic comics tradition thrives and is increasingly a focus in both popular and academic studies. Canada's landscape and its hockey ethos, its long history of colonialism and instances of cultural appropriation, as well as its ironic self-identification as "not American" are just some of the preoccupations of Canadian comics, according to Chris Chikuma-Reyns and Gail de Vos (12–13). Candida Rifkind and Linda Warley's excellent collection *Canadian Graphic: Picturing Life Narratives* (2016) explores the long and varied history of life narrative (memoir, confession, autobiography, biography) in the Canadian alternative comics scene.

---

3. Canadian superheroes are not frequent in mainstream comics, with a few notable exceptions. Bart Beaty (2006) explores four in detail: Superman, Johnny Canuck, Nelvana of the Northern Lights, and Captain Canuck. Superman joins this list because he was created in part by Toronto-born Joe Shuster. Johnny Canuck (created by Leo Bachle) and Nelvana were heroes of World War II and were characters associated with the "Golden Age" of Canadian comics production. *Captain Canuck* (created by Richard Comely and Ron Leishman), which debuted in 1975, was the first Canadian superhero comic to be published in color. Beaty points to the irony that the most successful Canadian superheroes have been all but exiled from critical commentary on superheroes (434). Fascinatingly, Canadian politicians have been cast as superheroes in mainstream comics. Prime Minister Justin Trudeau appeared in *Alpha Flight*, a Marvel comic in 2017 written by Toronto cartoonist Chip Zdarsky and illustrated by Ramón Pérez, engaged in a friendly boxing match with Iron Man Tony Stark. Issue #5 of *Civil War II: Choosing Sides* features a variant cover that depicts Trudeau in a boxing ring, wearing a red-and-white uniform with a red maple leaf at its center, visually evoking the boxing match against Conservative senator Patrick Brazeau in 2012 that set victor Trudeau on the path for the prime minister's office. His father, then prime minister Pierre Elliott Trudeau, also appeared in Marvel's *Uncanny X-Men* #120 (1979).

Canadian content has begun to achieve more prominence in mainstream superhero comics of late. The team Alpha Flight (created by Canadian expat John Byrne of Marvel) appeared in more than 150 issues of this American-produced comic and was composed of Canadian superheroes Sasquatch, Northstar, Shaman, Aurora, and Puck, each representing a distinct part of Canada and a specific (if clichéd and stereotypical) ethnicity. DC's Equinox, a sixteen-year-old Cree girl from Moose Factory, appears in a five-issue story arc in the *Justice League United* series (2014). Most recently, Marvel Comics revealed its newest superhero: Amka Aliyak, also known as Snowguard, an Inuk teen from Pangnirtung, Nunavut, Canada. She was introduced in *Champions* #21 in late June 2018. Her abilities, powered by the Inuit spirit/force "Sila," allow her to shapeshift. To develop the character, Marvel writer Jim Zub reached out to Nyla Innuksuk, founder of the Toronto-based virtual reality production company Mixtape VR, who is Inuit and grew up in Igloolik and Iqaluit. Innuksuk provided guidance about various aspects of Inuit life in northern Canada ("Meet"). With Amka, Marvel attempts to complicate Indigenous representation in mainstream American and Canadian comics and to acknowledge the oppression that Indigenous women in North America endure in particular.

In their introduction, Rifkind and Warley note that cartoonists of color and Indigenous cartoonists in particular are underrepresented in comics scholarship (4). As this chapter explores, comics and graphic narratives written specifically for children and youth in Canada about Indigenous characters and Indigenous political and cultural issues began in 2008 with the publication of David Alexander Robertson's *The Life of Helen Betty Osborne*, a comic about the 1971 abduction and brutal murder of a Cree high school student in The Pas, Manitoba, by four white men. The very diverse field of Indigenous comics in Canada expands on an annual basis, extending beyond life narratives into genres including myth, fantasy, realism, and speculative fiction. Although this chapter focuses primarily on stories that educate readers about Canada's troubled colonial past and present, I wish to acknowledge the many Indigenous comics in circulation that reject narratives of victimization, celebrate Indigenous futurism, and are humor oriented.

In keeping with theorizations of the term by Hillary Chute ("Retracing"; *Why*) and Michael Chaney, I continue to use the term "graphic narrative" rather than "graphic novel" in the description of this exciting new field of visual literature because the latter term emphasizes the inherent fictionality of some of the more autobiographical or truth-telling Indigenous visual texts, which, in the process, distances or, worse, negates the often difficult lived realities that some of these creators describe. Instead, the term "graphic narrative" alludes to the multiple affordances that image and word bring to these particularly explicit testimonies about the intergenerational legacy of Canadian and European colonialism. I use the term "Indigenous" and "Indigenous peoples" to refer to the First Nations, Métis, and Inuit sovereign nations living in what is now called Canada to honor the hundreds of culturally and linguistically distinct nations, and those of mixed ancestry, that inhabit North America and especially Canada. As much as possible, when discussing individual creators and their works, I clarify tribal and national identities as designations in a determined effort to resist further racial essentialisms.

This chapter on Indigenous comics for young people explores the affordances of word and image, myth and worldview, in making use of the healing power of language and visual storytelling to address the long-lasting legacies of systemic racism in the country of Canada. As with the two previous chapters, the texts that this section features narrativize information about marginalization and suffering; they resist narratives of victimhood in their depiction of Indigenous practices and the principles of resurgence and renewal that they communicate in the process. With this emphasis on healing and reemergence in mind, this chapter is organized according to the

Touchstones of Hope applied to reconciliation in the child welfare process—Truth Telling, Acknowledging, Restoring, and Relating—in its exploration of Indigenous comics for young readers. Of particular focus in this chapter is Cree author David Alexander Robertson's oeuvre, which encourages youthful readers to challenge official historical accounts, forcing readers to see the violence of colonialism, the Indian Residential School (IRS) system, and the gender violence that persists insidiously in Indigenous communities. The publication of comics and graphic narratives *by* Indigenous writers and creators *for* young Indigenous readers is another focus of the chapter, harnessing the power of storytelling to acknowledge past injustices and empower Indigenous youth in the present.

## Visual Storytelling as Living Resistance: Indigenous Picture Books and Publishing

In recent years, Indigenous comics in Canada have become more of a priority for publishing houses, and the increased cultural legitimacy of the graphic narrative as an artistic and literary form with which to address the multiple legacies of colonialism has produced many exciting synergies in the industry. Such texts as *A Girl Called Echo* (2017–), *7 Generations* (2012), and *Red: A Haida Manga* (2009), are especially powerful because, for the most part, they are created by Indigenous writers about their own communities for educational purposes and actively resist the perspectives of settler culture with its attendant colonial ideology. Michael Nicoll Yahgulanaas's *Red: A Haida Manga*, for example, is a Haida oral narrative that employs the hybrid form of Haida manga, a new visual genre that "reframes classic indigenous imagery and narratives into populist graphic literature" (author blurb).[4] Manga in and of itself is already a hybrid art form, mixing Indigenous traditions with European printing innovations brought to Japan in the 1860s (Levell 7). Yahgulanaas turned to Japanese manga specifically because it was not part of the settler tradition of North America but rather had its roots in the South Pacific (as does Haida art; "Notes" 54). In making much of the hybridity of Haida manga, Yahgulanaas interweaves characteristics and styles from varied cultures and places in his epic tale of Red, his heroic rage, and his quest for revenge. Consisting of 108 hand-painted pages that feature the bold, primary colors and geometric forms of traditional Haida art as well

---

4. Michael Nicoll Yahgulanaas, born in Prince Rupert in 1954, grew up alongside Delkatla, a slough near the fishing village of Masset on Haida Gwaii. He is part of the Haida Nation.

as its bentwood box design, Yahgulanaas's text combines the panels and gutters of comics art and the expressionistic formline of Haida art to produce a visually dynamic and avant-garde approach to an epic story.

As *Growing Up Graphic* argues, comics have the potential to provide information and build knowledge while educating young readers about their rights or about alternative histories. Indeed, comics are especially useful tools with which to address entrenched Canadian and European colonialism, the "biopolitical and geopolitical management of people, land, flora and fauna within the 'domestic' borders of the imperial nation" (Tuck and Yang 4). Métis writer Patti LaBoucane-Benson's graphic narrative *The Outside Circle* (2015) harnesses the power of the visual to address the overrepresentation of Indigenous people in the criminal justice system and of Indigenous children in government care. Inspired by Chester Brown's graphic biography *Louis Riel* (2003),[5] LaBoucane-Benson collaborated with illustrator Kelly Mellings on this comic that endeavors to communicate more than twenty years of historic trauma research into a format that could reach a broader (and younger) audience. LaBoucane-Benson affirmed that in producing *The Outside Circle* she "wanted to create a graphic novel so her research could appeal to more people." "My goal was to write this for my son's generation," she clarified ("Edmonton"). Particular visuals in this comic powerfully address the individual and collective healing that must take place before Indigenous and non-Indigenous peoples can move forward on the path to reconciliation (see figure 3.1). An entire splash page is devoted to the blood that runs down his arm after protagonist Pete Carver receives a tattoo from his gang. The vivid and visceral image suggests that this blood has roots in a long history of colonialism and intergenerational trauma dating back to the 1850s and leading up to the IRS system and the "sixties scoop," countless examples of the colonial legislation and practices that have attempted to assimilate Indigenous peoples. "The timeline implies that historical knowledge should play an important role in explaining these challenging situations" (Borkent 291). The blood that pours from historical wounds also has ties to contemporary gang violence. "My goal in this project was to tell the truth," LaBoucane-Benson insisted, "not to sensationalize gang activity, but to help Canadians understand what drives Indigenous men into prison, feel

---

5. Chester Brown's *Louis Riel: A Comic-Strip Biography* tells the history of the Red River settlement, the 1885 Northwest Resistance by the Métis people, and the charge of treason and eventual hanging of their leader, Louis Riel. Originally serialized in ten separate issues between 1999 and 2003, it was published in book form in 2003. Katherena Vermette takes a more contemporary approach to the history of the Métis and First Nations of the Northwest who face hunger and uncertainty as their way of life is threatened by the Canadian government.

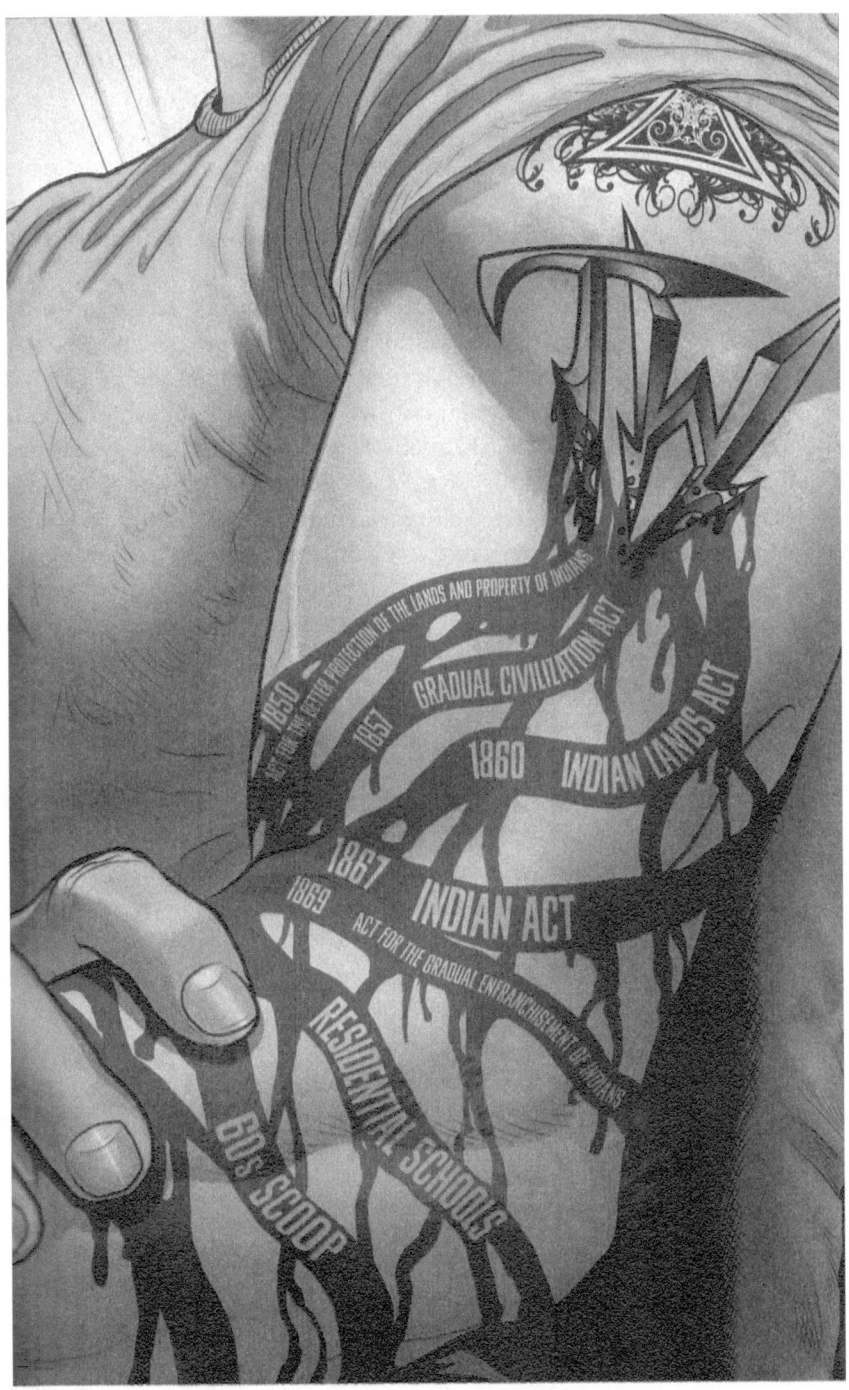

FIGURE 3.1. Pete Carver's tattoo. Patti LaBoucane-Benson, *The Outside Circle: A Graphic Novel*. Art by Kelly Mellings. House of Anansi Press, 2015.

the gut-wrenching process of healing and believe that change is possible" ("Truth, Dialogue"). In an interview with the Canadian Broadcasting Corporation (CBC), LaBoucane-Benson spoke about a group of grade 10 boys (characterized as "resistant readers") who devoured this comic. From them she witnessed firsthand the values of truth, storytelling, and the dialogue that were inspired by the text—values that Indigenous comics like hers can help foster among Indigenous and non-Indigenous youth, which are so important to the collective reconciliation journey.

This increase in the production of Indigenous comics in Canada is even more recent than the publication of Indigenous children's picture books, which, as postcolonial critic Clare Bradford notes, continue to be "a high priority for indigenous publishing houses, which seek to offer indigenous children experiences of narrative subjectivity while enabling non-indigenous children to engage with cultural difference" ("Race" 45). Writing and drawing are important strategies for self-representation. Publishing for young people is a crucial means of decolonization, Bradford suggests ("Prisms" 30). Indigenous writers have worked in fiction, autobiography, poetry, drama, and now in comics, not just harnessing the power of words to address colonial and assimilationist crises head on but also using visual representation to educate younger generations of readers about the past. Many graphic texts by Indigenous authors in Canada emphasize the spatial diaspora that occurred with the forced removal of Indigenous peoples from their ancestral lands and, as a countermove, the importance of community and family, specifically the influence of older generations (elders, parents, and grandparents), in helping Indigenous children establish or deepen their knowledge of cultural traditions and traditional knowledges.

Doris Wolf and Paul DePasquale argue that education about cultural traditions is an important component of the kinship relations that were destroyed by the influence of the European bourgeois patriarchal family (94). For Mississauga Nishnaabeg scholar Leanne Betasamosake Simpson, Indigenous storytelling is a crucial aspect "of returning to ourselves, a reengagement with the things we have left behind, a reemergence, an unfolding from the inside out" (17). Such stories about rebuilding, struggle, and self-determination are not all crisis-based narratives or victim-based narratives, she reminds readers; these stories rely on a "return to self-determination and change from within rather than recognition from the outside" (Simpson 22). Many Indigenous picture books, such as Jan Bourdeau Waboose's *Firedancers* (1999) and Deborah L. Delaronde's *Flour Sack Flora* (2015), and comics, like David Alexander Robertson's *Will I See?* (2016), focus on the renewed importance given to matrilineal genealogy and the maternal to help counteract the "double dispossession" that Indigenous women have suffered because of the colonialist heteropatriarchy that emphasizes the primacy of men, the fraternal links between Indigenous and colonial men, and the consequent subordination of Indigenous women to both groups (Wolf and DePasquale 96). These Indigenous picture books and comics specifically counteract contemporary stereotypes about Indigenous peoples by producing positive images of themselves "grounded in principles of self-representation and self-determination" (Wolf, "Seductions" 180). In their depictions of nurturing Indigenous families and communities, Indigenous picture books and Indigenous comics provide a visual and narrative response to colonial history and emphasize cultural affirmation, renewal, and hope in the process.

## Truth Telling:
## Visualizing Colonialism and Gender Violence

Specific genres of written discourse—the captivity narrative, the travel narrative, and European eyewitness accounts of "authentic" Native communities—have traditionally been used by Euro-Americans to characterize Indigenous peoples (Bradford, *Unsettling* 72). In turn, these genres have naturalized the conquest, removal, and further marginalization of Indigenous communities. These genres and texts often represent Indigenous peoples stereotypically, as sage figures, or as "at risk" peoples such as the urban homeless, people struggling with addictions and mental illness, alienated people caught between cultures, and so forth. In their complex deployment of word and image, Indigenous comics are bearers of important knowledge that can hopefully effect change at the very least at the educational level, if not at the political and ideological levels. In this way, they function as the visual embodiment of "wordarrows," a term coined by Anishinaabe writer and member of the Minnesota Chippewa Tribe Gerald Vizenor in 1978 to designate the "transformative power" of words as they are shot at colonial narratives in an effort to reclaim Indigenous epistemic ground (McLeod 31). Just as wordarrows help to establish discursive spaces for Indigenous peoples that resist colonial violence, comics offer spaces in which to share Indigenous stories and knowledge geared toward younger audiences. This is the decolonializing work of storytelling. More specifically, in the creative process and the reading experience, these visual texts are agentic and participatory in knowledge production, emphasizing the personal and political importance of connectivity, transmission, and cultural inheritance in a desire to restore a sense of belonging and balance to Indigenous communities and to the larger Canadian populace.

Stories bind communities together spiritually and relationally, both in the telling and in the reading process. Stories grounded in the material realities of the peoples whose lives are marked by the scars of colonialism bear witness to the traumas that land struggles, historical erasure, and the many other violences inflicted by global colonialism have produced, as we have seen previously with the comics that examine particular conflict zones around the world. Storytelling functions "as a crucial element in establishing new identities of longing (directed toward the past) and belonging (directed toward the future)" (Schaffer and Smith 19). Indigenous comics like *Sugar Falls* (2011), *Lost Innocence* (2013), and *A Girl Called Echo* (2020–), among many others, respond to and critique the longstanding assimilationist policies of the government of Canada. They acknowledge and validate Indigenous peoples' experiences of violence and racism by filling in historical gaps and correcting falsehoods and omissions. More specifically, they are valuable educational resources that mobilize the power of the visual to deepen young readers' knowledge about Canada's all too violent past. By challenging the Canadian colonial "master narrative," these graphic texts provide a visual "counterstory" to the benevolent peacemaker myth of settler Canada (Regan 34) and offer opportunities for critical reflection and catharsis in the hopes of facilitating the healing process. As testimonials of trauma, they also use Indigenous principles of "interrogation, critique, and theory [. . .] as the intelligence system that instigates resurgence and is the process from which grounded, real world, Indigenous alternatives are manifest and realized" (Simpson 34).

Historically, Indigenous literatures have struggled against Canadian cultural and language barriers, ethnocentrism in the academic establishment, competition from non-Indigenous authors, and feelings of estrangement in the Canadian publishing industry, which is still dominated by Eurocentric values. Indigenous storytellers have endured the forced alienation from their ancestral stories, a removal "from the voices and echoes of the ancestors," which Cree writer Neal McLeod describes as an "attempt to destroy collective consciousness" (19). Because of the problems of cultural appropriation and/or misrepresentation in the Canadian publishing industry, Indigenous authors have advocated for the need for Indigenous editing and publishing principles and practices as a solution. Independent presses that specialize in Indigenous comics, picture books, and stories in general are crucial to address the diaspora that emerges from a colonial presence in the production of cultural and literary texts. Small presses and publishing houses in Canada—Pemmican and HighWater Press (both located in Winnipeg, Manitoba), Theytus (located in Penticton, British Columbia), and The Indigenous Story Studio (located in Courtenay, British Columbia)—help to minimize the alienating process that Indigenous writers often experience in the writing and publishing industries. Pemmican Publications, the only Métis publishing house, specializes in children's texts; since its establishment in 1980, it has published thirty books for young readers. *Li Minoush*, written by Bonnie Murray, illustrated by Sheldon Dawson, and translated by Rita Flamand in 2001 (part of the Michif Children's Series published by Pemmican), is a dual-language book in English and Michif (the mixed language spoken by Plains Métis, comprising French nouns in conjunction with Plains Cree verbal systems), affirming the importance of the Michif language to young readers. Theytus Press's name emphasizes this particular principle. A Salishan word that means "preserving for the sake of handing down," Theytus publishes Indigenous texts that document and preserve language, rituals, songs, narratives, and cultural practices. It has published both a dual-language Cree–English text and a Cree symbol version of Beth Cuthand and Mary Longman's *The Little Duck* (1999), for example.

These small presses advocate for a culturally based editorial process that incorporates specific guidelines that do not follow European-based rules and practices. Some of the practices that govern their publication choices include making use of oral tradition principles within the editorial process; respecting, establishing, and defining Indigenous colloquial forms of English (a developing area of study that is termed "Red English" or "Rez English," Indigenous patois); incorporating Indigenous traditional protocols in considering the appropriateness of presenting particular aspects of culture; and consulting and soliciting the approval of elders and traditional leaders in the publishing of sacred cultural material (Young-Ing 236). The works they produce counteract the distancing experiences Indigenous young readers can have while reading texts that are written by white writers, predominantly focus on white children, and are framed according to European editorial principles.

HighWater Press, an imprint of Portage & Main Press, has published most of Swampy Cree writer David Alexander Robertson's impressive oeuvre, including *Sugar Falls* (2011), *7 Generations* (2012), and his *Tales from Big Spirit* series (2014–16), texts that will be explored in this chapter. Most of the comics that HighWater publishes focus broadly on education about diversity and more specifically about the theme and practice of reconciliation.

HighWater published Dogrib writer Richard Van Camp's *A Blanket of Butterflies* in 2015, illustrated by Scott B. Henderson. *Butterflies* is part of the Debwe Series, named in the spirit of the Anishinaabe concept of *debwe* (to speak the truth). This comic follows the story of Shinobu, a stranger who visits Fort Smith, Northwest Territories, to retrieve his family's samurai suit of armor and sword from the local museum, which were mistakenly sent to the Northwest Territories instead of Fort Smith, Arkansas. In Van Camp's narrative, Shinobu is from Nagasaki; he positions himself and his Japanese community as similar to the Indigenous peoples of Canada. This worldly comparison accomplishes several functions: It stresses the community of human loss in the global history of colonialism, it specifically addresses an organized and systematic attack on an entire population by a dominant country, and it offers an accusation of the colonial power—the dropping of the atomic bombs on Japan by America (and its European Allies) is compared to the colonization of the Indigenous peoples in Canada. *A Blanket of Butterflies* focuses on communities: the process of reconciliation that must take place among members of the Fort Smith community itself and even more broadly between colonized peoples in Canada and in Japan. As *A Blanket of Butterflies* imagines, the spirit world has a tremendous ability to heal rifts and to help people recover from the scars of global wounds.

Comics like these are important tools for truth telling. They could be used to facilitate intergenerational exchange in and among Indigenous communities and to emphasize the personal and political importance of connectivity between Indigenous and non-Indigenous communities.

## Reframing History:
### *Tales from Big Spirit* and *Will I See?*

Although many Indigenous comics focus on life-writing, increasingly these texts are expanding into fantasy, myth, realism, and speculative fiction. Cree author David Alexander Robertson and Métis writer Katherena Vermette are central figures in this growing field of Indigenous comics in Canada produced for young readers; their narratives are frequently illustrated by Scott B. Henderson. Since the early 2000s, librarians and teachers have begun to incorporate literature in comics into the curriculum as opportunities "for schools to promote student engagement with history" (Cromer and Clark 575). Michael Cromer and Penney Clark suggest that historical accounts in comics are more accessible to students because they are comparable to the hypertext and multimodal formats with which many students are already knowledgeable, thanks to their familiarity with social media interfaces (586). Comics about history might even encourage students to question or challenge official historical accounts—institutional and national histories and knowledges—that they encounter in text-only versions. Robertson believes that the visual elements of the comic are its particular strengths as a teaching tool: "In a text perspective, we're asking students to just imagine things. When we're presenting them with images, it forces them to be there and see it, rather than imagine it. And I think that is a far more important way to experience things that happened in history" ("David Alexander Robertson Calls"). Robertson employs the graphic medium to interrogate the violence of colonialism, the IRS system, and its legacy of intergenerational trauma in *Sugar Falls* (2011) and *7 Generations* (2012), written for young readers in hopes that his stories will lead to change.

In each of the seven comics by Robertson grouped under the series title *Tales from Big Spirit* (2014–16), for example, an important figure in the history of Indigenous peoples and in Canadian history is the focus.[6] Intended for students in grades 4 to 6 as part of the social studies curricula in Canada, the comics align with the framework created by the Historical Thinking Project, a Canadian nonprofit educational initiative that uses research to promote critical and historical literacy. Young readers can dip into Robertson's series and read only one or several of the seven self-enclosed comics, or they can read them all to gain a deeper understanding of the diversity of Indigenous figures that complicate Canada's official history. In their literary-visual format, these comics reclaim epistemic ground that was appropriated by colonialism, affirming "that the subjectivity of Indigenous peoples is both politically and intellectually valid" (Sium and Ritskes iv). Each comic begins with a contemporary frame in which a child engages directly with history (through visions, dreams, and sometimes even time travel), encouraging Indigenous and non-Indigenous readers to situate themselves in relation to that reclaimed history.

*The Ballad of Nancy April* (2014) focuses on Shawnadithit, the last remaining member of the Beothuk people. It catalogues the long, bitter struggle of the Beothuk against European expansion into Newfoundland and Labrador,

---

6. Robertson's series includes *The Ballad of Nancy April: Shawnadithit* (2014), *The Land of Os: John Ramsay* (2014), *The Peacemaker: Thanadelthur* (2014), *The Poet: Pauline Johnson* (2014), *The Rebel: Gabriel Dumont* (2014), *The Scout: Tommy Prince* (2014), and *The Chief: Mistahimaskwa* (2016). Most of the narratives are illustrated by long-time collaborator Scott B. Henderson, though *The Land of Os* and *The Peacemaker* are illustrated by Wai Tien and *The Rebel* by Andrew Lodwick. Throughout the series, attention is given to gender equity: There are an equal number of Indigenous women and men who are the focus of each historical narrative, both in past and contemporary time periods.

FIGURE 3.2. Indigenous Beothuk people encounter Europeans. David Alexander Robertson, *The Ballad of Nancy April: Shawnadithit*. Illustrated by Scott B. Henderson. HighWater Press, 2014, p. 6.

but its historical survey is bracketed by a contemporary frame narrative about Jessie, from Big Spirit First Nation reserve, who has a vision of Shawnadithit while walking home from school. Jessie's vision deepens her sense of cultural heritage. As Jessie wades deeper and deeper into the forest, the panels of the page transform into tree branches, and she falls back through history to 1475, allowing her to bear witness to the beginnings of the European incursion (see figure 3.2). The black gutter that separates the "white-skinned" from the Beothuk on this page emphasizes visually the insurmountable divide that separates colonizer from colonized, right from the first point of contact. As an extension of the wind, Jessie witnesses the lengthy process during which the Beothuk are systematically eradicated in Newfoundland and Labrador during the course of four centuries. Jessie gains firsthand insight into the innumerable slave expeditions mounted by the Portuguese and the Spanish who wanted to bring Beothuk people back to Europe as gifts for the king or as slaves for the black market. By means of Robertson's comic, and thanks to Henderson's vibrant visuals, contemporary younger readers are encouraged to understand how the land in Newfoundland and

Labrador was taken over by the Europeans and how the Beothuk began to starve. Making use of the comic's visual potential, Robertson reframes history from a distinctly Indigenous perspective and brings this forgotten (or silenced) history into the present by means of young Jessie, who awakens from her vision wearing Shawnadithit's traditional beads. Robertson's main conceit of using a contemporary youth on the way to school to juxtapose past and present through "lived" experience deepens his idea of living history whereby a young person learns the value of reclaimed history. As with *Zenobia, Baddawi,* and *They Called Us Enemy,* the comic represents complex information about cultural displacement and suffering and, by means of the child witness, solicits sympathetic readings from its audiences.

Thanks to their verbal/visual interface, comics have an ability to "speak beyond linguistic, cultural, and intergenerational gaps," to translate across cultures in an effort to bring up issues for "diffusion and discussion" between and among many audiences (Henzi 24): young people, adults, teachers, scholars, activists. They have a particular ability to bridge disciplines, to address the political, social, and cultural aspects of community. Teachers and librarians have come to view comics as a partial response to falling literacy rates, as a way to attract reluctant readers to texts, and as a supplement to multiliteracies since they make use of word and image. As alternative and often subversive forms of storytelling, Indigenous comics also present visual and narrative opportunities to truth-tell, to reflect on and resist Canada's history of colonialism, allowing readers to immerse themselves in vivid verbal and visual sensory fields. Frequently, they speak a language of resistance and resurgence. As Sarah Henzi argues, comics partake in the "creation of a new space to [. . .] reaffirm experiences, histories and memory, and to rectify the falsity of colonial imagery" (36–37). Even more importantly, they abstain from pushing Indigenous peoples to the peripheries of national narratives and public discourses. They specifically reinsert figures or important narratives into the wider historical and national fabric of Canada. Mi'kmaq writer Brandon Mitchell's graphic narrative *Lost Innocence* and Robertson's *7 Generations* saga, among others, call into question the benevolent peacemaker myth that Canada uses to bolster its national and international identity. More importantly, comics have a direct and immediate impact, linking one generation to the next and the past to the present. In allowing the reader to "mask" themselves in its representational figuration, comics encourage "the reader to connect to other experiences and other communities that might otherwise have been unfamiliar" (Parker Royal, "Coloring" 10). Their accessibility and adaptability ask readers to question narrative in a way that youth might not feel as comfortable doing with a canonical literary text or historical textbook.

Indigenous comics, now emerging at a rapid rate, are responding to the call made by Canada's Truth and Reconciliation Commission (TRC) in its 2015 Executive Summary to educate. "Using the power of the graphic medium to both show and tell" (Wolf, "Unsettling" 221), they tackle vital issues that affect Indigenous populations across Canada, such as chronic poverty, social exclusion, suicide, homelessness, violent death, substance and solvent addiction, disease, incarceration, colonialism, and cultural dislocation. Almost all of these texts resist the epistemology of victimhood.

Currently, the approximately 1,200 Indigenous girls and women who have disappeared and/or who have been murdered across Canada, an occurrence that James Anaya, UN Special Rapporteur on the Rights of Indigenous Peoples, has characterized as "disturbing" and "epidemic," are also a focus in Indigenous comics for young people (de Finney 171). "In Canada, Indigenous girls have the highest rates of sexual exploitation, racialized violence, incarceration, poverty, underhousing and homelessness, and underservicing in health and education" (171). An estimated 25 to 50 percent of Indigenous young women experience child sexual abuse, and they are also more likely to be trafficked in the sex and drug trades (171). Statistics like these speak to a dominant attitude about Indigenous women in Canada as being somehow exploitable and dispensable, a conception that stems from early assimilative colonial practices that governed who could be enrolled as members of First Nations, Métis, and Inuit communities. Women in particular were affected by the paternalistic gender framework that sustained the Indian Act of 1876. This act and its amendments institutionalized gender discrimination, helping to erode women's traditional rights and responsibilities within their own communities and families by regulating their status, excluding them from political governance, and forcing their children to attend residential schools. Until 1985, for example, an Indigenous woman who married a non-Indigenous man lost her membership in the community and her identity (i.e., her status) as an "Indian," whereas if an Indigenous man married a non-Indigenous woman, his female partner gained Indian status automatically. Bill C-31, passed in 1985 as an amendment to the Indian Act, was intended to bring the act into line in terms of gender equality under the Charter of Rights and Freedoms and reverse this sexually discriminatory policy. Yet gender discrimination persists, insidiously.

Nehiyaw and Trinidadian creator Tasha Spillett's *Surviving the City* (2018–20) is the most recent comic that deals explicitly with missing and murdered Indigenous girls, women, and two-spirit people. David Alexander

Robertson responds to institutionalized gender discrimination and the continuing epidemic of gender violence among Indigenous communities in at least three of his graphic texts: *The Life of Helen Betty Osborne: A Graphic Novel* (2008), *Betty: The Helen Betty Osborne Story* (2015), and *Will I See?* (2016). For Leanne Betasamosake Simpson, "Gender violence and the destruction of Indigenous families are the fundamental dividing and dispossessional issues of our times" (54), serving as colonial tactics to harm, humiliate, and shame. The murder of high school student Helen Betty Osborne in The Pas, Manitoba, in 1971 is at the center of two of Robertson's comics and informs two others. In these texts, Osborne is a visual synecdoche for the missing and murdered Indigenous girls and women across Canada. By means of its frame narrative of a young man reading stories about Indigenous women on social media, *Betty: The Helen Betty Osborne Story* (2015) encourages readers to reflect on what they can do to raise awareness about this horrific occurrence. On Facebook, the male character reads of yet another request from the police in Winnipeg for help in locating a missing sixteen-year-old Indigenous girl. This is followed by a splash page of his computer screen, featuring photos of other missing Indigenous women from all across Canada. Osborne's vicious murder and the contemporary frame character's realization that this reality of missing and murdered Indigenous women and girls dates back decades inspire him to "share" the missing girl's story on social media so that more people can become educated about racialized gender violence.

For Paulette Regan, a former residential schools claims manager, the foundational myth of Canada as a benevolent peacemaker must be destroyed, a process that can only be undertaken through the "restorying" of the past. This "restorying" process occurs in three ways, Doris Wolf argues: telling the stories that refute this peacemaker myth and focus instead on the violence that lies at the heart of Indigenous–settler relations; acknowledging Indigenous histories of law, diplomacy, and peacemaking to uncover how such Indigenous histories have been silenced; and reestablishing Indigenous practices as powerful possibilities today ("Unsettling" 208). This crucial need to imagine and act otherwise informs *Will I See?* (2016), a collaborative project by David Alexander Robertson, Cree/Dené musician IsKwé, and settler illustrator GMB Chomichuk. *Will I See?* begins with a rhetorical question for May, the Indigenous adolescent whose perspective shapes the narrative, and all young readers. The interrogative invites and challenges readers to confront the reality of the Missing and Murdered Indigenous Women, Girls, Trans, and 2-Spirited People (MMIWGT2S) across North America. Robertson's comic is based on a multimedia project by IsKwé, Chomichuk, and digital artist Erin Leslie about the murder in August 2014 of fifteen-year-old

Tina Fontaine, a member of the Sagkeeng First Nation in Manitoba. Robertson's comic panels present May as she walks home across the city, finding keepsakes and totems in different places along the way. When May and her Kookum string these totems into a necklace, May experiences visions of violent acts committed against Indigenous girls and women in her city. Present, past, fantasy, reality, colonial establishment, and Indigenous heritage are juxtaposed from the very first page as May's shrewd eyes seemingly look back to the epigraphs that open the text, epigraphs that reference the MMIWGT2S and invite readers to reflect on "the seen and the unseen [. . .] the forgotten and the remembered."

Chomichuk's aesthetic is as haunting as the subject matter of the text. The pages consist of black-and-white sketches, at times photo negative impressions that enhance the narrative's dreamlike, shadowy, and threatening atmosphere. Cree syllabics are superimposed over the pages haphazardly as though knowledge about these mysteries lurks just out of reach. The visuals envision a cold, hard, dangerous city, with splashes of red that stand out in harsh relief. The vivid red color distinguishes the items (a stone, an earring, a pendant, a key on a chain, a ring, a braided leather bracelet, an arrowhead, a leaf ornament) that May finds on her way home, the red in turn evoking danger and blood and linking the ephemeral images of violence toward spectral Indigenous girls and women that emerge in May's visions. These found objects communicate memories or suggest links to the women who lost them: "I wear it [the pendant] and it reminds me . . . It's like carrying a memory," May muses to herself. Images of Indigenous girls and women being shaken or beaten by men are unfocused. Smears of red grow larger and more expansive as the comic progresses, stretching across entire pages, across the affectless city (of Vancouver, presumably, and even across North America; see figure 3.3). On a two-page spread, the entire city is eventually painted red, with trails of blood stretching across the images and these found objects, suggesting the legacy of gender violence that stains all of North America. Young readers encounter this page horizontally, as the bird "spreads" over the cityscape below, and vertically in relation to the four inset panels that link a victim of gender violence and May herself, as she encounters totems of these victims across the city. The black hand (symbol of the Missing and Murdered Indigenous Women, Girls, Trans, and 2-Spirited movement) located in a bottom inset panel, out of which blood runs, symbolizes at once the voices of the women who have been silenced by sexual and gender-based violence, a legacy that May (and young readers) is invited to see. It is also May's hand that releases the blood from the amulet, figuratively insisting that stories cannot be silenced and sharing the blood-history to help ensure that the spirits of the dead are released.

FIGURE 3.3. May encounters legacies of violence. David Alexander Robertson et al., *Will I See?* Art by GMB Chomichuk. HighWater Press, 2016.

A transition occurs in the comic when May arrives at her Kookum's house. One of the few pages that does not feature individual comics panels, it uses the entire page to characterize the ideas that swirl around May and her Kookum as they discuss May's tardiness and her grandmother's worry about her, the objects that May found on her way home, and the missing girls and women whose spirits seemingly hover in the air around them. May's Kookum softens the horror of their trauma by telling May a story in which their spirits return to Mother Earth after death: "When we lose them, they blossom again, from Mother Earth. Their spirits do, you see?" Her Kookum continues to reassure her: "They become animal spirits, and everything those spirits represent. They become one. They are beautiful, always. They create flower blooms with every step they take. They leave flowers everywhere. And when we pick them, they share their spirit with us." As her Kookum tells this story, the girls and women transform into an eagle, a bear, a deer. Robertson, IsKwé, Chomichuk, and Leslie collaborated on this multimedia project to focus on Indigenous conceptualizations of life, the "cycles of creative energies, continual processes that bring forth more life and more creation and more thinking" (Simpson 24), in the face of the gender violence—past and ongoing—with which Indigenous communities live. As Candida Rifkind and Jessica Fontaine argue, instead of teaching about the pain inflicted by colonial violence on Indigenous communities, Robertson's comic and the multimedia project emphasize the continued spiritual presence of these missing Indigenous women after their disappearance (358).

The connections that the spirit guides offer May are not always happy, however. As these lost Indigenous girls and women gain focus in her visions, they begin to affect May deeply during the day and populate her nightmares. Chomichuk captures this idea vividly: Visions burst through the panels on the page and culminate with an entire splash page that depicts a frightening man (without pupils, but a predatory smile) hiding in the bushes, overlain by the ominous color red. May "sees" haunting images of a woman being prevented from screaming, pushed into a car, her face pressed up against the window as the car speeds off. Image after image convey the threat, the danger, the terror, and the helplessness that May feels when confronted by the willful blindness of the city's inhabitants to members of her community. Eventually, however, May finds strength in her visions, and it is by "seeing" these women—women in turn visualized on the comic's page—that she can release their spirits. By the end, these spirits are more clearly rendered than May herself, especially in the image in which May watches the spirit crane and bird fly off over the city. Finally, her horrific visions are transformed into beautiful, organic images of life and flight. The final page culminates with Kookum's quiet affirmation, "I see." May and her Kookum both vow to share the necklace and what it means so that the vision and the terrible reality of this gender violence are not forgotten. Robertson's comic "sees" this horror that targets Indigenous girls and women and encourages readers to see it too. *Will I See?* concludes with the peaceful image of a crane with outstretched wings hovering over May as she hugs her mother closely, affirming their love, community, and vitality.

In their arresting visual truth telling, in the open exchange they foster regarding Canada's controversial past, Indigenous comics for young readers like *Betty* and *Will I See?* resist the tendency to erase the violent history of colonialism through willful ignorance, an ignorance that in turn ensures that racial stratification remains and that systematic injustice continues. Instead, the comics deploy the accessibility and adaptability of the visual format as a form of living resistance to specific crises that affect Indigenous populations across Canada and North America.

## Acknowledging:
## Learning from the Residential School System

"We need to look at the past to teach others our stories and then look forward, together, with knowledge and healing" (40), affirms Betty Ross, elder from Cross Lake First Nation, at the end of *Sugar Falls* (2011), a residential school story that is Robertson's follow-up to *The Life of Helen Betty Osborne*. Although the practices of child removal and forced assimilation were classified as acts of cultural genocide by the United Nations in 1948, the IRS system was not fully abandoned in Canada until 1996. Recognition by Canadians of the profoundly negative impact of the schools on Indigenous peoples, and of the effects that these "stolen" and "lost" generations continue to have on Indigenous cultures, is ongoing. The recent discoveries in 2021 and 2022 of bodies of Indigenous young people found in unmarked graves at former residential schools across Canada remind people in Canada and around the world of the long history of erasure that distinguishes Canada's history and the ongoing systemic violence committed against Indigenous children and youth.[7]

Relocations of Indigenous peoples and even whole communities in Canada have been frequent since contact. In 1991 the Royal Commission on Aboriginal Peoples (RCAP) report enumerated the terrible consequences that these relocations have had for Canada's first peoples: They severed Indigenous people's relationship to the land and weakened their cultural and communal bonds; dispossessions led to a loss of economic self-sufficiency, including increased dependence on government transfer payments; they have also resulted in a decline in standards of health and changes in social and political relations within the relocated population (Vowel 191). After the

---

7. The remains of more than 1,000 people (mainly children) were discovered on the grounds of three former residential schools in British Columbia and Saskatchewan in May 2021. In June 2021, the remains of another 751 people (again, mostly children), were discovered at another former residential school in Saskatchewan. In the national TRC report, the commission estimated that at least 4,100 students had gone missing or had died in these schools. The Honourable Murray Sinclair, a former member of the Canadian Senate and Indigenous lawyer who headed the commission from 2009 to 2015, said in an email that he now believed that the number was "well beyond 10,000" (Austen).

Confederation of Canada in 1867, the new Canadian government practiced internal colonialism in the biopolitical and geopolitical management of its people: It used modes of control (like prisons, reserves, schools, policing, and minoritizing) "to ensure the ascendency of a nation and its white elite" (Tuck and Yang 5). Policies were formulated that displaced Indigenous peoples, who were seen as obstacles to settlement, and that controlled the proliferation of Indigenous languages and stories. To "help" Indigenous members to adapt to contemporary life, they were encouraged to sign treaties, move onto reserves, and take up farming—thereby disrupting kinship and governance systems further and removing Indigenous peoples from their traditional economies and sources of food.[8] After engaging in 178 days of public hearings, visiting ninety-six communities, doing research, and consulting with experts, the conclusion of the report filed by the 1991 RCAP reads as follows: "Our central conclusion can be summarized simply: *The main policy direction, pursued by [sic] more than 150 years, first by colonial then by Canadian governments, has been wrong*" ("Highlights," emphasis added). Even after the publication of this report, Indigenous populations have continued to be at risk of removal from what remains of their homelands (to enable bourgeoning urbanization and the corporate exploitation of natural resources like oil and gas pipelines). And they continue to suffer the highest rates of poverty, suicide, homelessness, violent death, drug and alcohol addiction, disease, imprisonment, and cultural dislocation (Fast and Collin-Vezina 127). Life's basics—clean drinking water, adequate housing, education, and child welfare—are still substandard, such that Canada has been admonished by the United Nations Economic and Social Council for the significant disparities that still exist between Canada's Indigenous and non-Indigenous peoples.

Commenting about the systemic injustices committed against Indigenous peoples, Doris Wolf argues that non-Indigenous Canadians must be involved in the truth and reconciliation process in ways that are genuinely intercultural. The "restorying" of the past, as she calls it—the dismantling of

---

8. In 1969 the White Paper (officially titled "Statement of the Government on Indian Policy") was circulated, a Canadian policy paper proposal made by Prime Minister Pierre Elliott Trudeau and his Minister of Indian Affairs, Jean Chrétien. The Canadian government wanted to finish the assimilation project by eliminating Indian status, abolishing the Indian Act, getting rid of the Department of Indian Affairs, converting communally held reserve lands to private property that could be sold by a First Nation or its members, transferring responsibility toward "Indians and lands reserved for Indians" from the federal to the provincial governments, appointing a commissioner to address any outstanding land claims, and gradually terminating existing treaties (Vowel 269). The racist policies of this White Paper were met with forceful opposition by Indigenous leaders in Canada.

the foundational myth of Canada as a benevolent peacemaker by focusing on the violence it has directed against entire communities—must be accomplished by *non*-Indigenous Canadians to understand and acknowledge that forced removals and relocations of Indigenous peoples and whole communities to make room for white settlement, as well as enforced education, were principal components of Canada's racist policies. Paulette Regan also insists that, before the real reconciliation process can begin, non-Indigenous Canadians must acknowledge that the IRS legacy is a settler problem rather than an Indigenous problem (63).

In Canada, residential schools operated for 150 years, beginning in the 1840s. By 1932 there were more than eighty schools in operation. More than 150,000 Indigenous children attended these schools; approximately 6,000 died in the system. Most schools were church affiliated: 67 percent were run by the Catholic Church, 20 percent by the Anglican Church, and the rest by other Protestant denominations (Vowel 171). In 1850 attendance at the residential schools became compulsory for all Indigenous children between the ages of six and fifteen; parental noncompliance was punishable by prison terms. And the quality of the instruction was substandard, since the children spent most of the day doing hard labor around the property. The residential school legacy is a story about racist and paternalistic educators, church officials, and a government who wanted to assimilate Indigenous children into mainstream Canadian society for "their own good." Young people were forcibly removed from their families by agents or police officers and forbidden to speak their own languages or practice their cultural or spiritual traditions. The other part of the story concerns the cultural, psychological, and emotional harms and traumatic abuses that were inflicted upon small children, "an intergenerational history of dispossession, violence, abuse, and racism that is a fundamental denial of the human dignity and rights of Indigenous peoples" (Regan 5).

A rash of apologies for the many types of abuse practiced in the IRS appeared from 1986 onward, as testimonies from survivors began to circulate: in 1986, from the United Church of Canada; in 1991, from the Missionary Oblates of Mary Immaculate; in 1993, from the Anglican Church; in 1994, from the Presbyterian Church; finally, in July 2022, Pope Francis formally apologized for the Catholic Church's role in Canada's residential school system. In 1988 then Minister of Indian Affairs Jane Stewart offered the first official apology from the Canadian government. On 11 June 2008, Prime Minister Stephen Harper offered an apology on behalf of Canada, but it was an apology that Cherokee writer Thomas King characterizes as "a stingy thing," limited only to the abuse that Indigenous peoples had endured in the residential school system (122–23), one that ignored the treaty violations, the theft of land and resources, and the institutional racism that Indigenous people have endured since contact. Harper's apology was made doubly insufficient on 25 September 2009 when, during the G20 Summit, he affirmed that "We [Canada] also have no history of colonialism" ("Every"). In stark contrast to Harper's convenient blindness, current Prime Minister Justin Trudeau has committed his Liberal government to full federal action on the TRC's final report. Although there is still much important work to be done to balance Indigenous rights and the creation of oil and gas pipelines on their traditional lands, the focus Trudeau has given to truth telling and historical acknowledgments is undeniable.

The repercussions of the IRS system are still very present. Although the last school closed in 1996, approximately 80,000 former students are still alive. The Indian Residential Schools Settlement Agreement (IRSSA) of 2006, the largest class-action settlement in Canadian history, responded to more than 12,000 individual abuse claims filed against the federal government and church entities. The IRSSA featured a number of components that addressed the needs of survivors. These included monetary reparations, an independent assessment process that adjudicated physical and sexual abuse claims and awards for financial compensation, a health support program for survivors administered by Health Canada, a commemoration program for memorial projects, and the creation of the TRC of Canada. The TRC, established in 2008 (the same year as Stephen Harper's apology), was charged with gathering testimony from former students, collecting documents relating to the schools, producing a report on the residential school system and its aftermath, and making recommendations to the government based on its findings.[9] The first paragraph alone of the TRC's Executive Summary is searing in its condemnation of Canada's long history of racist policies toward the Indigenous peoples whom it has dispossessed:

> For over a century, the central goals of Canada's Aboriginal policy were to eliminate Aboriginal governments; ignore Aboriginal rights; terminate the Treaties; and, through a process of assimilation, cause Aboriginal peoples to cease to exist as distinct legal, social, cultural, religious, and racial entities in Canada. The establishment and operation of residential schools were

---

9. The TRC issued an executive summary in the summer of 2015, eventually releasing six volumes of its final report on 15 December 2015. Its work has been transferred to the National Centre for Truth and Reconciliation housed at the University of Manitoba, which is now the permanent home for all statements, documents, and materials gathered by the TRC.

a central element of this policy, which can best be described as "cultural genocide." ("Truth")

Although the Executive Summary specifically identifies "education institutions and what they have taught, or failed to teach" (Vowel 175) as the source of the troubled relations between Indigenous peoples and non-Indigenous Canadians, the commission maintains that education is also key to reconciliation. In a national benchmark survey conducted in May 2008, results confirmed that although Canadians were somewhat familiar with the physical and sexual abuse that occurred in the IRS system, very few had any substantive knowledge about the policy goal of assimilation that motivated it (Regan 41–42). Truth and Reconciliation Commissioners warned in their Interim Report: "The Commission continues to face huge challenges in raising awareness, among non-Aboriginal Canadians, of the residential school history and legacy. This presents an enormous limitation to the possibility of long-term understanding and meaningful reconciliation" ("Truth").

## Visualizing Intergenerational Trauma: *7 Generations*

In response to this lack of awareness, education has become a primary concern and focus of Indigenous comics in Canada that are directed at young readers—education about Canada's past and present and education among communities, Indigenous and non-Indigenous alike. As the comics industry testifies, Indigenous experiences and acts of resistance have become "narratable" as a valid and valuable testimonial discourse. Indeed, they are "necessary interventions" (24), claims Sarah Henzi, whose Indigenous knowledge provides an antidote to the conventional history of the Americas and calls for an urgent change in worldview. Métis writer Jo-Ann Episkenew argues that contemporary Indigenous literature serves two transformative functions: "healing Indigenous people and advancing social justice in settler society" (15). For Indigenous creators and readers, these stories can bring healing by giving voice and validation to their collective experiences (Episkenew 16). They can also affect healing by advancing social justice, by educating settler readers about Indigenous perspectives and knowledges in Canada, and by challenging settler myths (17). Even more importantly, the transformation of trauma into narrative can enable Indigenous creators and readers to begin to distance themselves from the trauma (70). "By re-experiencing these emotions in a safe environment and by expressing them in language," Episkenew optimistically suggests, "we are often able to come to terms with emotional injuries and then move our emotional lives forward to a place of health and contentment" (70). In this way, Indigenous stories offer opportunities for critical reflection and catharsis.

David Alexander Robertson's *7 Generations: A Plains Cree Saga* (2012) is a persuasive educational tool to excavate the legacy of intergenerational trauma that European and Canadian colonialism, as well as the IRS system, have imposed on Indigenous peoples. Aimed at a grade 9–12 reading audience, *7 Generations* visualizes how identity is shaped by the relations of past and present ancestors and argues that reconciliation between past and present is needed to begin the intergenerational healing process. Beginning with the cover of the comic, contemporary protagonist Edwin gazes into the river and sees his father reflected there, the mirroring device suggesting that their identities are both united and separate and that "the entire narrative may be read as Edwin's healing journey to reconcile with his father" (Dudek 42). Endorsed by the chair of the TRC, Senator Murray Sinclair, a member of the Ojibway people, *7 Generations* is a powerful saga about the "cumulative emotional and physical wounding across generations" (Vowel 172), culminating in the renewal of the emotional bonds between Edwin and his absentee father, James. In the first section, *7 Generations* juxtaposes the experiences of Stone, Edwin's ancestor, and Edwin, the contemporary protagonist, whose suicide attempt in the opening pages immediately introduces readers to the psychological trauma, despair, loss, and loneliness that so many contemporary Indigenous peoples endure. As Edwin recovers in the hospital, his loving mother (who watches by his side) reminds him, "Our past has shaped us all. You, me . . . all of us. [. . .] You should know where you came from" (6–7). Edwin is very resistant to hearing about the past: He knows that the past can be and has been used to explain or justify poor behavior in the present (as he feels his father has done for years). His mother Lauren, however, uses this recovery time to educate him about his ancestors, from the beginning of the nineteenth century to the present. "Stone" is thus a powerful title for this first segment, referring as it does to Edwin's ancestor from two hundred years before. "Stone" also alludes to the amulet in the shape of an eagle's head that Stone found during his vision quest, a totem that has since traveled down the seven generations of his family to Edwin himself. The narrative suggests that the inspiring warrior story will help to weaken the "stony" silence that currently exists between Edwin and the missing father whom he craves.

A central tenet of Robertson's *7 Generations* saga and of Plains Cree Indigenous philosophy in general is that family relationships are central to the wellbeing of a people (see figures 3.4 and 3.5). On these mirrored pages, Robertson juxtaposes past and present yet links time and place, providing visual parallels between Stone's emotional tie to his brother, Bear, and Edwin's connection with his mother, Lauren (who watches over his recovery in the hospital). Both Stone and Edwin wake to emotional trauma: Stone, when he realizes that Bear has been killed by the Blackfoot during an ambush, and Edwin, when he realizes with disappointment that he is not dead after overdosing on pills. While Stone is tormented by the murder of his brother, Edwin does not fear death. He craves it. Henderson juxtaposes their different emotional states by means of polyptychs, parallel and mirrored pages, that each feature six frames, the central oval-shaped frames contrasting Edwin's current state of pain and despair with Bear's peaceful warrior's death. "I don't know what I want. I'm confused. This is pain," Edwin whispers into his hospital pillow (18). By means of these images, illustrator Henderson juxtaposes the vibrant colors of Bear's passing (his "good" death, being killed by a Blackfoot, a "warrior's death [22]), with the muted, jaded colors of Edwin, who remains reluctantly alive after the suicide attempt, still tortured by his many levels of suffering.

Edwin's failed suicide attempt leaves him open to his mother's storytelling about their past, about the six generations of Cree people that preceded him and helped make him who he is. Stone embodies the warrior ethic and spirit, and his precontact story has the potential to remind Edwin's family and community of the heroism and spirit that once defined who they were as a people. The visual and literary trope of the calling river continues this idea, emphasizing the connection that Lauren wishes to forge between Edwin and his ancestors to remind her son of the powerful emotions of love, grief, and courage that Edwin and Stone share, even though they are separated by two centuries of colonial upheaval. Lauren uses Stone's story to remind her son that hope energizes people when they know they have someone to fight for: "Maybe you will know that someone is fighting for you, too," she suggests to him quietly (31). Lauren breathes life into these stories from the past, the vibrant colors of the narratives pre- and postcontact emphasizing their liveliness. Significantly, these flashbacks occupy the majority of the visual narrative, inserting themselves into Edwin's lived reality and helping to transform his turbulent present.

So much of this text is about learning from the past and embracing the knowledges that Indigenous ancestors taught. Eventually, readers realize that Lauren's opening words, "Come on, pick up," are not to Edwin at all but to Edwin's father, with whom Edwin is eager to reconnect (3). "Scars," the second section of *7 Generations*, visualizes the devastating impacts of

FIGURE 3.4. Edwin awakens in the hospital. David Alexander Robertson, *7 Generations*. Illustrated by Scott B. Henderson. HighWater Press, 2012, p. 18.

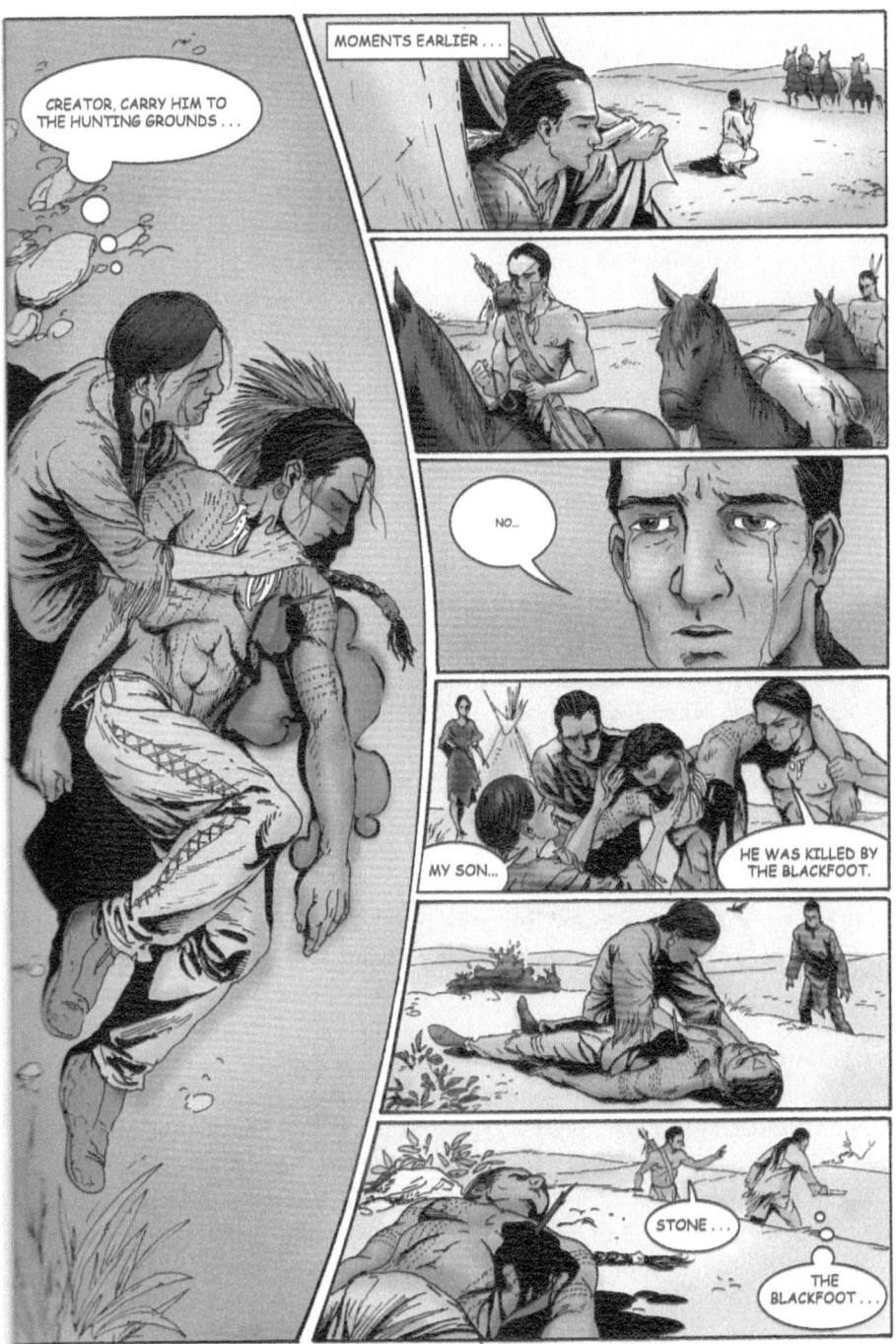

FIGURE 3.5. Bear's death. David Alexander Robertson, *7 Generations*. Illustrated by Scott B. Henderson. HighWater Press, 2012, p. 19.

colonialism that continue to affect the present. The title is again extremely evocative. "Scars" refer to the physical traces that the smallpox epidemics left on the bodies of Indigenous peoples after contact with settler societies, to the physical and metaphorical traumas that continue to affect Indigenous peoples in Canada, and to the emotional scars that abusive experiences in the IRS system left on Edwin's father, which he in turn feared to inflict on Edwin (see figure 3.6). This page of the comic makes evident that the father's guilt about the abuse he suffered at school is destroying his son. The fragments of the cracked picture of Edwin's father on the bedside table are echoed in the panel frame that features Edwin after his attempted suicide, reminding readers of the intergenerational shattering of families. Lauren teaches Edwin the important lesson about loving someone so much and having to let them go (a decision we learn that Edwin's father made in the past and that has scarred his son deeply). To do this, Lauren focuses on another ancestor, White Cloud, who lived in 1870 and endured the arrival of smallpox. "In many ways, it was the end of our way of life as a people. The end of the time we called paradise" (38), Lauren tells her fragile son. The only one left of his tribe after the smallpox wiped them out, White Cloud sets off on his journey of survival. A difficult choice to return to save a Cree girl whom he, his cousin, and his uncle found alone and sick further isolates White Cloud when his uncle and cousin abandon him out of fear of catching the deadly disease. Returning for her, White Cloud discovers that she has hanged herself in despair. The devastation he feels knowing that he was involved in that suicide decision, coupled with his realization that his newfound family has abandoned him as well, threaten to undo him (see figure 3.7). On the page, the white of the birch trees echoes the fragments of the broken picture frame in the first book, visually linking Edwin and White Cloud in their frustration and despair. "Memories were hard to lose. Like scars, you see," Lauren muses. "There, always. Always a part of you. Even amongst the thick and endless trees" (56). At this point, the change in narration from Lauren to Edwin signals both an acknowledgment of the past and a fragile but newfound feeling of peace. Thanks to Lauren's storytelling and White Cloud's vision of his father, who reminds him that he must live to ensure that his people are not forgotten, Edwin and White Cloud search deep within themselves for strength. Seeing this, Lauren gives Stone's eagle amulet to Edwin, telling him, "It has the power of our culture within it. It will help you on your journey to healing" (60). Henderson's illustrations link White Cloud's smallpox scars with the scars of Edwin's self-cutting, both visual reminders of colonial oppression. These scars, however, do not have to continue to define Edwin in the present, a truth he comes to realize.

FIGURE 3.6. Edwin confronts an image of his father. David Alexander Robertson, *7 Generations*. Illustrated by Scott B. Henderson. HighWater Press, 2012, p. 35.

FIGURE 3.7. Edwin and White Cloud are juxtaposed. David Alexander Robertson, *7 Generations*. Illustrated by Scott B. Henderson. HighWater Press, 2012, p. 56.

The third section of Robertson's graphic narrative, "Ends/Begins," demonstrates that the intergenerational nature of the dysfunctional family is rooted in a system that wanted to assimilate all Indigenous peoples. The backslash that separates the words in the title is mirrored in the diagonal gutter that separates Edwin from his father in the final two frames of "Scars." This literal and metaphorical backslash separates yet links these two men, at once severing a link yet solidifying the connection between them. The nature of this connection is something for the present, and the rest of *7 Generations*, to clarify. This third section focuses on the traumas of Edwin's father, James, and his father's brother, Thomas, in the IRS and the scars they bear because of the abuse they endured in a system that attempted to suppress "the Indian in the child." Edwin's father is triply scarred by the crippling guilt he carries with him because he could not save Thomas from death. Finally, he decides to leave his family so that he will not inflict his past traumas on them. His actions are misguided, however. Edwin's feelings of abandonment contribute to his suicide attempt. Henderson's color palette darkens once James and Thomas arrive at the residential school, emphasizing the stark contrast between life before and after, juxtaposing their happiness at home and the sadness, terror, and abuse that they experience at school. The boys become visually interchangeable once absorbed into the system; they are stripped of their clothes, their language, and their Cree identity. The regularity of the panels that depict life at the school emphasizes the surveillance that the system practiced on the children, the rigid cycle of Christian prayer, "manual training" (79), and the school lessons that they endured every day. The terrific beating that James gives the priest when he discovers him brutally whipping Thomas propels Thomas out into the snowy landscape, dressed only in his pajamas, running in terror. Tripping on a rock, Thomas strikes his head and dies instantly in the snow. A visual analogue is made between the white priest brutally strapping Thomas and the aggressive position of James standing over toddler Edwin years later, on the verge of strapping him with a belt when he finds him playing in the road (and in danger of being hit by a car). Thus, the cycle of abuse and trauma "ends/begins," as Robertson and Henderson remind us literally and visually.

"Ends/Begins" and "The Pact," the fourth segment of 7 *Generations*, feature the confession narrative of James as he tries to acknowledge his grief, guilt, and despair and begin the process of reconciliation with his son. Robertson and Henderson draw a visual parallel between Stone tripping over a stone in his vision quest, which leads to him finding his eagle stone (and his warrior identity), and Thomas tripping over a stone, hitting his head, and dying, a moment that in turn haunts James for much of his adult life. Both events are powerfully jarring but equally instrumental in providing these men with direction and focus. Seven generations into the future, Stone's leadership and spirit inspire James to assume agency over his life and emotional well-being. Robertson's comic depicts the experiences of colonization as "systemic, personal, intergenerational, and, significantly, genocidal" (Wolf, "Confronting" 341). In one panel, the position of young Thomas lying dead in a snowbank mirrors the image of Edwin lying in his hospital bed shortly after his suicide attempt, with James looking on, seeing and feeling his complicity in these events. Propelled by Lauren's love, James invites Edwin on a journey of reconciliation, eventually bringing him back to the river: "One of the things that helped me was coming to know our ways again, finding those things I'd lost when I was young," James tells his son. "Those parts of us help to make us whole, son. They're pieces of who we are" (125).

James speaks about "blood memory," the connection between and among past and present ancestors that makes a person who they are in the present, which in turn contributes to the well-being of a people. Edwin generously returns the eagle amulet to his father with the hope that James will continue on his healing journey. Edwin sets off on his own vision quest, as did Stone seven generations before him. The vision he eventually experiences merges his past ancestors into a stronger identity for himself. The ending of Robertson's *7 Generations* is thus optimistic, an affirmation of the healing power of the spirit world and a reminder for readers of the powerful forces of family, ancestry, and community.

*7 Generations* features the reconciliation of two men (a father/husband and a son) by means of the intervention of their wife/mother. The education that Lauren offers them both is instrumental in bringing them back together. Although her terror and despair at the thought of losing her son and husband are depicted visually, the predominant focus of the narrative is on her hope and belief in the power of Indigenous community, ancestry, and storytelling. Significantly, the comic juxtaposes Lauren's decision to go to university to study psychology with a frame that depicts James drinking his life away, emphasizing the measured decisions she makes for the betterment of herself and her family (which in turn produce powerful effects for her community as a whole). Throughout, Robertson depicts Lauren as a loving and devoted partner, a wife who had to let her husband go because he was tormented by his demons, and a mother and provider for Edwin. Robertson's comics acknowledge time and time again the power of women vis à vis the well-being and self-determination of their Indigenous communities.

## Restoring and Relating: Indigenous Comics for Indigenous Readers

A major component in the reconciliation process is acknowledgment. Increasingly, initiatives at the community, provincial, and federal levels of government are attempting to make procedural and legal changes to ensure that systemic racism and assimilationist politics are undone. Education is at the forefront of reconciliation measures. Yet, "the fact remains," Métis critic Chelsea Vowel argues, "that the Canadian system of education does not provide adequate space for the widespread development of an Indigenous system of education" (280–81). Since the 1970s, treaty First Nations have assumed administrative control of schools on reserves, but they must follow provincial curriculum and federal policy guidelines. Doris Wolf agrees: "Regardless of some good changes in curriculum content in reserve schools, the system itself remains a form of cultural racism" ("Seductions" 183).

One of the initiatives that is being used to "restore" Indigenous child and youth well-being is the publication of comics *by* Indigenous writers and creators *for* young Indigenous readers. These Indigenous comics (published mainly by small, independent presses) harness the power of storytelling to acknowledge past injustices and thereby empower youth in the present, with an eye to the future. The Indigenous Story Studio (formerly known as the Healthy Aboriginal Network) is one such nonprofit press. Located in Courtenay, British Columbia, the Indigenous Story Studio (ISS) is producing comics written specifically for Indigenous youth to provide readers with positive images of themselves grounded in self-representation. These publications provoke reader identification with the story's characters, in the process affirming an agentic vision of the child (young characters take an active role in responding to the events that shape them personally). But they are also persuasive tools for knowledge building and can educate Indigenous readers about the rights that they are due in Canada. Most importantly, the texts affirm the subjectivity and knowledges of Indigenous peoples and confirm that they are politically and intellectually valid.

Established in 2005 and funded by various governmental bodies and agencies (the British Columbia Ministry of Health's Aboriginal Health Division, the First Nations Inuit Health Branch, and the Canadian Council on Learning), ISS has published comics (*An Invited Threat, Lighting Up the Darkness, Lost Innocence,* and sixteen others) that explore health and social issues that are particularly topical for Indigenous youth. Topics are wide-ranging and include living with fetal alcohol spectrum disorder (FASD; *Drawing Hope*), gang awareness (*Path of the Warrior*), youth in care (*Lighting Up the Darkness*), sexual health (*Kiss Me Deadly*), residential school trauma (*Lost Innocence*), maternal health (*It Takes a Village*), mental health (*Just a Story*), financial literacy (*The Game Plan*), family violence (*Clear Skies*), community justice (*Making It Right*), bullying (*Drawing Hope*), alcohol and drug dependency and child protection (*Emily's Choice*), smoking prevention (*River Run*), diabetes (*An Invited Threat*), and dog bites (*The Gift*). Roughly forty pages in length, with sturdy binding and glossy pages, the production values of ISS comics are high. They have an

> art magazine feel[;] the comics' four-color glossy format signifies value and permanence. Implied here is that the value of HAN's comics is not simply

related to immediate symptoms of physical or social dis/ease to be readily fixed with the right health information. Rather, they function as a wider social critique that aims at gaining its power and longevity by offering its primary readers, Aboriginal youth, the critical skills to identify root causes and solutions. (Wolf, "Seductions" 193)[10]

These texts function as "communal sharings" (Sium and Ritskes v) that link communities through their resistance to centuries-old colonialist violence and foster a resurgence of Indigenous knowledge.

Many of the comics created by Plains Cree Steven Keewatin Sanderson have been published by ISS. His work focuses on creating awareness of topics that are relevant to Indigenous populations: diabetes, foster care, careers, suicide, and identity. Sanderson uses his art to keep stories alive and to bring Indigenous youth and elders together, as well as to help increase awareness of these issues among Indigenous populations—in the process moving them from the margins to the center of political discourse. His comic *Just a Story* (2012) is particularly meaningful since it addresses the power of storytelling to restore cultural health and well-being to a community. Protagonist Wendy tells her little brother stories that help him to relax before bed and that help them both cope with the toxic atmosphere in their household (their parents are constantly fighting). Storytelling becomes a coping strategy for the youth and in turn an effective device that communicates the nature of Wendy's tumultuous relationship with her parents to her concerned teachers at school. More generally, this technique accounts for the approach ISS takes in creating sustaining stories both to educate and entertain.

A few of the comics are more explicitly didactic than others, using the accessible medium to reach as many young readers as possible about topics that have an immediate and practical value to Indigenous communities. Canadian Heiltsuk/Mohawk creator Zoe Hopkins's graphic narrative *It Takes a Village* (2012), illustrated by Canadian Chilean artist Amancay Nahuelpan, emphasizes the circular nature of the multigenerational community of support that a new mother needs. A young woman with a baby on her back serves as the narrative's mouthpiece to communicate important information about maternity, such as the importance of eating healthy foods, avoiding alcohol, breastfeeding, and bonding with the baby. By means of rhetorical conversations that Lara, a self-involved young, pregnant woman, has with Danis (who turns out to be, as readers come to learn, Lara's daugh-

---

10. ISS's comics have a modest circulation: 10,000 copies of Richard Van Camp's *Kiss Me Deadly* (2011) were distributed for free across the Northwest Territories; 20,000 copies of Van Camp's *Path of the Warrior* (2009) were distributed across British Columbia. E-copies are available for free download on ISS's website.

ter in the future), Lara is taught the correct behaviors to adopt during her pregnancy and as a new mother. Presumably, by reading this comic that validates the experiences of Indigenous women and mothers, readers would gain practical information about motherhood. Likewise, Mi'kmaq writer Brandon Mitchell and Jane Dickson-Gilmore's *Making It Right: A Community Justice Story* (2016) describes the conflict resolution assistance that Community Justice Committee volunteers can offer members of an Indigenous community on a reserve when it comes to minor and nonviolent offences. This comic is more didactic than some of the other ISS publications: It provides an in-depth look at how volunteers shepherd members of the community through the peacemaking circle and encourage each person to take personal responsibility for their role in the problem. Strength of community in conflict resolution is stressed.

The predominant values of these Indigenous comics published by ISS are change and empowerment, family and community, forgiveness and self-love, and they specifically point to the young person's responsibility to bring this self-determination to their respective Indigenous communities. Sean Muir, founder and executive director of ISS, explains the selection and production process that all of the creative content undergoes: ISS tests all of the draft stories in focus groups (online with professionals and in-person with Indigenous youth) for authenticity and relevancy. Videos are made from rough storyboards so that, after the focus group testing, the story and visuals can be edited easily and cheaply ("Indigenous Story"). Many of these comics carry an image of three crows with the caption, "Certified Indigenous," which reinforces the reliability of these narratives as teaching tools for an audience of Indigenous youth.

Sometimes playfulness offsets the educational purposefulness that many ISS publications display. *An Invited Threat* (2013), Steven Keewatin Sanderson's comic about diabetes prevention, comments metatextually on the superhero comics genre, redeploying the traditional North American superhero as a commercial threat to the physical well-being of Indigenous communities.[11] So-called superhero Captain Zaz is the figurehead for a new cola drink that has emerged on the markets. Zaz is a symbol of corporate capitalism that has infiltrated the reserve and now influences the choices of food that Dennis, owner of the store on the reserve, must stock simply to

---

11. It must be said that the luring of children and adults by transnational corporations to eat unhealthy and expensive food is not particular to Indigenous peoples. It is a worldwide phenomenon. What is singular is the correlation of multiple factors that intensify the problem for Indigenous people—poverty, isolation, unemployment, the expense of bringing fresh produce to remote areas, and so forth—exacerbating a problem and making it life-threatening, literally, as Sanderson's comic visualizes.

break even financially. By means of this comic, Sanderson argues that diabetes is a systemic problem on reserves because of the cheaper, carbohydrate-laden processed foods that inhabitants crave (thanks to the seductions of corporate advertising) and that Dennis must supply. Keewatin's graphics emphasize how impressed young Ricky is by the primary colors of the fast-food options in front of him: The reflection in Ricky's eyes of the cereal high in sugar content emphasizes how mesmerized he is by commercial messaging. The tentacles of corporate capitalism are far-reaching; Ricky is overpowered by them on the reserve, consuming high-fat, processed foods under the unseeing eyes of his busy mother and father. Restricted to the reserve and encouraged to buy groceries at the band store, Ricky and his family are governed in this way by the capitalist structure imposed by settler culture.

While walking home in a snowstorm after a meeting at band council, Ricky, Dennis, and Diane (Ricky's mother) experience separate visions about their dietary choices, each of which provides horrifying insight into the future that awaits them if they continue to eat this way. Ricky, for example, walks off with Captain Zaz, who proudly takes him to meet all kinds of animated sugary foods that inhabit Candy Land, rendered as conventional cartoon characters named Bubble Snake, Crazy Crunch, and Atomic Drops (see figure 3.8). In this vision, Sanderson's color palette is vibrant and the figures clearly parodic, evoking the television commercials for these sugary foods that Ricky has been watching. In this vision, Ricky gorges himself to such an extent that he makes himself sick, the too-bright colors and the sickly sweet candy snacks eventually overwhelming him. Finally, he realizes that the snacks that these candy creatures are forcing on him are not healthy. Captain Zaz is no hero, but rather a mouthpiece for capitalist messaging and sales. Meanwhile, Diane has a vision of Ricky grown up and overweight, leading a sedentary lifestyle. Ricky tells her that her husband has died of a heart attack because of his unhealthy dietary choices. In a nightmarish scenario, Diane is pursued by a monster who threatens to saw off her legs with his bandsaw arm because she, too, has developed diabetes. In this terrifying vision, Sanderson visually references early American horror and sci-fi comics in the gruesome alien that pursues Diane, desperate to amputate her legs, a procedure sometimes necessary in dire diabetes cases.

Dennis's vision, in contrast, addresses the traditional Indigenous values that have been called into question by the capitalist economy that governs the reserve. The past offers no promise for the present since the community of exchange in the past was already circumscribed by colonialist exploitation. In his dream, Dennis returns to a traditional Indigenous village and bears witness to the rotten food that a chief brings for his people to share, spoiled food that was the only thing left after settlers took the best

FIGURE 3.8. Captain Zaz and Ricky in Candy Land. Steven Keewatin Sanderson, *An Invited Threat*. The Healthy Aboriginal Network, 2013, p. 18.

from the land. The rancid, maggot-ridden meat is like the high-fat foods Dennis sells his people in his store: poor nourishment that emerges from settler relations. Not only do all three characters experience visions that speak to the responsibility they bear to make healthy choices for themselves, but their visions in turn show how this responsibility translates into community accountability. Doris Wolf points out that Dennis's newfound determination to buy healthy food carries with it an even greater significance than simply combating diabetes: It "emphasizes the importance of self-determination as the fundamental building block to establishing a new form of citizenship for Aboriginal youth, in this case one that rejects a consumerist ideology symbolized by the Captain Zaz figure for a collectivist one based on the idea of wider community good" ("Seductions" 193).

The ISS publications educate Indigenous youth about past problems with an eye to the future. As *An Invited Threat* demonstrates, when an Indigenous family learns about the long-lasting effects of fast food on the reserve, comics can empower and educate readers, giving them the critical skills with which to determine both cause and solution.

The right to self-determination on the part of Indigenous peoples was affirmed at the international level by the ratification of the United Nations Declaration on the Rights of Indigenous Peoples in 2007. Although Canada ratified the UNCRC in December of 1991, thereby committing itself to upholding the rights of *all* children in Canada, as of January 2010, Canada, the United States, and New Zealand had not signed this particular declaration about the rights of Indigenous peoples (and children, more specifically). As recently as May 2016, Minister of Crown–Indigenous Relations and Northern Affairs Carolyn Bennett affirmed that Canada had finally become a full supporter, without qualification, of the UN declaration. As this policy change attests, however, there is still an urgent need to challenge the Euro-Canadian colonial status quo, and these Indigenous comics are effective tools with which to do so. By making use of the visual and linguistic possibilities of unsettling commonplace frames of difference and thematizing the practices of truth telling, acknowledging, restoring, and relating, these comics establish new modes of representation and interpretation.

As Kate Cregan and Denise Cuthbert remind us, the "status of a nation's children stands as an index for the development and advancement of the nation" itself (113). That so many Indigenous people still do not have access to clean drinking water, adequate housing, education, and child welfare is a terrible example of Canada's prioritization of settler issues and concerns over its Indigenous peoples. As the Commission for Truth and Reconciliation makes clear, education is "an effective peacemaking tool" and, perhaps even more importantly, a "weapon" (Regan 99). Indigenous comics for young readers exemplify the power and possibility of comics in helping to align the needs of Canada with the worth of *all* of the children who inhabit its lands.

CHAPTER 4

# Space and Orientation in LGBTQ+ Graphic Narratives

> It wasn't until I discovered Alison Bechdel's *Dykes to Watch Out For* that I really understood what I was looking for, a queer world with stories and characters that I could recognize, that I could laugh with and care about.
>
> —Lana Wochowski, foreword to *No Straight Lines*

Hillary Chute identifies queer comics as the "fastest-growing area in comics right now" (*Why* 349). Queer comics—that is, comics that articulate the experiences and ideas of LGBTQ+ (lesbian, gay, bisexual, transgender, and/or queer) people and characters—are flooding the market and represent one of the most exciting subgenres in the comics industry. In 1989, with the softening of the Comics Code Authority's rules about the representation of sexuality in comics,[1] comics juggernauts Marvel and DC began to introduce openly queer characters into their storylines. In *Alpha Flight* #106 (1992), superhero mutant Northstar broke new ground when he proclaimed, "I am gay," a first in mainstream comics. With greater frequency, Northstar's storylines addressed homophobia and the mentoring of gay teen superheroes; in 2012 *Astonishing X-Men* #51 featured his marriage to boyfriend Kyle Jinadu.

---

1. Several principles enshrined within the original Comics Magazine Association of America's Comics Code governed sexuality and marriage. According to the 1954 Code, all sex must lead to marriage, and all treatments of "love-romance stories shall emphasize the value of the home and the sanctity of marriage" (Kvaran 144). "Sex perversion"—a term employed to refer to homosexuality—was "strictly forbidden"; consequently, almost every aspect of sexuality disappeared from mainstream comics. With the revisions of the code in 1989, rules concerning the representation of homosexuality began to relax.

Marvel's *Runaways* series (2003–) includes transgender character Xavin, a gender-shifting alien. *Archie Comics* introduced Kevin Keller, the first openly gay character in that universe, in 2010. Since 2003 DC Comics has included two lesbian characters with significant character development and storylines: Hispanic detective Renee Montoya and Montoya's sometimes girlfriend, lesbian socialite and future Batwoman, Kate Kane. Marvel's latest superheroine, America Chavez, is queer and Latina. Once a character in *Young Avengers*, she later became the star of her own comics series. In the past, comic books were the subject of the US Senate's attempt to censor reading material for young readers because of comics' allegedly perverse and violent content; now, they explore the experiences of LGBTQ+ people openly. Queerness has gone mainstream for adult and young readers alike.[2]

Filmmaker Lana Wochowski observed at the beginning of Justin Hall's groundbreaking LGBTQ+ comics compendium *No Straight Lines* (2015) that Hall's collection gave her what she was looking for in queer comics: politics, social commentary, adult sexuality, and a queer world full of complexity, ambiguity, and humanity that she could recognize and in which she could find herself. While queer comics for adult readers are printed and circulated more and more freely among prominent publishing houses, and their subject matter has become more accepted among general readers, comics that focus specifically on LGBTQ+ topics for young readers are much more common but by no means less controversial. In a survey of recent comics for a younger reading demographic, queerness is now an openly acknowledged topic in the narrative proper—and frequently in the texts' reception histories—even as many remain some of the most challenged book titles by North America's public and school libraries.[3]

---

2. Eve Kosofsky Sedgwick (1993) defines "queer" as "the open mesh of possibilities, gaps, overlaps, dissonances and resonances, lapses and excesses of meaning when the constituent elements of anyone's gender, of anyone's sexuality aren't made (or *can't be* made) to signify monolithically" (7). I enjoy the term "queer" because it also allows unruly articulations that cross borders of gender and sexual identities, communicating multiple aspects of one's self and the world around them. Sexual and gender queerness in this way intersect with ethnic, racial, class, and national particularities.

3. In general, one to five books with LGBTQ+ content appear on each year's Top Ten Most Challenged Books lists, compiled by the American Library Association's Office for Intellectual Freedom. The *New York Times* recently published an article that examined the increasing stress American librarians experience to remove LGBTQ+ books from the shelves so as to protect young readers from the books' so-called "dangerous" moral content (Harris and Alter). Canada experiences similar challenges regarding the censorship of queer topics in texts for young readers. In an article entitled "12 Canadian Books That Have Been Challenged," Mariko Tamaki reminds readers: "Overwhelmingly books in these lists are there for LGBTQIA themes and content." *This One Summer* and *Skim*, two of Tamaki's own graphic narratives, are frequent targets of challenges either for their sexual and/or queer content.

This chapter approaches North Americans' continued investment in the myth of childhood innocence (specifically, the myth that separates innocence from any knowledge of sexuality) by highlighting how LGBTQ+ comics for young readers provide powerful representations of the complex lived realities of young queer people and, more importantly, highlight the importance of desire in their declarations of self and identity as they navigate the challenges of adolescence. Yet, I move past viewing the process of "coming out" per se—in the sense of arriving at a sense of one's "conclusive" sexual identity—as the definitive experience that these comics showcase because this tendency codes all manifestations of sexuality as a personal and narrative "problem" that can/must/will be overcome with a satisfying sense of closure. Such an assumption is necessarily flawed: Human beings (and literary characters) are much more complex than that. The notion of arriving at an ostensibly "stable" sense of sexual and gender identity is also defied by the complex range of experiences that current LGBTQ+ comics for young people visualize, narratives that focus on a young person's continuous process of growth as opposed to an emergence at a final stage of fixed identity. In keeping with other comics that *Growing Up Graphic* has examined, texts like *Laura Dean Keeps Breaking Up with Me* (2019) and *Always Human* (2020) visualize the adventures of young queers, specifically not in relation to a narrative of rescue or self-rescue. Indeed, the LGBTQ+ comics that this chapter studies resist the temptation to characterize LGBTQ+ people as necessarily "at risk" and at the margins of public discourse. Emphasizing the active role that young people take in the events that shape them personally, LGBTQ+ comics visualize instead the distinctive lived experiences of youngsters as a determined and politicized response to stereotypical representations of young people in the process of "becoming" adults, a position of privilege that is so frequently valued as being more significant than that of a young person. Intervening against a "culture of invisibility" (Chute, *Disaster* 5), these comics describe the particular experiences that young queers undergo, the moments around a personal life change or predicament that carry a significant impact. These crises can include the break-up of a relationship, a new life experience, or a traumatic event, such as the suicide of a peer, among many others. Some of these occurrences are more serious than others, certainly. They are a far cry from the personal narratives based on physical and emotional abuse and suffering that young people across the world endure in armed militias, displacement camps, and residential schools. Most of these LGBTQ+ comics, however, validate the particular experiences of young queers enduring hardship or breaking new emotional ground, while at the same time attempting self-consciously to align themselves along and against the sociopolitical systems that create the hierarchies they inhabit and the social expectations that they encounter on a daily basis. The protagonists at the center of these stories are often drivers of personal change who model this behavior for young readers. LGBTQ+ comics offer a world full of complexity, ambiguity, and humanity in which young queer readers like Lana Wochowski can recognize experiences that align with their own.

Opportunities for recognition begin with, and are conditioned by, the narratives' spatial orientation, as Sara Ahmed argues in *Queer Phenomenology*. These are the principal locations that typically have an impact on the lives of young people and in which many of these crises occur: home, school (elementary, middle, and high school; college or university; extracurricular activities), and summer camp, among others. As this chapter explores, *Adrian and the Tree of Secrets* and *Tough Love* depict educational institutions as particularly oppressive locations of trauma and deep interpersonal conflict, frequently surveilled by adults who ignore the bullying and torment that occur right in front of them. More recently, Mariko Tamaki's *Laura Dean Keeps Breaking Up with Me* situates the school as a mere backdrop for the interpersonal opportunities that await young queers and the struggles they face, with their queerness as but one of many challenges that they undergo. Extracurricular activities, according to other graphic texts for young readers, offer opportunities for personal and sexual empowerment. Comics like *Drama*, *Check Please!*, and *The Avant-Guards* present the drama studio, the hockey arena, and the basketball court, respectively, as empowering spaces that are supportive and queer-positive. These texts generally "normalize" queer lived experiences by reorienting narrative conflict away from sexual difference in favor of interpersonal relations. Summer camp also appears to be a space in which young people push back against the norms and expectations that govern their daily lives at home and at school. *Honor Girl*, *As the Crow Flies*, and the *Lumberjanes* showcase the informal worlds of young people and their social experiences that develop away from the oversight of parents, caregivers, and the education system. These experiences are equally positive and negative, emphasizing camp as a place of gender presentation as much as a mode of performance.

In the last five years, there has been a notable movement in the queer comics field away from viewing LGBTQ+ experiences as problematic in and of themselves or as providing particular sexual and gender concerns that must be dealt with conclusively.[4] Instead, the narratives feature young queer subjects who take an active role in the events that continue to shape them personally over a large span of time, not necessarily limited to the years associated with childhood and/or adolescence. Queerness, in these texts, is simply one part of their complex identity. LGBTQ+ comics like *As the Crow Flies* (2017) and *Adrian and the Tree of Secrets* (2013) visualize the protean range of young people's queer experiences in spaces typical of youth, making use of the inventive visual and textual practices of comics to do so. To appreciate how distinctively these comics provide readers with affirmative and encouraging literary experiences, a brief survey of past practices in young adult literature (and its reception) is first required.

## Sexuality and Queerness in YA Literature and Comics

Young adult (YA) literature—and I include the comics that this chapter explores under this rubric—is certainly no stranger to queer subject matter. Queer sexuality, however, has often been framed within this field in terms of crisis. As Roberta Seelinger Trites and Kenneth Kidd have each observed, YA narratives have been especially receptive to lesbian and gay characters and themes for several reasons. First, because "coming out" is often described in relation to adolescence and captures that period "as an intense period of sexual attraction, social rebellion, and personal growth" (Kidd, "Introduction" 114). Second, YA's openness to queer content centers on its use of "sexual potency" as a common "metaphor for [youthful] empowerment" (Trites, *Disturbing* 84). And yet, representations of sexuality and queerness in YA literature (and comics for young readers) frequently unleash firestorms as intense as those provoked by comics in the 1950s (the ones that led to

---

4. This supportive tendency stands in marked contrast to recent disturbing developments in American society. The passing of Florida's Parental Rights in Education measure (commonly known as the "Don't Say Gay" law) in July 2022, which bans discussion of sexual orientation or gender identity in the classroom, has established a very dangerous precedent in American society, setting the stage for half a dozen or so other conservative-led states to impose similar versions. Similarly, the banning of gender-affirming medical care for trans youth by Texas Republicans points to significant anti-LGBTQ+ propaganda and legislation that are cropping up with new and increased frequency in American society (Kane). Likewise, the appearance of the Proud Boys, a right-wing hate group, at a Drag Queen Story Hour at a library in San Francisco and the arrest of thirty-one members of the right-wing white supremacist Patriot Front at a Pride event in June 2022 speak to escalating anti-LGBTQ+ aggression across American society (Winter).

Senate subcommittee hearings that examined the alleged links between comics and juvenile delinquency). Judy Blume is one of the most frequently challenged YA authors of the twentieth and twenty-first centuries, whose oeuvre remains a target for the "religious Right" in the United States because of its sexual content, a blanket term used to refer to anything from menstruation, breasts, masturbation, wet dreams, birth control, and sexual intercourse. Phoebe Gloeckner's comic *A Child's Life and Other Stories* (1998, 2000) was initially held back by the publisher because of its realistic representation of a young girl's sexual abuse. By virtue of its unapologetically vivid representations of rape, Gloeckner's text challenges the tendency to ignore the sexual precarity of young girls and women. As Elizabeth Marshall and Leigh Gilmore argue, "Gloeckner's images are graphic: explicit and published, they stake a claim to public knowledge about 'a child's life.' She chooses to depict violence rather than imply it in deference to propriety" (103). *A Child's Life* was banned from public libraries in San Joaquin County, California, after it was checked out by an eleven-year-old reader. In 2004 Gary Podesto, mayor of Stockton, California, called the book "a handbook for a pedophile" (Jones). Sexual content in reading material for young readers provokes immediate and visceral responses from adults, specifically around the interpretation of what "a child's life" *should* look like.

Raina Telgemeier's *Drama* (2012), a comic that targets a younger reading demographic, found itself enmeshed in a similar example of adult gatekeeping that attempts to regulate young readers' knowledge of homosexuality. Since its release in 2012, *Drama*, which visualizes two adolescent boys' developing a relationship in and around the staging of the annual school play, has received the Stonewall Book Award for excellence in LGBTQ+ fiction for young people. In spite of its many accolades, however, *Drama* has frequently been at the center of debates about why not to allow young people to read it ("Case Study"). The American Library Association announced that among the 311 reports about attempts to remove or restrict materials from school curricula and library bookshelves that they received, *Drama* was #10 on their list for its alleged sexual explicitness, even though Telgemeier's comic contains no explicitness whatsoever.

Narratives about childhood and adolescent experiences of sexuality routinely raise red flags among parents, teachers, and librarians at the same time as they appeal to young readers who look for forms of representation that speak to them as readers. For much of the twentieth century, attempts to "protect" childhood innocence dovetailed with efforts to shield young readers from sexual knowledge and to discourage any interest in sex—especially alternate expressions of sexuality—by associating them with transgression and punishment. The representation of sexuality as a problem per se is therefore typical of the YA genre and suggests that knowledge about sex and sexuality is more to be feared than celebrated, a strategy employed by Western adult culture to "control adolescent power by simultaneously designating adolescent behavior as deviant and redirecting its energies to approved ways of behaving" (Reynolds 116). Connecting sexuality and shame has often been an effective way to encourage young people to "avoid sex or sexual knowledge as long as possible [, . . .] ensuring that they see it as something unpleasant and dirty, as not for them or about them" (Tribunella 646). At their roots, such efforts to separate innocence from a knowledge of sexuality also seek to preserve adults from the discomfiting idea of childhood sexuality and youthful experiences of queerness.

Much of the controversy around allegedly "inappropriate" topics of sexuality and queerness in YA fiction and LGBTQ+ comics for young people can be traced back to the pervasive myth of the implied Romantic child reader, whose purity is necessarily incompatible with sexual awareness and experience. The reader at the heart of many such censorship debates is a contradiction, one who is imagined by adults as passive, someone "deeply susceptible to indoctrination. [. . .] Someone without agency, someone who can be overpowered by a book" (Owen 117). Even though adolescence is often yoked in theory to rebelliousness, the search for identity, and a disrespect for elders and the social order, adolescence is a stage where a teen's resistance and rebelliousness are expected and yet where their behaviors are still somewhat managed and controlled (Owen 120–21). Roberta Seelinger Trites points to the tendency employed by YA literature to use sexuality as "an ideological tool [. . .] to curb teenagers' libido" (*Disturbing* 85). Thus, young readers find themselves being represented as essentially asexual at the same time as they are being "vigorously gendered" (Reynolds 115) by means of this literature. Frequently, an adult moralism asserts authority over the narrative and, in turn, over young readers, subjecting them to consistent messaging that encourages the regulation of their experiences of sexuality by repressing them. Alan Moore and Melinda Gebbie's triple-decker graphic text *Lost Girls* (2006)—although not written for young readers by any means—visualizes how such impulses to repress childhood sexuality and an early knowledge of queerness can lead to dysfunction in adulthood. Moore and Gebbie's deliberate sexualization of Golden Age children's classics (*The Wonderful Wizard of Oz, Peter Pan,* and *Alice's Adventures in Wonderland*) make clear that the "'innocent' child grows up to be a damaged adult" (Tribunella 631) because of this suppression. The value of positive and diverse sexual representation in literature for young readers should not be underestimated:

Such reading material creates opportunities for readers to gain insights into themselves and those around them in the hopes of creating long-term social and emotional benefits (such as candid discussions about sexuality). Comics are persuasive tools for knowledge building, providing stories that can inform and educate readers about issues that are pertinent to their personal experiences (Reynolds 120). Perhaps even more importantly, young readers can explore accounts of sexual experiences through the private act of reading, something that in turn validates their own learning experiences (Reynolds 117).

Representations of sexual encounters in YA fiction, however, have traditionally been heteronormative, reinscribing the performativity and materiality of gender in binary terms, terms that struggle to value queer experiences at all and that do not begin to recognize the gender complexities of polymorphous or alternatively gendered children. Steven Bruhm and Natasha Hurley note that panics about childhood and sexuality frequently erupt around suggestions of queer sexuality or the queer child, "the child whose play confirms neither the comfortable stories of child (a)sexuality nor the supposedly blissful promises of adult heteronormativity" (ix). Lee Edelman observes that the abstract figure of the child (white, middle-class, heterosexual) is at the center of many American political campaigns, not to mention books for young readers (1). This abstract child is vital to social, political, and literary narratives of compulsory heterosexuality as well as normative sociality, Edelman argues, and is synonymous with so-called family values and a "reproductive futurism," the prevailing telos of a social order that is motivated by a belief in and a desire for creating better futures for (heterosexual) children (4). Tison Pugh extends Edelman's argument. Since heterosexuality is the assumed and expected sexual identity of many YA and children's literature protagonists, Pugh identifies as "queer" this complete disavowal of sexuality in children's literature "through celebrations of [childhood] innocence" (1). J. M. Barrie's classic fantasy *Peter and Wendy* (1911) signals this paradigmatic tension between "purging sexuality from a text to preserve childhood innocence while nonetheless depicting some form of heterosexuality as childhood's desired end" (Pugh 2). The text's eponymous character willfully remains in a state of arrested development in Neverland, ignorant of the social and sexual expectations that Tiger Lily, Tinkerbell, and Wendy Darling have of him. "All children, except one, grow up," the novel's opening words promise (Barrie 1). Barrie's novel culminates with a vision of Wendy Darling, now a grown mother, who sends her own daughter off to Peter in Neverland every year during childhood to revel in her innocence and purity until the shades of heterosexual motherhood invariably begin to close around her as well. For Pugh, Peter Pan's queerness lies in his obstinate refusal to acquire sexual knowledge and the homosocial existence he leads with his crew of Lost Boys, all the while being surrounded by female characters who look to him to satisfy (or at the very least acknowledge) their emerging sexual desires (5). Barrie's rejection of aging and concomitant nostalgia for childhood innocence attempts to forestall a young person's experiences of sexuality. The particular "queerness" of this paradigm rests, first, on the generalized expectation of sexual heteronormativity among all children and, second, on the shaping of heterosexuality through the homosociality of young people's first friendships (Pugh 6).

Positive queer representation in literature for young readers is still in its formative phase. Queer characters and themes present in pre-1980s YA fiction raised limited awareness of a lived reality without necessarily providing a younger reader with transformative (or even realistic) narratives. Stories of HIV/AIDS, the closet, and gay shame dominated the genre early on. Novels with LGBTQ+ content from the 1970s and 1980s—John Donovan's *I'll Get There: It Better Be Worth the Trip* (1969), *Sticks and Stones* (1977) by Lynn Hall, and *Annie on My Mind* (1982) by Nancy Garden—are generally stories of "homosexual visibility" in which a character who had not previously been considered gay or lesbian "comes out either voluntarily or involuntarily" (Jenkins and Cart xiv). Narrative tension develops around what happens when this invisible challenge becomes visible. In such stories, a "previously homogeneous society is interrupted by the appearance of a character who is clearly *not* 'one of us'" (Jenkins and Cart xiv). Worse, in such stories there was often a disturbing correlation made between homosexuality and death. Gradually, however, YA books (such as Norma Klein's *Breaking Up* [1980] and Aidan Chambers's *Dance on My Grave* [1982]) began to feature LGBTQ+ people as secondary characters (that is, friends, gay/lesbian parents, teachers, older siblings, mentors, etc.), presenting them at a safe distance from the protagonist while still including them in the narrative proper (Jenkins and Cart 48). Often, however, isolation was still common among queer characters in these texts. This distancing served a dual purpose: While it likely reduced the possibility of "emotional involvement by the reader" and in the process diminished the "authenticity of the LGBTQ+ experience," it might have also provided "an easier point of access" to the story for heterosexual readers, as Christine Jenkins and Michael Cart suggest (70). Thus, in these early texts, the default prioritization remained an implied heterosexual reader.

Gradually, however, "gay assimilation" stories emerged in the 1990s that assumed the existence of "a *melting pot* of sexual and gender identity" (Jenkins and Cart xv) with few to no narratives that explored the intersections of sexuality, ethnicity, and race. Frequently such assimilation stories strove to "normalize" homosexuality or lesbianism by means of the tautology "love is love," which suggests that there are no inherent differences between heterosexual and LGBTQ+ relationships. This tautology had a "bibliotherapeutic intent" as Roberta Seelinger Trites called it, in the sense that readers—queer or straight—would come to "feel a sense of catharsis or validation or acceptance of homosexuality after reading such novels" (*Disturbing* 113), once again striving to "normalize" an experience for youngsters. Most often, in such YA fiction, the "corporeality of homosexuality"—the physical pleasure of queer characters—is downplayed in favor of characters' personal experiences of homophobia (114). Trites argues that this tendency to deny the pleasures of homosexuality further "disempowers gay sexuality" (114). Oftentimes in such YA fiction, narrative closure also relies on an arrival point where the character finally experiences a moment of self-realization or self-actualization, "whereby the struggles of finding one's 'true' identity have been overcome" (Mallan 7). This narrative paradigm depends on an implicit assumption that an "essential" self can emerge. "Such a narrative resolution provides readers with a reassurance that things will work out for the best in the end, which is an enduring feature of the genre and part of liberal-humanism's project of harmonious individuality" (7).

Comics for young readers are powerful at evoking LGBTQ+ childhoods, thanks to their particularly visual register. Even so, early twenty-first-century graphic texts are similarly limited by a tendency to "normalize" queerness or provide insight into a so-called marginal demographic. Judd Winick's *Pedro & Me: Friendship, Loss, & What I Learned* (2000) is a memoir of his friendship with Pedro Zamora, the HIV-positive AIDS educator who appeared on MTV's reality show *The Real World: San Francisco*. While it is a heartfelt testament to Zamora's important social advocacy work, Winick's text itself is emblematic of YA fiction that defines gay people in relation to disease and death. Alison Bechdel's memoir *Fun Home: A Family Tragicomic* (2006)—albeit not a text written specifically for young readers—also deserves mentioning because it is central to the LGBTQ+ comics canon. An early queer graphic text, the challenges in *Fun Home* center on identity and sexuality, anatomizing the emergence of eponymous character Alison's sexual and gender identities, which are diametrically opposed to her father's closetedness (which, the narrative implies, might have contributed to his death/suicide). A brilliant graphic memoir, *Fun Home*'s narrative is organized around a knowledge of sexuality (lesbianism, homosexuality); its resolution in social activism and creative fulfillment, or accidental death or suicide, align it with the tendency in YA fiction to identify the performance of sexuality as the particular problem of the narrative. Ostracism, illness, and death are tropes that continue to crop up in LGBTQ+ graphic narratives for young readers, even into the twenty-first century. Jul Maroh's *Blue Is the Warmest Color* (French, 2010; English, 2013) explores the life and loves of two young lesbians in France. Maroh's text affirms the agency that protagonists Clementine and Emma exercise over their bodies and their sexual choices. The text's visualizing of lesbian sex is groundbreaking in its corporeal anatomization of queer sexuality: It renders in explicit detail the sexual dreams that torment Clementine and the first sexual encounter between the young women. In spite of this, the text is limited by its stereotypical characterization of lesbianism in terms of personal loss (the loss of family and friends due to ostracism) and death (the eventual death of Clem to a heart complaint). Every narrative event is organized around the construction of lesbianism as a problem that Clem and Emma endure. The text concludes with Clem's death in hospital.

It is in part due to these early stereotypical representations of youthful LGBTQ+ lived experiences that Kathryn Bond Stockton's ideas in *The Queer Child, or Growing Sideways in the Twentieth Century* (2009) are so refreshing. Strikingly, the book offers fresh opportunities for thinking about young people (actual and literary) outside the gender binary. Stockton's metaphor of "growing sideways," as a way of thinking about and seeing the queer child and character, steps aside from the adult focus on growing "up" vertically and into an implied heterosexual adulthood, wholly governed and policed by adults. This horizontal approach is most apposite because it suggests an alternative mode of thinking about queer children and queer young readers. If a vertical process of growing "upward" implies that there is an end to growth (i.e., adulthood), a sideways movement does not imply that sense of finality at all: "'Growing sideways' suggests that the width of a person's experience or ideas, their motives or their motions, may pertain at any age, bringing 'adults' and 'children' into lateral contact of surprising sorts" (Stockton 11). In thinking about and reading sideways, queer children and young readers can at last operate outside both the adult-child hierarchy and the outdated binary paradigm of gender. This sideways growth does not make queer "normal," human, or recognizable within privileged structures but helps to disrupt the very systems that created the inside and outside in these traditional hierarchical relations in the first place. Recent LGBTQ+ comics "grow sideways," both in terms of form and content, by showcasing narratives that complicate visualizations of queer sexuality; that gesture toward intersectionalities of class, race, ethnicity, and ableism; and that deploy crisis as something other than a young person's process of "coming out." Comics invite young readers into new narrative worlds that do not need to justify the validity of queer experience and agency—they take them as givens.

## Children's Spatialities and Sexual Desire

In response to the limitations of many of these early LGBTQ+ graphic texts, the queer comics for young readers that began to flood the marketplace in the 2010s presuppose that queerness is a given and feature youth who are dealing with crises that are no more significant or extraordinary than those experienced by heterosexual youth. Like Stockton's theory of the queer child who grows sideways, "graphic texts engender literal ways to read sideways, that is, in non-*straight*forward ways" (Howard 286), in ways that step aside from traditional binary notions of gender and sexuality. Recent texts such as Liz Prince's *Tomboy: A Graphic Memoir* (2014), Victoria Jamieson's *Roller Girl* (2015), and L. Nichols's *Flocks* (2018) depict the lives of young people who challenge normative expectations of feminine and masculine identities. *Tomboy*, for example, depicts Prince's struggles with gender dis-ease, her desire to dress and behave like a boy, to present herself as a boy at home and at school. A major focus is the stress that peer groups and school administrators place on a student's alignment with traditional gender binaries. Similarly, L. Nichols's *Flocks* is a fierce memoir about the turbulence a person feels as they experience gender dysphoria while growing up in a strict Southern Baptist household. Throughout childhood and youth, and even into early adulthood, L. wrestles violently with the expectations of the "flocks" among which she moves, specifically the religious "flock" of her youth. Eventually L. leaves the flock behind through the process of gender transition. Both of these visual texts move toward narrative resolutions that involve and invoke the "arrival" at and acceptance of the subject's self and sexual identity that I have already critiqued. Yet, their visualizations of the social pressures that locations exert over a young queer person are what distinguish these texts from other early twenty-first-century LGBTQ+ comics for young readers.

Young people's spatialized experiences have drawn the attention of researchers in a number of disciplines in recent years: Literary scholars, architectural and social historians, social scientists and psychologists, geographers, and anthropologists have all examined how children and young characters interact with and are enmeshed in the worlds around them.[5] Commentators are particularly interested in exploring how spaces shape children's actions, in turn influencing how young people choose to live their lives. The locales prescribed for children are "political and ideological" in the sense that "children's freedom is often constrained through access to

---

5. See, for example, Hackett et al.; Doughty and Thompson; Foley and Leverett; Goodenough; Gutman and de Coninck-Smith.

space" or in turn through the ways that locations condition their interactions (Hackett et al. 5). In some instances, adults have created spaces for children (e.g., Kozlovsky's exploration of early twentieth-century playgrounds); the use and experience of these facilities inevitably vary among young people according to factors such as ability, age, gender, class, race, and culture. Stephen Leverett employs the term "institutionalisation" to describe the establishment of boundaries, rules, and regulations of sites for young people and their cultures. In turn, places create and "reproduce dominant discourses and the 'social order'" (10). The relationships between young people and the locations that they inhabit are inherently dynamic: They are both producers and products of these spaces. In turn, spaces provoke powerful feelings associated with belonging, exclusion, safety, and/or danger, affecting young people in profound ways.

How locations influence sexuality and gender can be seen most specifically in the public restroom debate that has emerged in recent years. Public bathrooms have become gender identity battlefields, provoking very powerful and polarizing feelings of belonging and exclusion among queer people of all ages.[6] By their very structural design, public washrooms reinforce and maintain the power structures of sex and gender performance dichotomies (Riggle 482). "Public restrooms have always been politicized, contested sites, based on race, ethnicity, sexuality, religion, economic status, and gender," Ellen Riggle argues. "The bathroom, as we know it, actually represents the crumbling edifice of gender in the twentieth century," J. Jack Halberstam presciently declared back in 1998 (*Female* 24). The familiar restroom signage featuring male or female silhouettes reduce gender identity to iconic representations of gender-specific bodies and clothing. Bathrooms also assume particularly gendered expectations of those who use the spaces. While women's restrooms are locations generally associated with the surveillance of gender conformity, men's public toilets operate as highly charged sexual spots, ones that are as likely to become sexual cruising zones as they are sites of homosocial interaction (Halberstam, *Female* 24). Not only do public toilets reinforce outdated gender stereotypes; in their segregation of the sexes they also fail to acknowledge trans and gender-diverse people. "More seriously, these symbols present trans and gender-diverse people within a climate of violence, interrogation and surveillance based upon their bodies, when

---

6. Access to public restroom facilities based on sex/gender identity is currently the subject of litigation, legislative and institutional debates, and social discourse (Riggle 484). Federally, in the US, while the Obama Administration issued regulations to support the rights of transgender individuals to use the bathroom that corresponds to their gender identity, the Trump Administration rescinded these protections (Riggle 493).

really, all anyone wants to do is use a toilet" (Castricum). The recent appearance of gender-inclusive bathrooms has begun to address the need for safe, neutral locations in which all people feel comfortable. Unfortunately, the controversies that have erupted around public bathrooms and transgender rights are conflicts imposed upon the trans and gender-diverse communities by cisgender interest groups. This polarizing problem about public facilities demonstrates how a specific place shapes a person's navigation of sexuality and gender in daily life—an awareness that LGBTQ+ comics showcase in their visualizations of the crises that young characters experience in the spaces around them.[7]

Crises that occur in locales central to youthful experiences explore the particular spatiality of sexual desire and gender performance. LGBTQ+ comics foreground the queer reorientation of bodies in sites typically associated with childhood and/or adolescence (home, school, summer camp) as the characters learn to "feel at home" in their changing bodies and identities. For Sara Ahmed, "If orientation is a matter of how we reside in space, then sexual orientation might also be a matter of residence, of how we inhabit spaces, and who or what we inhabit spaces with" ("Orientations" 543). Bodies are shaped by their dwellings and take shape by the act of dwelling. The process of becoming reorientated (i.e., of becoming queer) therefore involves encountering the spaces of the (heterosexual) world differently (Ahmed, *Phenomenology* 69). "To become straight means that we not only have to turn toward the objects that are given to us by heterosexual culture, but also that we must 'turn away' from objects that take us off this line," Ahmed argues. "The queer subject within straight culture hence deviates and is made socially present as a deviant" (*Phenomenology* 21). Thus, for Ahmed, "queer" alludes to that which is oblique, off-line, or "wonky," as she describes it ("Orientations" 565). Seen this way, sexuality and gender are not simply determined by object choice but also by one's very relation to the sites that one inhabits. "If orientation is about making the strange familiar through the extension of bodies into space, then disorientation occurs when that extension fails" (*Phenomenology* 11).

So many of the LGBTQ+ comics that this chapter explores are about the characters' disorientation from conventionally heterosexual scripts and norms and how that sideways movement in turn shapes their lived

---

7. In *Feminist, Queer, Crip* (2013) Alison Kafer writes about public toilets as "sites of exclusion and activism" (154). Access to bathrooms has been segregated along racial, classist, and ableist lines, policed for "inappropriate behavior or inappropriate users" (154). "Thinking through access can then become a way of thinking through questions of disability [and gender] identity" (157).

experiences. As Peter Hopkins argues, home is the first such location, assumed to be a safe location, "where the closest relationships of our lives are lived, and away from outside pressures such as those associated with hanging out with friends or at school" (26). As some of these texts prove, however, home can be a very difficult or unsafe location for young people to inhabit, especially because of family dynamics, not to mention particular social, economic, and political elements. School also has a profound influence on young people's "sense of belonging, level of self-esteem and social and emotional well-being" (P. Hopkins 29). The school is generally made up of two zones: the zone of the educational institution (the adult-controlled school world of official structures, with its timetables and lessons) and the informal zone of young people, friendship groups, gangs, and social experiences (29). As locations in which children and youth spend a considerable amount of time, schools have the potential to exert tremendous power and influence over them.[8] Through the control of time, for example, schools dictate where young people should be and how educational locations should be used. As Peter Hopkins observes,

> The implementation of school rules and regulations often involves the monitoring and control of particular spaces, such as entrances and exits and rooms being out of bounds, such as the staff-room. Schools are therefore places where young people learn at firsthand about how certain adults and certain children can assert dominance, and the ways in which power and control operate in society. (29)

These sets of power relations vary in intensity among different schools across the globe; gender, race, class, ability, and age are only the most obvious determinants.

As LGBTQ+ comics visualize, locations for extracurricular activities (the gym, the drama studio, the sports field, the ice rink, etc.) also offer significant opportunities for growth and self-awareness among young people. Summer camps—a fascinating and noteworthy preoccupation of many recent LGBTQ+ comics—engage with conventional associations of children, young people, and nature (associations that reach back to philosophers like

---

8. The important role that school plays in the daily lives of young people will become especially pertinent during the COVID-19 pandemic, as discussed in the conclusion, when young people had to isolate at home and were not able to attend in-person school for extended periods of time. Mental health challenges were just some of the many repercussions that occurred once the daily structure of school was removed from the everyday lived experiences of young people.

John Locke and Jean-Jacques Rousseau and Romantic poets like William Blake and William Wordsworth) for their visualizations of how and where youth endure and even thrive in (often) intensely heteronormative locales. Summer camp—a location traditionally associated with idyllic if robust innocence, and subsequent nostalgia—can be an enabling or oppressive site for some of the young people, especially for youth who might not necessarily embody the white, middle-class norms that govern this location and experience. In many of these comics, summer camp also carries with it the power of the performative, in terms of the opportunities for gender play that the texts offer characters and readers.

Young people can enjoy tremendous agency and freedom or, at the other end of the spectrum, experience terrible oppression and loneliness in public and private locations. In each case, they move through and even mobilize space to organize themselves as affective social, sexual, and distinctive agents of change. These comics describe the life experiences that young queers experience, the moments immediately before, during, and after a life change, emergency, or predicament that carries a significant impact. Frequently representing and narrativizing complex information about gender identity presentation, these LGBTQ+ comics almost always feature a protagonist at the center of the story who is a driver of personal change.

## School as a Place of Visible Invisibility:
*Tough Love, Adrian and the Tree of Secrets,* **and** *Laura Dean Keeps Breaking Up with Me*

As previously discussed in relation to Leila Abdelrazaq's *Baddawi*, the school is a vital setting and context for young people, one that can have negative and positive effects. While the residential schools in *7 Generations* are oppressive and violent, institutional tools mobilized by the Canadian government to eradicate Indigenous cultures and ethnicities from the larger population, the school in the Palestinian refugee camp (more so than the school in Beirut) offers Ahmad in *Baddawi* an opportunity to gain the knowledge and grades he needs to apply to universities in America that would eventually offer him an alternative to his experience of precarity in the refugee camp in northern Lebanon.

Among the first comics to visualize LGBTQ+ experiences in schools, Abby Denson's *Tough Love: High School Confidential* (2006) and Hubert and Marie Caillou's *Adrian and the Tree of Secrets* (2013) depict educational institutions as particularly oppressive places where difference and homosexuality are frequently linked to self-harm and/or suicide. *Tough Love* tells the story of Brian, a new student at high school, and his budding romance with Chris, a classmate. Religious doctrine often hovers in the background of these early LGBTQ+ comics, providing the basis for a young person's ostracism by their peers and a parental and administrative justification of homophobia. In *Tough Love*, for example, former boyfriend Li's fundamentalist Catholic Chinese family sends him back to China once they discover his relationship with Chris. Li attempts suicide by slitting his wrists. The text emphasizes the terrible cost of prejudice on a young person's well-being. In this particular comic, the Catholic religion and the institutionalized homophobia that is part of the school community are specifically identified as being responsible for feelings of inadequacy and self-hatred that define the lived experiences of some queer children who struggle to align themselves with the social and cultural expectations that give shape to this educational space.

Frequently, the school becomes the setting for social rituals that young people cherish, value, or dread. The prom—the end-of-year formal dance—has emerged as a North American sociocultural event in real life and in literary/visual narratives that carries with it particular expectations or understandings of gender and sexuality. The prom or formal dance is the staging ground for the performance or revelation of a young's person "true" self as they come of age, their "arrival" so to speak at a moment on the cusp of adulthood. This carries through into contemporary LGBTQ+ comics, as can be seen in *Tough Love* and *Skim*. In *Tough Love*, the epilogue features new couple Brian and Chris attending the prom together. The final page of the text visualizes them—literally and figuratively—on the brink of entering into a socially significant venue (the school's gymnasium) and in so doing "coming out" publicly as gay to the student population and supervising teachers and administrators, a dangerous choice given the community's proven heteronormativity. Interestingly, the text concludes with a freeze-frame panel that depicts the powerful moment *before* their actual arrival at the prom, with no indication of how Brian and Chris's experience goes afterward.[9]

In Hubert and Caillou's beautifully illustrated *Adrian and the Tree of Secrets* (2013), a French all-boys' Catholic school figures as a place of oppression

---

9. The end-of-year formal dance and the prom are culturally resonant—and predominantly heterosexual—social events and public spaces, as can be seen even more currently in Matthew Sklar's 2018 Broadway musical and Ryan Murphy's film adaptation (2020) of *The Prom*. In these texts it is a female student, Emma Nolan, who wants to take a girl to the dance, prompting the school's PTA to organize a separate prom for her so that her queerness would not "taint" the heterosexual norms governing the event itself.

FIGURE 4.1. Barriers erected at Adrian's school. Hubert and Marie Caillou, *Adrian and the Tree of Secrets*. Arsenal Pulp Press, 2013, p. 9.

and ostracism, where the changeroom becomes a site of particular anxiety for protagonist Adrian because of the confusing mix of homophobic and homoerotic behavior it encourages among the male students. Worse, the school's administration condones displays of hatred toward anyone who might appear to be different (as when Father Kemeneur tries to "toughen" up Adrian by having the boys tackle him in rugby, and when the principal, in response to the queer-bashing that Adrian experiences, tells him that he is "sick" and that he must pray that his illness will be cured by the church). Early on, the text offers a powerful commentary on the disturbing correlation Adrian (and so many queer youth) makes between school and desperation (see figure 4.1). As he travels to the Notre Dame school on public transit, Adrian reflects on the barrier that has been erected outside to prevent people (students) from attempting suicide, a safety measure instituted in response to student Terry Abjean's tragic act of self-harm. The small figure in the distance in each of the panels suggests the presence of another young person who struggles to reorient themselves in relation to this heteronormative location. The toxic school atmosphere reveals an institutionalized hatred from which no physical barrier could protect a young person: Hazing and queer-bashing from the students, and blatant hypocrisy on the part of the administrators who protect the abusers while condemning the marginalized, are common, everyday occurrences at Notre Dame.

School becomes an extension of society in the small French town in which they live; the oppression Adrian endures at school is similar to what he experiences from his conservative mother and her heteronormative assumptions and expectations about Adrian's future. As with the idealized ending of *Tough Love,* however, the conclusion of *Adrian and the Tree of Secrets* moves into the realm of the fantastical, suggesting that there is no plausible alternative to the prejudice that Adrian endures at school and at home. The final sequence depicts Adrian climbing down a hill and immersing himself in the sea, cleansing himself symbolically after his beating at school and the emotional trauma he has experienced as well as being shunned by his lover, his peers, and finally his mother. Fantasy, it seems, offers the only alternative to a traumatic lived experience of queerness and to the crisis of "coming out." Although Hubert and Caillou's text offers no real consolation for young readers who suffer ostracism at home and at school, it bears mentioning here because of its detailed and all too believable visualization of homophobia.

Although *Tough Love, Adrian and the Tree of Secrets,* and Mariko and Jillian Tamaki's *Skim* (2005) depict the school as an oppressive institution that positions young queers in opposition to racial and heterosexual norms, this approach begins to shift in more contemporary graphic texts in which the school's rules and regulations become less oppressive, and the site functions more as a backdrop for the interpersonal opportunities that await young queers. *Laura Dean Keeps Breaking Up with Me,* for example, distinguishes itself from these three earlier texts by separating the process of coming of age from the experience of sexual difference.

Mariko Tamaki's comic *Laura Dean Keeps Breaking Up with Me* (2019), illustrated by Rosemary Valero-O'Connell, tackles complex issues such as toxic relationships, teenage pregnancy, and abortion. School, as an institution that shapes the experiences of young people, is noticeably different in this text published fourteen years after *Skim,* reflecting the awareness and social supports that have grown in the public education sector, as well as the establishment of peer groups for youth at schools, such as Gay-Straight alliances and LGBTQ+ Youth Groups. In contrast to the schools represented in the previous three comics, Berkeley High School is welcoming and queer-positive in *Laura Dean*; LGBTQ+ topics are de rigueur in protagonist Frederica "Freddy" Riley's classes. The curriculum in history class, for example, includes discussion about the first openly gay elected official in California,

Harvey Milk, which in turn inspires a productive debate among the students about whether to describe him as "homosexual" or "gay" (31), a debate that signals the strides young people and some educators have made in terms of cultivating more complex theorizations of queer identity. In contrast to the homogeneous school community in *Skim*, the high school population in *Laura Dean* is diverse, reflecting Tamaki's determination to depict complicated love relationships along a spectrum of queer people. Tamaki's text features a refreshing group of primary and secondary LGBTQ+ characters from a range of racial, ethnic, and gender types, all featured against a backdrop of American high school culture.

Tamaki's visualization of LGBTQ+ experiences is complex and multigenerational, a far cry from the gay assimilation or homosexual visibility stories that were typical of early YA fiction and early LGBTQ+ graphic narratives like *Pedro & Me* and *Blue Is the Warmest Color* and a reminder that queer experiences are anything but homogenous and no longer overdetermined by heterosexist expectation. At home, Freddy's family is wholly accepting of her lesbian identity: Her relationship turmoil with her ex-girlfriend Laura is a topic that her parents oversee with a humorous (and respectful) tolerance. Freddy's home is a much safer location than it was for Li, Adrian, and Kim, for example, where her gender identity and sexual activity are not perceived as threatening by her parents. Importantly, Freddy and her peers no longer need to reorient themselves away from the heterosexual world; instead, the high school world that Tamaki's text depicts is one where queers dwell freely and openly. As the text takes pains to emphasize, *Laura Dean* is not about *being* queer, specifically, so much as it is about the turbulence of adolescent relationships in general, queer and straight. "It was important to me that in part of the book there wouldn't be a lot of resistance from the world that these queer characters live in," Tamaki clarifies in an interview. "There's no conflict about that. Peripherally, there's internal and external conflicts, but the majority of it is not about the process of coming out or struggling with identity, it's that identity is just there" (Orr). *Laura Dean* captures the social media frenzy of teen culture, as well as the small moments of public humiliation in school when the intricacies of one's relationship become common knowledge. Becoming the subject of public discussion among one's peers following a series of bad relationship decisions forms the crux of this comic.

Freddy Riley attends high school in Berkeley, California, surrounded by a dynamic and supportive group of LGBTQ+ peers. As this is a text about escaping the "mark" that labels impose on a person (a theme *Laura Dean* shares with *Skim*), Tamaki's text visualizes an intersectional queer peer group, one in which sexual and gender identities go largely undefined. In terms of symbolic spaces, the school forms a mere backdrop for the students' escapades as opposed to functioning as an institution that shapes and regulates their day-to-day lives. The title expresses the text's main concern: Freddy's frustrated and yet resigned assertion that "Laura Dean keeps breaking up with me." As the title emphasizes, Freddy defines herself in relation to Laura, first as her girlfriend and then as her ex-girlfriend, and always, more to the point, as the passive recipient of Laura's disrespectful behavior. Visually reminiscent of James Dean, Laura's leather jacket and floppy hair evoke a self-absorbed, devil-may-care attitude that is initially captivating for Tamaki's protagonist. Freddy is repeatedly disrespected by Laura, who is elusive and flirtatious with other girls. Laura withdraws emotionally whenever Freddy asks her to account for her behavior: for not following through on a promise, for kissing another girl at the Valentine's Day dance, for breaking up with her (again) over text message, and so on. In this way, the title evokes Freddy's hurt, frustration, and resignation to the unpleasant "reality" of toxic relationships that all too many young people experience. In contrast to *Tough Love* and *Adrian and the Tree of Secrets*, the crisis in this text is neither Freddy's lesbian identity nor her process of "coming out," but rather the emotional heights and depths of early love that a young person experiences as they decide what they will accept and not accept in a partner. Freddy finds her confidence shattered repeatedly by the damaging relationship that she shares with Laura. Laura Dean's all-pervasive influence on Freddy—and in turn, on how Freddy comes to view herself—is communicated visually in pages that capture moments of ecstasy and connection for Freddy, precious moments of time, often washed over by a whimsical pink color that suggests nostalgia for a past and a relationship ideal that she longs for but that is no longer possible (or never was).

More pertinently, Tamaki depicts the emotional challenges that young people can experience in high school by means of the text's focalizing lesbian character, Freddy. *Laura Dean* is about defining what "healthy" relationships are by visualizing what they are not, as Freddy learns to feel at home in her body and in her identity as a confident young queer woman. Laura's emotional manipulations bring out the worst in Freddy, who remains so obsessed with Laura that she is disrespectful to her peers. Valero-O'Connell calls attention to Freddy's process of reorientation, as she moves beyond the tribulations of first love and, fascinatingly, reorients herself, not away from the heterosexual world and its spaces but rather toward an authenticity of self and thought that is not necessarily codified as queer. The predicament that Freddy faces is one with which many young people struggle and one that is not specific to queers (see figure 4.2). Once Freddy takes control of

FIGURE 4.2. Freddy breaks up with Laura. Mariko Tamaki, *Laura Dean Keeps Breaking Up with Me*. Illustrated by Rosemary Valero-O'Connell. Groundwood Books, 2019, p. 277.

the situation and decides to break up with Laura, she begins to exceed the parameters of the page, visually reflecting the developing agency she demonstrates. Laura, on the other hand, remains boxed in by the comic's panels. The top part of this page represents an "unmoored moment" (Postema, *Narrative* 40)—one that readers can consume at their leisure—that emphasizes the importance of Freddy's choice to end it with Laura.

*Tough Love*, *Skim*, and *Laura Dean* all culminate with the end-of-year formal dance. In *Laura Dean*, however, the prom has lost all cultural resonance, becoming a mere backdrop to the more important decision Freddy makes to value herself and the integrity of her friendships over her desire for Laura. At the dance, Freddy chooses to be "a good date" and a "better friend" rather than the "ex-girlfriend of Laura Dean" (287)—thus re-marking and reorientating herself—and in turn modeling this crucial assumption of agency for young readers.

School as an institution that governs the lives of characters becomes less of a focus in more recent LGBTQ+ comics. Instead, the focal point shifts to the choices that young queers make that affirm personal integrity and their chosen peer groups, as well as the struggles that young people in general face, with their queerness being but one of many different challenges.

## Queer "I" for the Straight Eye: *Drama* and *Check Please!*

If, as *Tough Love* and *Adrian and the Tree of Secrets* suggest, school can be a metaphorical closet, then extracurricular activities can offer opportunities for personal and sexual empowerment, as some of these more recent LGBTQ+ comics depict. In these comics, extracurricular activities host the informal worlds of young people with their friendship groups, and social experiences enable the orientation of the queer body to the world around it in a more positive fashion, outside the constrictions of the school environment. Comics like *Drama* (2012), *Check Please!* (2018–), and *The Avant-Guards* (2019–) present extracurricular activities as supportive, empowering, and queer-positive, although this representational strategy might not always accord with the actual lived experiences of young queers. In the case of *Check Please!* and *The Avant-Guards*, for example, the suggestion that organized sports like hockey and basketball—and their attendant spaces, the ice rink and basketball court—allow queer youth to reorient themselves away from heterosexist paradigms seems rather implausible, given the contemporary reluctance of recreational, varsity, and professional athletes to come out in the public eye. In striking contradistinction from previous LGBTQ+ comics, these particular comics mobilize distinctive portrayals of queer youth, ones that seek to "normalize" their lived realities and approach crises as moments in the lives of young people immediately before, during, or after a personal life change or predicament that carries a significant emotional impact. Perhaps not coincidentally, such depictions come from LGBTQ+ comics collectives and allies, eager to carve out accepting stories for queer characters in literature as much as for young North American readers. The material at hand is noticeably lighter and less intense emotionally than in earlier LGBTQ+ comics. The conflict is not necessarily oriented around sexual difference.

James Tynion IV and Rian Sygh's *The Backstagers* series (2017–19) and Raina Telgemeier's *Drama* (2012) depend upon the understanding that dramatic productions offer extracurricular opportunities (spatial and social) for people who are queer. "Drama" as a title thus evokes the stage and performance, as well as the tumultuous interpersonal politics that govern school life and the theater tech crew at Eucalyptus Middle School. As with *Laura Dean*, queer relationships are not presented as the central "problems" of the narrative. Instead, Telgemeier "treats being gay as a normal part of life, not something exceptional" (Abate 356). The predicament per se revolves around the love triangle among peers Matt, Callie, and Greg: Callie is fixated on Greg, while Matt longs for Callie from afar. Matt's passive aggressiveness toward Callie because of the time she spends alone with twins Justin and Jesse offers a lesson to young readers about decoding social and sexual codes of behavior. Warning Callie about getting too "attached to the performers" (*Drama* 68), Matt's jealousy and homophobia escalate as the production progresses and as Callie spends more time with the brothers, finally erupting in the discriminatory criticisms he unleashes on Jesse ("What guy sits around studying a woman's role in a musical?" [194]) and his sneering advice to Callie that she needs to start "chasing after *real* men" (195). *Drama* addresses a series of challenges that young people face in school, from anxiety and depression, to overbearing parental expectation, heteronormativity, interpersonal relationships, and, in this case, sexual prejudice. Telgemeier does her best to "normalize" queerness to show that LGBTQ+ peers are as common in schools as they are in society at large. In a similar way to *Check Please!*, *Drama* offers a lesson for young readers to recognize and understand the subtleties of sexual difference.

In Telgemeier's comic, the LGBTQ+ storyline surfaces with the twins, Jesse and Justin, who see the flyer about tryouts for the play and express interest in participating. In the first panel in which they are introduced, they appear to be almost mirror images of one another, with Justin demonstrating the more stereotypically gay attributes (flamboyance, exuberance, extroversion, interest in the spotlight, a love of singing, etc.; see figure 4.3). The narrative, however, discourages readers from wondering about Jesse's sexual orientation by directing attention to the more exaggerated behaviors of his brother. Telgemeier goes on to deploy the gay character Justin as comic relief in the narrative proper as well as in the school musical (where he is cast as the fool, Colonel Scrimshaw), once again relying on stereotypical representation to distinguish the twins. In the process, readers are so preoccupied by Justin's demonstrative behavior that Jesse flies under the radar. Justin's "coming out" moment to Callie is extremely matter-of-fact, Telgemeier openly addressing queer sexual identity after visualizing stereotypically queer behavior. Set against very regular paneling, swirling dialogue boxes link Callie and Justin in this moment of confession. "Gay? You can

FIGURE 4.3. Justin and Jesse meet Callie. Raina Telgemeier, *Drama*. Graphix, 2012, p. 30.

say it! I don't mind" (65), Justin declares, unashamed and calm in front of his friend. Callie accepts without question Justin's declaration, generously asking him questions about the boys that he thinks are cute in the school, an example of an "appropriate" response to queer youth that Telgemeier models in her graphic text.

Telgemeier's more subtle didacticism occurs in her characterization of Justin's twin, Jesse. A careful reader will note early on in *Drama* that Jesse reveals that he can gender-bend, that he is willing to sing the female lead, Maybelle, to Justin's male lead. When Callie successfully convinces Jesse to join the stage crew, he breaks into song, floating away on the notes of Maybelle's melody. "Maybe we'll cure him of his stage fright yet!" (60), Justin tells Callie hopefully, signaling to younger readers (and to Callie) that Jesse is struggling to accept who he is and that their father's expectation that he will become an engineer restricts his freedom. Part of the so-called narrative "drama" of Telgemeier's LGBTQ+ comic is the misinterpretation of these subtle social and sexual cues. Callie, for example, worries about why Jesse has not asked her to accompany him to the eighth-grade formal, discounting her friend Liz's suggestion that he might be gay because he does not display any of the allegedly "typical" behaviors that his twin Justin does. Similarly, Jesse struggles against the norms of hegemonic masculinity as well as his father's rigid beliefs, torn between his sexual attraction to West Redding and social expectations about masculine behavior. In spite of Telgemeier's determination to "normalize" queerness in middle school culture, heteronormativity reigns, as the flyer advertising the musical reminds readers (as it features a male and female kissing). The climax to Telgemeier's LGBTQ+ comic occurs at the end-of-year formal—heteronormative rite of passage. The evening begins with Jesse and Callie, Justin and Liz, performing the expected heterosexual roles emblematic of this rite—going for dinner, arriving at the dance, and dancing—in spite of Jesse's increased discomfort with playing this role. Eventually, Jesse uses the excuse to use the washroom and disappears altogether, leaving Callie alone at this event that carries with it so many social expectations. Jesse gravitates to heartthrob West, who sits outside on the steps of the school, but does not know how to express his intentions to Callie or even what those preferences might mean. Telgemeier chooses not to spell out Jesse's moment of realization; Callie successfully decodes his behavior, finally. Fascinatingly, Jesse's moment of personal and sexual awakening is navigated wholly in relation to this heterosexual young girl.

In this popular text for young readers, Telgemeier invokes visual stereotypes about homosexuality while ostensibly teaching younger readers to decode more subtle sexual cues and social expectations about behavior and identity, "normalizing" them by not explaining them explicitly. Such representations of queer youth offer distinctly straightforward views of the challenges that young queers experience while navigating heterosexual spaces and learning to dwell in them. Queers are a "normal" part of the social fabric that white, heterosexual, and middle-class characters like Callie are bound to encounter in middle school and in society, or so *Drama* reasons. At the center of the narrative lies Callie, whose experiences stand as the social norm. In *Drama* Telgemeier has provided a vision of middle school that is visually diverse—sexually and ethnically—in terms of its student demographic. In spite of this diversity, however, Michelle Ann Abate argues that Telgemeier's comic sentimentalizes a nostalgia for the antebellum South, glorifies plantation life, and whitewashes American racial history through its evocation of *Moon Over Mississippi* as the school musical, which is a loose adaptation of *Gone with the Wind* (375). Abate astutely suggests that the narrative at the heart of *Moon Over Mississippi* is in effect a reconciliation story, one that features a relationship between a Northern man and a Southern belle, whose union serves as a synecdoche for the political union of the US after the Civil War. Such reconciliation stories were interested in uniting North and South, but white supremacy was still the ground on which to build national unity. Telgemeier's *Drama* "demonstrates the limitations of LGBTQ+ youth advocacy that does not remain cognizant of intersectionality, while it also highlights the problem with millennial forms of liberal multiculturalism that omit critical discussions of race" (Abate 357). I would suggest that Abate's claim about "millennial forms of liberal multiculturalism" applies also to *Drama*'s depiction of gender and sexual orientation. In *Drama*, although Telgemeier features characters who are visually diverse in their ethnicities and sexual orientations, deeper, more complex understandings of race and queer experiences are not addressed in a meaningful way, and the text can appear to be dangerously homogenizing in its determination to "normalize" difference.

Ngozi Ukazu's *Check Please! Book 1: #Hockey* (2018) is another example of this tendency to "normalize" queer experiences in graphic literature for young people. Hockey and "bro" culture are an unlikely setting for LGBTQ+ content, one would imagine. As soon as Ukazu introduces protagonist Eric "Bitty" Bittle as a freshman joining the hockey team at Samwell University, readers are struck by the collision of stereotypical "queer" characteristics and hypermasculine hockey culture. Bitty has a background in figure skating, is obsessed with baking pies, and records vlogs in which he provides baking advice and updates on his experiences at college. In a daring move, Ukazu "normalizes" queerness by situating it within one of the most hypermasculine and heteronormative cultures in North American society: hockey. The juxtaposition of Bitty's gentle and stereotypically effeminate demeanor with his teammates' aggressive masculinity is a source of (uncomfortable) humor in the narrative as Ukazu implies that each set of behaviors balances the other out. In his vlogs, Bitty visualizes "bro" culture for readers: Teammate Shitty's vernacular is littered with vulgar expletives; Holster and Ransom are flagrant in their misogyny; and the frat "haus" that the boys inhabit revolves solely around alcohol consumption, poor decision-making, and the loss of virginity at keggers. Not surprisingly, Bitty's initial enthusiasm about joining the team wavers after meeting his teammates, who do not share his standards for hygiene and who do not treat his pecan pie with the respect that it deserves.

Ukazu adeptly visualizes Bitty's anxieties about playing for Samwell's racially homogeneous hockey team, his worry about body-checking, and his stress about not having what it takes to succeed as a varsity athlete. The vlog format of the panels allows Bitty to connect with young readers directly about these feelings. Yet, Ukazu attempts to sanitize the experience of an effeminate young queer trying to fit into a hypermasculine team, avoiding the expected traumas of initiation and hazing. According to the narrative's argument, Bitty must learn the social codes to fit into "bro" culture and come to terms with the misogyny that undergirds the masculine behaviors of his teammates, just as his teammates must learn to appreciate his gentleness and effeminacy. On this page, Bitty's cultural misstep—not being able to identify a well-known hockey player—suggests that he is different from his teammates, while his clever adaptation of this misstep in terms of queer icons (Michelle Kwan, Lucille Ball, Beyoncé) reminds young readers of his "feeling at home" in his body and identity. By "braiding" their similarities and creating an "associative logic" (Postema, *Narrative* 69), Ukazu implies that "bro" culture and queer culture are more similar than one might expect, given their respective performances of masculinities, both of which are equally valued within the narrative proper. Bitty can learn from his teammates just as his teammates can learn from him, the narrative reasons idealistically. While several pages detail Bitty's worry about coming out to his motley crew of teammates, the eventual revelation comes and goes with relatively little anxiety for Bitty. "There's no big coming-out scene, no 'convert the lone homophobe' drama, no storyline cooked up just to educate the reader about the gay experience. Bitty doesn't need any of that, and Ukazu gives the reader credit for not needing it either" (Lehoczky). When Bitty comes out to Shitty, Shitty reminds him that friendship and team camaraderie are more important in the grand scheme of things than one's gender identity. Thus, in *Check Please!*, Bitty's crises are those of social acceptance by his teammates and success at college rather than acceptance of his sexuality. He becomes the team's backbone, winning the Carlisle Award for his enthusiasm and devotion to the team. *Check Please!* is in this way emblematic of a trend in LGBTQ+ comics that returns to the "love is love" tautology typical of YA fiction in the 1990s, in which readers experience a cathartic acceptance of homosexuality upon reading the text, in which the corporeality of queerness is downplayed, and in which closure brings completion and a satisfying sense of "arrival" at a stable understanding of identity (Trites, *Disturbing* 114; Mallan 7). The lack of realism, however, undercuts the persuasiveness of *Check Please!* as a representation of authentic queer experience. Etelka Lehoczky characterizes Ukazu's "glowing, antiseptic bubble for her hero to fall in love inside" as "banal," a "convenient" choice that is entertaining, if "unaffecting." In actual life, neither the hockey arena nor the frat house is a space so easily negotiated or mastered.

Primarily in response to representations of young people experiencing marginalization and ostracism, contemporary LGBTQ+ comics (like *Check Please!*) depict extracurricular activities as ones that are distinguished by a collectivist ethos, ones that provide supportive communities that incorporate all types of young people, queer and straight. *The Avant-Guards* (2019–), a collaboration by Carly Usdin, Noah Hayes, and Rebecca Nalty, is a tale of friendship and love, featuring an intersectional group of young people who have formed an NCAAA Division IV women's basketball team at Georgia O'Keeffe College of Arts and Subtle Dramatics. Again, a sporting facility is the emblem of cooperation and respect. Balancing out the series' focus on the team's dynamic, as well as on its training for competitions, is the relationship that Olivia (Liv) and Charlie develop on and off the court. Importantly, *The Avant-Guards* offers young readers visions of intersectional queer subjectivities in a series that features LGBTQ+ identities as a fact of life. There are possibly four queer characters on the basketball team, three of whom have had relationships with women in the past. Another character, Jay, uses they/them pronouns. The comic does not spend any time clarifying those pronouns and individual identity labels: Instead, Jay's nonbinary or gender-queer identity is merely alluded to in passing. *The Avant-Guards* also distinguishes itself as a series by featuring an ethnically and religiously diverse cast of characters (see figure 4.4). No two characters are represented in the same semantic and visual way in the series, a noteworthy change that chooses equity in representation over true conflict in the narrative. According to the first issue, the basketball court offers a space in which young people learn to feel at home as much in their own bodies and identities as they do in their peer group; importantly, the challenges they navigate (in their love relationships and in their training) are no longer oriented around sexual and gender identification.

These creators employ extracurricular activities to explore opportunities for queer characters to step outside the heterosexist binary that can govern school life in North American culture and society. Locations—like the

FIGURE 4.4. An ethnically and religiously diverse cast of characters. Carly Usdin, *The Avant-Guards*. Vol. 1. Illustrated by Noah Hayes. Boom! Box, 2019.

theater, the hockey rink, and the basketball court—become idealized sites to visualize and value the lived experiences of queer people. The hockey rink and the basketball court, especially, are represented as spaces that are relatively uncomplicated to negotiate and where young protagonists can choose to dis-orient themselves from conventional heterosexist norms that have otherwise governed their daily lives. While such narratives are rather unrealistic in their argumentation, perhaps their strength lies in their insistence that queerness is not the central problem with which young people struggle. These three texts certainly encourage young readers to develop compassion and empathy for all members of society, queer and straight, in the process provoking reader identification with the story's characters. As previous chapters of this study have demonstrated, comics are persuasive tools for knowledge building, encouraging young readers to think more broadly about many issues, including gender and sexuality. The comics analyzed in this section affirm for young readers that people who identify as LGBTQ+ are "just like them," with similar problems and preoccupations.

## Camp Narratives:
### *Honor Girl*, *As the Crow Flies*, and *Lumberjanes*

Extracurricular activities like dramatic productions and varsity sports offer opportunities in which young queers can enjoy a freedom from heteronormative expectation and a supportive community that incorporates all types of young people, as a number of LGBTQ+ comics visualize. Contemporary LGBTQ+ graphic narratives increasingly focus on another culturally resonant space—the summer camp—as a site in which young people can push back against the norms that govern their everyday lives at home and at school. In such texts as *Lumberjanes* (2014–20), *Honor Girl* (2015), *As the Crow Flies* (2017), and most recently, *Camp Spirit* (2020), the summer camp offers a temporary alternative to home and school, one that has an equally profound influence on young people's social and emotional well-being. Summer camp comics showcase the informal worlds of young people, friendship groups, and social experiences, both positive and negative, that develop away from the oversight of parents and the education system. What is particularly powerful about the summer camping experience is its evocation of camp as a location, a place of gender presentation, as well as a mode of performance and flamboyance.

When thinking about camp in relation to LGBTQ+ texts, one must acknowledge the double meaning of the term: both a "wilderness" experience for (mostly) affluent teens and an allusion to an aesthetic style and sensibility that is ironic and excessive, along with its key elements of artifice, performance, frivolity, and naïveté. Central to the camp mode is the assumption that all identities are roles. That is what Susan Sontag discusses in her 1964 essay, "Notes on Camp": "Camp sees everything in quotation marks. It's not a lamp, but a 'lamp'; not a woman, but a 'woman.' To perceive Camp in objects and persons is to understand Being-as-Playing-a-Role. It is the farthest extension, in sensibility, of the metaphor of life as theater" (280). In *How to Be Gay* (2012), David Halperin also discusses camp as a mode and as a creative impulse that does not cover up or deny the pain of a marginalized person living in a society of white, heteronormative privilege; nor does it make fun of things from a position of moral or aesthetic superiority. Instead, camp lovingly demeans. "But it doesn't demean some people at other people's expense," Halperin explains. "It takes everyone down with it together" (190–91). In its practices of cultural appropriation—its recycling of bits of mainstream culture—camp is a creative impulse and a "strategy for dealing with social domination" (Halperin 203). Deflating pretension and dismantling traditional hierarchies and binaries, camp is inclusive and democratic, both "presum[ing] and produc[ing] community" (207). In this mode, humor coexists with horror, and human calamities (like the HIV/AIDS epidemic, for example) can become vehicles for parody without any suggestion of cruelty or disavowal. "To make your own suffering into a vehicle of parody, to refuse to exempt yourself from the irony with which you view all social identities, all performances of authorized social roles, is to level social distinctions," Halperin claims (187–88). "The ability to identify a particular object or style as camp and to encourage others to share that view creates a basis for community" (189). Camp is thus all-inclusive: It allows no possibility for distance or disidentification. Halperin invites readers to consider camp as offering opportunities to level gender hierarchies, challenge the authenticity of naturalized identities, and question the conventional scale of values that determine degrees of social dignity and personal agency. A number of these LGBTQ+ texts about summer camp visualize this exciting dismantling of traditional binaries and hierarchies, inclusive deflating of pretension, and engagement with performativity.

From *Lumberjanes* to *As the Crow Flies,* many comics choose summer camp as a particular location in which young protagonists explore their nascent sexual and gender identities as well as a mode with which creators think reflexively on how to express those identities. As such, summer camps become sites for crisis—not for "coming out" per se—but for larger questions about identity, faith, belonging, and a more general collectivist ethos, with some of the protagonists in the process modeling agentic behavior for the texts' young readers. Kenneth Kidd and Derritt Mason's collection *Queer as Camp: Essays on Summer, Style, and Sexuality* (2019) breaks new ground in its examination of camp in YA literature as a style and an expressive mode, a location, and a place of presentation for young queers. Kidd and Mason identify summer camp "as a queer time and/or place" (10), evoking Halberstam's identification of the queer "way of life" as one that embraces subcultural practices, alternative methods of alliance, forms of transgender embodiment, and practices of representation that capture willfully eccentric ways of being. Time spent at day- and sleepaway camp can, in many instances, allow young queers to explore "the potentiality of a life unscripted by the conventions of family, inheritance, and child rearing" (Halberstam, *Queer* 2), temporarily at least. Traditionally, the summer camp was scaffolded on the Romantic ideal of childhood innocence while ostensibly preparing the young person for adulthood (and by implication, heterosexual romantic relationships). More contradictory is the idea that while camps often discouraged same-sex intimacy, they also created a location for such attachments because of the intense, immersive experiences they offered young people (Kidd and Mason 10). As these comics visualize, summer camp offers habitual activities that shape the bodies of young people and their particular friendship worlds, frequently against a backdrop of interpersonal growth and challenges. Many of the young characters' experiences of dwelling in those locales optimistically visualize the gradual process of reorientating oneself away from heterosexual and heterosexist norms of behavior.

Queerness and camping did not go hand in hand, however. The camping craze for young people began in the United States in 1861, when the headmaster of the Gunnery School in Connecticut, Frederick William Gunn, took his entire student population for a two-week excursion into the wilderness (Kidd and Mason 10). The earliest summer camps were not-for-profit experiments in alternative living directed by educators who saw opportunities to provide urban young people with outdoor education possibilities that schools did not offer (Thurber et al. 242). They looked to "correct" city children and adolescents who were not necessarily familiar with strategies to cope with the challenges of the outdoors and to instill in them valuable team-building skills. Thurber and colleagues argue that camp settings were uniquely suited for positive youth development, offering experiences in community living; being away from home; a holistic experience that included physical exercise in an outdoor, recreational setting; mental challenges (cooperative problem-solving); social skill development (making friends); and spiritual events (outdoor worship; 242). Originally, summer camp had a history of "promoting egalitarian ideals" (Gillard et al. 95), and as such "campers who would be marginalized in other settings [had] decreased feelings of isolation as well as increases in self-esteem, familial acceptance, personal security, and social skills" (Bialeschki et al. 778). Writing about summer camps in the US as being based on a view of nature as a "munificent, restorative, character-building agent" (88), Michael B. Smith also describes them as places in which young people could "adjust to the conditions of the outside world without having to confront them directly. They could adjust as individuals within groups, benefiting from intimate, controlled encounters with other personalities, yet hopefully without undue pressure to conform" (85). The summer camp experience quickly grew to become one of the most popular activities for middle- and upper-class, predominantly white young people in the United States. Between 1900 and 1918, for example, the number of summer camps in the US increased more than tenfold (Eveleth 192). By the 1930s, however, summer camps began to move away from the notion of "roughing it" in favor of more "civilized" pursuits: watching films, listening to radio broadcasts, playing tennis, and textile weaving (192). As Kyle Eveleth notes, critics came to lament the lack of actual "camping" in these camps, as daily activities and amenities eased the rigors of the wilderness that were once their mainstay. Camps now have many different iterations—Scout Camp, bible camp, sports camp, science camp, weight-loss camp, sailing camp, and so forth—but most invoke similar associations of escape and pleasure.[10]

Many LGBTQ+ comics hinge on the idea of "summer camp as a location and as a venue for adolescent growth" (Eveleth 192). The irony relies on the enforced segregation of male and female lives—intended to quash adolescent desire—while only appearing to enhance this desire in the process. The three summer camp narratives that this section explores feature single-sex communities that celebrate girlhood and womanhood and place importance on a community for and by women. Each comic distinguishes between vastly different orientations of the queer bodies within these locations, demonstrating how wide the spectrum is of queer experience in this socially resonant space. *Lumberjanes* occupies one end of this spectrum, with its naturalization of various manifestations of the queer experience; *Honor Girl* occupies the other. A common complaint about single-sex summer camps is that they "reinforce essentialist conceptions of sex and gender," specifically the idea that "biological sex always informs gender identity" (Musinsky 55). In their segregation of the sexes, they can reinforce gender differences as well as stereotypes of expected norms of masculinity and femininity.

*Honor Girl* (2015), Maggie Thrash's memoir about her summers spent at Camp Bellflower, visualizes her experiences at age fifteen when she becomes acutely aware of her gender-queerness in an environment that is predicated on rigid and binary notions of gender and sexuality. Maggie attends sleep-away camp in the heart of Appalachia at a summer camp dating back to 1922 that her mother and grandmother attended as well. This all-girls' camp has all of the conventional attributes—campfires, outdoor activities, crafting, and talent shows, among others—as well as an atmosphere and ideology that is firmly rooted in conservative, Southern "family values" and biases. Maggie spends the summer outdoors, enjoying nature and the supposed freedom it offers from the routine of school life. Her primary goal during the summer in question is to earn her Distinguished Expert certification in shooting, the highest award offered by the National Rifle Association. At this camp, the campers spend their days daydreaming about Luke (the camp's dishwasher), Little Jim (the lawnmower guy), and Danny (the garbage

---

10. I acknowledge the obvious contrast that such North American summer camps have with the displacement camps, refugee camps, and concentration camps to which chapter 2 refers. Although summer camps in the US and Canada are generally associated with pleasure and escape, camps throughout history and into contemporary times are tools used for the geopolitical ordering and control of people.

collector). In contrast to their obsessive mythologizing of these dubious examples of masculinity, the girls' homoeroticism is overt: They jump on each other on the beds in the cabins; they hold hands openly; they shave each other's legs and call each other sweetheart (Thrash 123). Yet, in spite of this implicitly sanctioned homoeroticism, Camp Bellflower is not queer friendly at all, as Maggie's memories of Beth and Ellie from two summers before prove. Ostracized by their peers because of their alleged lesbianism, neither returned to the camp. Consequently, Maggie is self-conscious of her emerging gender-queerness, frequently isolating herself from her peers, an isolation that is visually reinforced within the comic's panels themselves.

Isolation is broken during one significant moment in *Honor Girl*, reminding readers of the opportunities for performance, the deflation of social pretension, and the common fellowship of shared recognition that performances at talent shows and such events offer campers (see figure 4.5). Maggie's inspired and inspiring "genderbent performance" (Stamper 115) as Kevin from the Backstreet Boys provokes Erin, one of the camp counselors, to notice her. Maggie's devotion to this boy band, her deep commitment to the role (even using a Sharpie to draw a goatee on her chin), her soulful crooning of the Backstreet Boys' pop lyrics, and her strong performance of the role of Kevin are quintessentially camp elements. Significantly, these two pages in *Honor Girl* are ones in which the colors are most vivid, and the pages' paneling diverges from their regular organization. In this way, Thrash calls attention visually and thematically to Maggie at her most authentic (which can only be expressed through a campy performance of a boy band star). Sontag describes camp as "a mode of seduction—one which employs flamboyant mannerisms susceptible of a double interpretation; gestures full of duplicity, with a witty meaning for cognoscenti and another, more impersonal, for outsiders" ("Camp" 281). In this dramatic performance reminiscent of "drag kinging" (Stamper 116), Maggie's tongue-in-cheek and wildly earnest performance lovingly demeans, as Halperin suggests; her performance inspires appreciation from all of the campers watching because of its intensity and commitment, empowering Maggie temporarily while managing to provoke Erin's desire. This is the only moment in this memoir in which Maggie appears to feel at home in her body and identity, when the allowances of the talent show enable her to step outside the camp's rigid gender ideology.

Maggie's budding relationship with Erin, one of the camp counselors, forms the backdrop for the insight *Honor Girl* provides concerning the heteronormativity at work in similar single-sex summer camps. Thrash's concern is to expose the oppression that such a camp can encourage young people to experience: a location that uses language and propaganda

FIGURE 4.5. Maggie performs as Kevin. Maggie Thrash, *Honor Girl*. Candlewick Press, 2015, p. 36.

around the concepts of "team" and "sisterhood" to encourage homogeneity and mediocrity rather than authenticity and exceptionality. Head Counselor Tammy, for example, schools Maggie in the importance of not "showing off" her rifle talents because they make fellow camper Libby feel uncomfortable. Instead, Tammy implies, Maggie should adopt more "typical" feminine behaviors such as modesty and faith, as well as the collectivist ethos that favors the group over the individual. Seeing a potential problem brewing between one of her counselors and campers, Tammy also works to separate Erin and Maggie physically. The brief moments of intimacy that the two share are missed with increasing frequency, as the strictures of the camp work to affect their separation. When Head Counselor Tammy searches

Maggie's wastebasket and finds drafts of love letters that Maggie has written to Erin, she confronts her and forces her to consider the potential legal implications of her queer behavior. "So it's gross. And illegal. Your parents could sue us. Do you know what statutory rape is?" Tammy asks her bluntly (171). Tammy frames her "concern" for Maggie's personal safety as a pretext for saving the other campers from Maggie's corrosive "lesbian influence," as she calls it, in the process reminding her of the American military's "Don't ask, don't tell" policy (172). Maggie's anxiety around coming out is well founded at this summer camp; the ideologically driven policies governing the camp work to marginalize her further.

The central tension of Thrash's text focuses on the intersection of "honor" and sexuality, however. The beginning of *Honor Girl* clarifies the collective identity that campers at Bellflower are expected to adopt, providing the framework against which readers measure the protagonist. Maggie reveals to the reader that on the first night at camp, campers serenade the Honor Girl, usually a sixteen-year-old camper appointed the previous summer and whom all of the girls idolize (Thrash 17). Maggie's sarcasm signals immediately to the reader her ironic dismissal of the camp's basic values. Throughout the text, she is openly contemptuous of this alleged "honor," seeing the award as one that endorses an inauthenticity about the camp experience and about one's personal (and presumably sexual) identity that she does not value. Ironically, by the end of her summer, and after her relationship with Erin is acknowledged (and ended) by Tammy, Maggie wins the "honor girl" award one year sooner than normal—not because it has anything to do with her honorable qualities but because it was intended to keep her quiet about her so-called "freakish feelings" for girls (212). Worse, Maggie does not win the award that she is due (Best Rifle Shooter), an award that she actively worked for, as she is schooled in the oppressive ethos of sisterhood over individuality. The other irony of the label "honor" is that it should signal that Maggie is being true to herself, but she is not. Her "honor," therefore, is compromised by the leaders' homophobia. Thus, the appropriately named camp, "Bellflower," calls attention to an example of a single-sex summer camp that dissembles homophobia behind a celebration of traditional feminine values. Maggie ultimately represses her queerness in this world, unable to turn away from the pressures of heterosexual culture. Thrash's memoir foregoes the depiction of a young person's empowerment by calling attention to the oppression that a communal space can have on the orientation of a young queer woman.

Melanie Gillman's *As the Crow Flies* (2017) also addresses the oppression that can be endorsed by single-sex, overnight-camping communities, but with a surprising twist. *As the Crow Flies* portrays a young queer who attends a religious summer camp (the Girls' Outdoor Adventure Backpacking Camp) while wrestling with questions about identity, faith, and belonging. Protagonist Charlie is a thirteen-year-old Black and queer-questioning camper whose faith in God has become complicated by her emerging sexual identity. Her parents have enrolled her in the Christian summer camp; Charlie immediately feels marginalized because she feels as though she is attending a camp predicated on white privilege. She takes exception to the use of the phrase "whitening our souls" (29) that Head Counselor Bee uses with regards to the spiritual purification that they were supposedly experiencing by means of their hiking excursions. Wrestling explicitly with her emerging identity and personal faith, in many panels Charlie recoils overtly from Christian symbols even though she holds conversations with God throughout the text. At first, Charlie finds herself out of step with the traditional elements of camp life: the appropriation of Indigenous languages, the team mentality, and the camp's "womanly" mythos that connects female empowerment with a communion with nature. Charlie's interior conflicts (her feelings about the racially inflected language, her faith, and her worry about standing up for what she believes in) come to a head when camper Therese uses the derogatory phrase, "That's so gay" (49). Fellow camper Sydney rightly challenges Therese for her homophobic language, and Charlie slowly begins to see that she might have found someone compatible to spend time with at the camp. Sydney's ironically dismissive questioning of the camp's ethos is a strategy that they both employ to cultivate a sense of community and camaraderie. Unlike Maggie in *Honor Girl*, Charlie in *As the Crow Flies* learns to see past herself and her own insecurities to recognize that perhaps Sydney feels excluded too. Initially missing the significance of Sydney telling her that she has packed mace because "not everybody's equally safe in places like this" (97), Charlie and Sydney find solidarity in their contempt for the pseudo-feminist ceremonies that structure the camp life and the exclusionary language and philosophy that it appears to be built on. Eventually, Sydney alludes to her process of gender transition to Charlie by describing herself as "in*trans*igent" (194) and encourages Charlie to become more aware of her own process herself, having assumed that Charlie was queer-questioning as well. Gillman in this way subtly "braids" together the young women's experiences.

The naturalization of Charlie's coming into a sense of gender and sexual identity is produced through the aesthetics of the text itself. Many of the panels for the first half depict Charlie walking alone in beautiful natural settings. Gradually, however, Charlie begins to inhabit panels with other campers, or at the very least with Sydney and her growing group of friends.

The soft, pastel colors in this colored-pencil graphic narrative communicate warmth and visualize the wilderness as welcoming even though undeniably physically (and emotionally) challenging. Charlie begins to smile in the second half of Gillman's text, as she becomes more comfortable with herself. As the story progresses, Gillman's camp offers surprising opportunities to level gender hierarchies and challenge the authenticity of naturalized identities. Realizing that the prospect of putting on a swimming suit makes Sydney uncomfortable, Charlie supports her emotionally. "Wanna go sit on the bank with just our feet in, like nerds?" she asks Sydney, sensing her discomfort (233). This important moment leads to a telling conversation with another camper, Adelaide, during which Sydney and Charlie use the gendering and racializing of God to talk about the need to pass beyond gender binaries and even gender entirely. "God almost never *looks like* most of the people on the planet," Charlie muses (249). The three friends go on to offer numerous interpretations of God as "a Peruvian grandmother," "a Black women's wrestling champ," "a kid in a wheelchair," and "someone who doesn't need a gender at all," all to shake up traditional depictions of the deity (251). Such musings speak more directly to their lived experiences of identity, sexuality, and gender. The text culminates with a panel that features Charlie and Sydney holding hands during the final fireside scene, smiling happily at each other, understanding and appreciating each other, and signaling that Charlie has come to terms with a newfound sense of a genuine feminist faith that values women's empowerment.

While *Honor Girl* and *As the Crow Flies* invoke and question essentialist conceptions of sex and gender, *Lumberjanes* (2014–20), with its focus on friendship and girl-power, creatively bypasses basic stereotypes of masculinity and femininity and provides multiple points of sexual and gender identification for its young readers. A series created by ND Stevenson, Grace Ellis, Shannon Watters, and Gus Allen, *Lumberjanes* focuses on the quirky adventures that young campers have (thereby consciously moving away from the memoir trend in LGBTQ+ comics like *Honor Girl* and *Gender Queer* [2019]). *Lumberjanes* offers a wonderfully liberating reading experience. Iconic elements of the summer camp experience are parodied, beginning with the scouting manual and the badges that campers traditionally earn over the summer, and in its queering of the traditional binaries of male/female, culture/nature, white/Black, queer/straight, and the like. This queer-friendly summer camp series is a huge hit with young readers largely thanks to its tongue-in-cheek lampooning of the scouting novel literary tradition.

*Lumberjanes* revitalizes and revises the scouting genre of popular fiction that was made lucrative by the Edward Stratemeyer Syndicate between the late 1910s and 1940s. As previously mentioned, the scouting movement capitalized on popular beliefs about the positive effects that the wilderness and outdoor education could have on young people. Widespread fears about the forces of modernity provoking a crisis of masculinity fueled the creation of the scouting movement, launched by Robert Stephenson Smyth Baden-Powell (author of *Scouting for Boys* [1908]) and Ernest Thompson Seton, creator of the Woodcraft Indians (1902; Eveleth 189).[11] Eventually girls were offered similar, albeit separate, opportunities for outdoor education, such as Luther and Charlotte Gulick's Camp Fire Girls (1911) and Juliette Gordon Low's Girl Scouts (1912; 189). These scouting groups aimed to solidify traditional—read, conservative—gender roles and expectations: "Though girls were allowed to be outdoors and take part in more strenuous activities than they would in, say, church groups, their excursions were always founded upon honing 'womanly qualities'—skills like social mediation, community activism, and housekeeping rather than riflery, archery, or wayfinding" (190). Thus, these scouting novels fell in line with conservative gender ideals and were a "marketing ploy" by the Stratemeyer Syndicate (producers of the *Nancy Drew* and *The Hardy Boys* series) to reach white, middle-class American youth audiences (190). The Boy Scout in these books was "a paragon of truth, justice, and the American way," whereas the Girl Scout was domestic, feminine, and heterosexual; her ultimate goal was to find a suitable husband (190–91). The *Lumberjanes* are diametrically opposed to this binary way of thinking. *Beware the Kitten Holy*, its first issue—and, in fact, all of its subsequent seventy issues—provides a parodic send-up of the adventure mode and its engagement with the summer camp collectivist ethos by privileging female-led narratives and showcasing cisgender, queer, and trans characters who are all on their own quests to learn how to feel at home in their bodies.

Importantly, *Lumberjanes* confronts the problematic gendering that is built into the very foundations of the scouting ideology and literary genre. The girls who attend Miss Qiunzella Thiskwin Penniquiqul Thistle Crumpet's Camp are a far cry from the shrinking violets and demure young women trained in early Girl Scouting camps. Instead, this camp is inhabited by self-proclaimed "Hardcore Lady-Types," a label that calls attention to the typology of young girls who each offer different ways of presenting for their young readers. April and Molly, for example, are outwardly cisgender; Mal is nonbinary; Jo is trans and has hit her growth spurt, towering over the

---

11. Camping and outdoor education were encouraged by President Theodore Roosevelt, as John Burroughs explores in a 1906 issue of *The Atlantic*. Roosevelt cultivated a rugged outdoorsman image to counteract the slick politico impression he projected. His interest, however, was also genuine: He helped to establish the national parks system.

rest of the girls; and Ripley is androgynous, all scrapes and childlike bravery (Eveleth 196). The series self-consciously resists explaining, excusing, or justifying these ways of presentation; instead, it emphasizes diversity (sexual, gender, and racial), focusing most of its attention on the predominantly speculative plots. As with *Laura Dean*, the *Lumberjanes* series self-consciously avoids situating the process of "coming out" as the challenge that young people must somehow overcome. Instead, characters' personal relationships are peripheral to the story proper, although they certainly add intrigue to the adventures. After the encounter with the River Monster, for example, Molly and Mal are physically affectionate with one another, hugging, holding hands, and "smooching," as April and Ripley call it, after Molly carries Mal out of the water, unconscious, and administers CPR. Molly and Mal are delighted by this development in their relationship once Mal awakens, although this plot development remains largely peripheral to their subsequent adventures. The series returns periodically to this storyline to show how Molly and Mal gradually reorientate themselves to the world around them. Camp, in this way, provides a space (for characters as well as young readers) that is accepting, intersectional, and nonjudgmental, focusing instead on the adventure-crises that the campers must overcome.

The creators of *Lumberjanes* parody gender essentialisms in their secondary characters as well. Camp Director Rosie is a mash-up of a lumberjack, Paul Bunyan–type with Rosie-the-Riveter hair and biceps (Eveleth 196), while the camp director of the neighboring Scouting Lads camp is an example of exaggerated masculinity: He wields an axe, insists that "cookies are for the weak" and that "real men should be splitting wood and smoking pipes," and performs ridiculous feats of masculinity like catching a fish by wrestling it away from a bear. Likewise, the boys who attend the neighboring camp appear to be perfect examples of scouting resourcefulness and camaraderie, whose love of baking, cleanliness, and order conceals a rabid propensity for violence, once activated. The creators self-consciously parody gender essentialisms, redeploying iconic elements of the scouting and camp experience in their construction of community. Even though many of the Lumberjanes display conventionally "feminine" traits, they also display attributes traditionally reserved for boys in scouting literature. Counselor Jen understands the natural world and has perfect plant and animal recognition as well as a great knowledge of astrology, which comes in handy in their adventures. Molly can handle a bow and arrow as well as solve complex anagrams. Mal is known for her shrewd attack tactics and sophisticated strategies. Even cisgender April has a tomboy streak: She defeats a stone god in an arm-wrestling match. Jo has a great understanding of mathematics, managing to decode the complicated Fibonacci sequence that in turn allows the Lumberjanes to escape a mysterious cave into which they have stumbled. In contrast, the boys at the neighboring camp have a knack for domesticity and nurturing, rescuing the girls when they fall into a grove of poison ivy and bringing them back to their cabin for freshly baked cookies. With its collective protagonists, this series was created to challenge the "token girl character" that is often found in mainstream comics, a character who is assumed to be a role model simply because she is the only girl in the narrative (Dean-Ruzicka 219). In contrast, the Lumberjanes pool together their deep knowledge of science, mathematics, and the outdoors to solve the particular challenges that face them, and their collectivist mantra ("Friendship to the Max!") reminds young readers about girl power. Moving conclusively away from the tokenism of mainstream comics, this series celebrates "a new kind of collectivist *and* intersectional feminism," one that prioritizes "group success over individual attainment" (Dean-Ruzicka 219). In its collectivist ethos, the series offers "multiple points of identification for young readers," intersectional representations of its principal characters, and campers who are all at different developmental stages (219–20). As the series clarifies, "girl" and "girlhood" do not mean the same point in time or experience in each character's life.

*Lumberjanes* shares with *Honor Girl* and *As the Crow Flies* a prioritization of group success over individualism, although *Lumberjanes* makes sure to point out that the group's collectivist ethos is one that is not predicated on the loss of each camper's personal and gender authenticity. The youngsters are all a part of the Roanoke cabin and form a strong bond together, largely in response to the surveillance practiced by Counselor Jen, who cannot seem to keep them under control. "Friendship to the Max!"—the camp's motto—speaks to the ethos that joins these young people, and yet each camper comes into an awareness of the world around them that is specific and authentic to themselves.

## Reading to the Max

Reading, for queers, is a form of "survival just as much as a way to gain pleasure, develop knowledge and skill, and make a mark on the world" (Fawaz and Smalls 171). LGBTQ+ comics are especially important, I would suggest, for visualizing the lived experiences of queer people as they develop an awareness of their sexual and gender orientations. "We read for many reasons," Ramzi Fawaz and Shanté Smalls remind us, "to cope, to figure out what to do next, to distract ourselves, to become informed, to develop our own voice, to gain a deeper understanding of the world in which we live or in which we aspire to live" (177). Importantly, these comics for young readers visualize the particular spatiality of sexual desire and gender performance that many young queers undergo as they orient themselves in relation to—and oftentimes, against—the heterosexual world. The protagonists at the center of these stories often become agents of personal change, in turn modeling this behavior for young readers. "Children's literature will not change the world," Kerry Mallan declares, "but it does make significant and often undervalued contributions to how its child readers see the world and their place in it" (3). Mallan's statement applies equally to the comics about physical impairments, learning challenges, mental disorders, visual and hearing impairments, and neurological disabilities that the following chapter will explore.

CHAPTER 5

# Young People and/in Graphic Medicine

> It's considered *normal* in this society for children to combine words and pictures, so long as they grow out of it.
>
> —Scott McCloud, *Understanding Comics*

Marjorie Liu and Sana Takeda's fantasy comics series, *Monstress* (2015–), tells the story of a war between Arcanics (magical creatures who can sometimes pass for human) and the Cumae (sorceresses who consume Arcanics to fuel their power). Maika Halfwolf, the eponymous character, is an Arcanic "but with a *fully* human appearance" (Liu and Takeda 6). Her left arm, however, has been severed, and a *monstrum* occasionally emerges from its stub. This demon, who periodically takes over her mind and body, is a source of great power but is challenging to control. The first issue of *Monstress* begins with a full splash page that features Maika, naked, her body on display, with a chain around her neck. She is a slave being sold at an auction. The apprising look that she directs at those around her is one of anger, repulsion, and even calm curiosity, establishing her already as someone to fear. In the following panel, Sir Conroy, who is looking to buy an Arcanic at the auction, asks about the amputation: "And her missing arm? That brand? Even if she is a monster, she's deformed" (6). In these two pages Liu and Takeda address a current trend in comics that focuses on individuals' embodied experiences and responses to health and health care, illness, and perceptions and experiences of disability. The series engages directly with stereotypical configurations of bodily variation as a marker of "difference" and "monstrousness." Throughout the series, Maika is characterized as a "freak," a "monster," and a "curiosity" (12) in large part due to this amputated limb. This "monstrousness," however, is her primary source of power, allowing her to access extreme violence and demonstrate agency over the adults that want or need to subdue her. The *monstrum* that resides within her and struggles to emerge also aligns power and amputation in a way that disrupts conventional ideas about childhood, identity, gender, and ability. Maika, in this opening image and throughout Liu and Takeda's series, embodies power and control in defiant contrast to this preliminary, demeaning evaluation of her by auctioneers and people around her as being somehow imperfect and flawed. As in many of these texts for young people about health and illness, Maika's youthful power resides in her particularly embodied experience of bodily difference.

## Comics, Health, and Graphic Medicine

Visualizing the body, representing its complex internal and external facets, has been a crucial part of medical history, as Leonardo da Vinci's anatomical drawings remind us and as textbook illustrations, photographs, and radiological images call to mind. This history in turn relates to comics culture. Many of the formative works in the field of graphic narratives were inspired by individual experiences of particular health crises. These include, among others, Al Davison's 1990 text, *The Spiral Cage*, about spina bifida; Harvey Pekar, Joyce Brabner, and Frank Stack's *Our Cancer Year* (1994), which depicts Pekar's treatment for lymphoma; and David Wojnarowicz's psychedelic memoir *7 Miles a Second* (1996; 2012), dramatizing the social alienation and pain associated with being a queer person living with AIDS in the early years of the epidemic. Since then, comics have visualized various lived experiences of health, illness, and disability: cancer (Marisa Marchetto's *Cancer Vixen*, David Small's *Stitches*, Jennifer Hayden's *The Story of My Tits*), epilepsy (David B.'s *Epileptic*), chronic pain (John Porcellino's *The Hospital Suite*), herpes (Ken Dahl's *Monsters*), sexually transmitted disease (Charles Burns's *Black Hole*), lupus (Julie Wertz's *The Infinite Wait*), Alzheimer's disease (Sarah Leavitt's *Tangles*), depression (Allie Brosh's *Hyperbole and a Half*), anorexia and bulimia (Katie Green's *Lighter Than My Shadow*), and bipolar illness (Ellen Forney's *Marbles: Mania, Depression, Michelangelo, and Me*). The list grows by the year. Not surprisingly, this trend is also gaining prominence in comics created for and about young people. Much of Raina Telgemeier's oeuvre (*Smile*, *Guts*, and *Ghosts*) as well as Cece Bell's *El Deafo*, Tory

Woollcott's *Mirror Mind: Growing Up Dyslexic,* Marie d'Abreo's *Beautiful,* and Marie-Noëlle Hébert's *My Body in Pieces* are just some examples of pathographies, a bourgeoning new genre for younger readers.

Graphic pathographies, "stories of illness conveyed in comic form" (Myers and Goldenberg 158), are an effective and affective form for readers, young and old. Often relatively quick to read, they are emotionally powerful and evoke sympathy among a variety of readers, including medical specialists and nonspecialists, creators and critics, casual readers and aficionados. At times depicting complicated medical experiences from the perspectives of health-care practitioners (including medical students) and patients, graphic pathographies can communicate quickly and directly to readers and have the potential to "transcend language and literacy barriers" (Czerwiec, "Medical" 200). For example, a hospital in Berlin recently developed a graphic version of its informed consent form for cardiac catheterization surgery and assessed afterward how effective the ten-page comics-style booklet had been in enhancing patients' knowledge of the procedure in comparison with the forty-page textual version. "The comic version did better at reducing pre-op anxiety, it had better post-op outcomes, it was better right across the board," Susan Squier reported. "People who got the long form would say, 'You gave me all that, I was just too anxious to read it'" (qtd. in Winner).[1] Studies have shown that the information gained through visual stories "is more likely to be retained" (Myers and Goldenberg 158). For a patient or family member who wants to learn about a health complaint issue, disease, or even medical procedure, comics can be "an inviting, nonthreatening way to familiarize oneself with a condition that is perhaps itself inherently threatening" (159). These first-person visual narratives can also provide a patient with a sense of community, lessening the isolation that they often feel and perhaps even helping patients "cultivate practical skills that might enhance their autonomy and moral agency" in relation to health challenges (158, 161). In turn, graphic pathographies can assist health-care professionals understand patients' personal and lived experiences of illness and can also help general readers who want to understand more about the illness or particular medical challenge from the perspectives of people who have lived it.

Graphic pathographies thus share with the comics previously explored the potential to build awareness, provide information, and raise consciousness about a significant event in a person's life. Sarah Leavitt, for example,

---

1. According to a study published in the *Annals of Internal Medicine* about this use of comics by a Berlin hospital to inform patients about the risks of this medical procedure, patients' levels of anxiety before cardiac catheterization were reduced and their understanding of the procedure was enhanced ("Why Comic-style").

employs the medium of the graphic narrative to represent her mother's experiences of Alzheimer's disease. Leavitt reproduces examples of her mother's handwriting in *Tangles* (2011) to memorialize her mother's presence even as she undergoes the gradual loss of memory and motor control associated with the progression of her condition. She also visualizes the MRIs, CAT scans, PET scans, blood tests, and urine samples that doctors employed as diagnostic tools to chart the process of cognitive and physical deterioration that Midge experiences during the six years that she lived with Alzheimer's. *Tangles* balances this cataloging of medical diagnostic practice with an empathic representation of an Alzheimer's patient. An important moment occurs early in the text when Leavitt employs an oversized blank page with a small representation of Midge located in the lower corner of the page along with the powerful statement, "I hate what's happening to me" (42). This predominantly blank page presents a startling contrast to previous pages, the panels of which are densely organized and crammed full of information, juxtaposing particular episodes of Midge's condition (moments of symptomatic behaviors, moments of everyday normality, and moments of connection or anger with family and friends) with medical diagnosis. On this particular page, the blank space that surrounds Midge conveys the horrifying experience of deterioration that mother and daughter undergo, in their respective roles as patient and caregiver. Spatial orientation, size, and composition are key elements of graphic pathographies in capturing the physical, social, emotional, and existential impacts of the illness or medical challenge, for sufferers and loved ones alike.

The attention given to diagnostic methods and medical procedures also fulfills a particular pragmatic need for readers, young and old. Pathographies' ability to be "diagrammatic," to sketch medical equipment and specific visual information about treatment and process, is particularly useful for patients or students looking for scientific accuracy (Chute, *Why* 241). In *Cancer Vixen*, for example, Marisa Marchetto draws the biopsy needle with realistic accuracy, along with the true size of the biopsied cancerous tissue, conveying vividly rendered details about breast cancer (*Why* 241). Some pathographies insert fragments of medical reports (such as audiograms) or images produced by digital-imaging technologies, at once calling attention to the personal perspective from which the comic was created as well as the comic's distinctively intermedial relationship with medical procedural details and diagnostic tools. Yet, just as the realistic mode of representation or the inclusion of medical intertexts in the comic can enhance the text's verisimilitude, iconic abstraction can also distance the medical experience and trauma from readers, in turn broadening the audience at whom the text is directed. Raina Telgemeier's comics, for example, feature emoticons (a smiley face; an angry face; a nauseated face) as the cover art, prompting a similar understanding or feeling among young readers of different backgrounds, ethnicities, sexes, abilities, and ages. "The smiley face is not specific to one group of people; rather, it is readily identifiable as universally human" (Myers and Goldenberg 159). Thus, graphic pathographies for readers have a broad use-value: Depending on their mode of representation, they are informational and can provide pragmatic information and details about medical experiences and procedures, or (in keeping with Scott McCloud's theorizations about the wide, even global appeal of the cartoon figure) they can invite readers to see themselves in that character.

For MK Czerwiec, Ian Williams, Susan Squier, and the other creators of the *Graphic Medicine Manifesto*, "Comics give voice to those who are often not heard" (2). Created in 2015 by six "pioneers" of graphic medicine (a new genre that uses comics to tell personal stories of health and illness), the *Manifesto* advocates for a "more inclusive perspective of medicine, illness, disability, caregiving and being cared for" (2). The creators resist the notion of the "universal patient" by encouraging multiple approaches to the representation of health and disease. Frequently, graphic medical comics are autobiographical or semifictional, dealing with the creator's own illness or that of a family member. In *Taking Turns: Stories from HIV/AIDS Care Unit 371* (2017), MK Czerwiec describes the events that propelled her to create. In the 1990s, while working as a nurse on the dedicated inpatient HIV/AIDS Care Unit at the Illinois Masonic Medical Center, she began to draw "as a coping method in a moment of need," adding that "making comics was a comfortable, enjoyable, and effective method of professional and personal expression" (Czerwiec, "Medical" 199). In many respects pathographies make use of the "curative utility of drawing"; drawing becomes an act of creation, a narrative technique, and/or a mode of therapy and meditation (Venkatesan and Peter, "Drawing" 104).

Comics about young people and/in graphic medicine, as this chapter argues, narrativize complex information about health, illness, and disability, encouraging empathetic identification among readers. Frequently told from the perspective of the young patient, whose voice is too often lost in medical dialogue, comics (like Telgemeier's texts *Smile* and *Guts*) can communicate how illness manifests in a young person's body and how that experience shapes their interactions with their sociocultural, and sometimes even geographical, environment. The graphic form's tactile quality, as expressed in the act of drawing and experienced by the reader as the trace of the creator's presence, enhances the subjective and affective abilities of its verbal-visual content. As Elisabeth El Refaie argues, "The artwork represents a way for artists to make invisible aspects of their subjectivity visible" (*Metaphor* 77). The particularly "haptic charge of drawing" (Scherr 24) pulls readers into the page and is used, in many cases, to awaken readers (young and old) to an affective medical reality beyond the page itself.

In keeping with many of the comics that this study has explored, these graphic pathographies figure "crisis" as a personal crisis of ontology on the parts of young people, as opposed to a predicament imposed by adults on their bodies and minds. In texts like *El Deafo, Mirror Mind*, and *Stitches*, among others, the young protagonists reflect on their everyday lived experiences, shaped by and at times overshadowed by illness and/or disability. Comics are also effective at representing the consciousness of someone suffering from a mental disorder and/or depression, as *Marbles, Fun Home*, and *Swallow Me Whole* demonstrate. A corresponding focus in comics (such as *My Body in Pieces, Tyranny*, and *Lighter Than My Shadow*) is one that examines eating disorders and the ways in which art and the act of creation are crucial to a young character's quest for bodily self-acceptance. The particular strength of these texts lies in their visualizations of medical episodes, but, more importantly, their representation of illness and/or disease as distinctly embodied experiences through which young bodies operate. Frequently, these texts refute the dominant tropes of unspeakability, invisibility, or inaudibility that have characterized traumatic narratives in the past (and even contemporary times) and challenge the ways in which bodily and mental "norms" are evoked to subjugate particular young people. As creators as diverse as Raina Telgemeier and Katie Green assert in paratextual material appended to their graphic narratives, comics about young people and/in graphic medicine seek to validate their experiences of medical crises and, most importantly, to value the particular insights they share about these lived experiences. "I just kinda look around me, and listen to what people say . . . Then I make comics about it!" Telgemeier observes at the end of *Guts*, her text about anxiety and phobias. The artistic process allows creators to assert some measure of control over that medical experience in order to "normalize" that life event and to resist the desensitization that can occur in the production of texts about bodies, illness, and bodily or mental variation.

This assertion of control over one's body occurs, undoubtedly, in the act of creation just as much as it does in the act of reading; an affective investment on the parts of creator and reader alike is involved. Building on Charles Hatfield's idea of "committed reading"—when readers become aware of themselves as collaborators in the visual text—Jodi Cressman emphasizes the ethical implications of reading comics about bodies and illness (23). Cressman borrows from Rosemarie Garland-Thomson's important theorization of "staring" as transformational and "generative" (10). Stares are "urgent efforts to make the unknown known, to render legible something that seems at first glance incomprehensible" (Garland-Thomson 15). The act of reading graphic pathographies and, in our case, comics about graphic medicine has the potential to position the reader as an "embodied witness who both sees and is seen" and who balances empathy and action, practicing a "vigilance against objectifying others" and resisting the tendency to become "desensitized to pain or finding pleasure in a relief that the suffering is not one's own" (Cressman 23–24). Frederik Byrn Køhlert concurs: The comics form "allows for the staging of a dynamic exchange of stares with the implied observer that has the potential to help the author elude the objectifying gaze commonly associated with looking at disability" (124). The personal perspectives from which many of these texts are narrated refute the spectacularization of illness and disability that can occur (as permitted by photography, according to Susan Sontag) and, instead, present affective experiences of health, illness, and disability for young readers. Readers, in turn, can read, learn, and think critically about the structures of power that govern the bodies and minds of people, young and old.

## Young Readers and Visual Representations of Health and Illness: *Smile* and *Guts*

The predominant approach to disease around the world is the biomedical model, according to which a state of health is defined by the absence of illness. This episteme focuses on disease as an "objective fact," defined and diagnosed by health professionals. Yet, "it tends to neglect the wider social, cultural, political and economic contexts in which [illness and disease] occur" (Ansell 251). Because of the prevalence of this biomedical approach to health, with its impersonal scrutiny and interpretation of the body, minimal attention has been given to subjective experiences of illness or disease, particularly among young people (252). Few studies look beyond "immediate mechanisms of causality to the wider political, economic and cultural contexts that shape people's experiences of health" (252). Significant gaps in the knowledge and understanding of young people's health have resulted, such that, as Nicola Ansell observes, "young children's voices are almost never heard in relation to their own health experiences" (286). Comics about young people and/in graphic medicine respond to this silence, often in the process emphasizing the definition of health (established by the World

Health Organization [WHO]) as "a state of complete sense of physical, mental and social well-being, not merely the absence of disease or infirmity" ("Preamble"). *Stitches*, *Swallow Me Whole*, and *Tyranny* visualize subjective connections between the young person's mind and body in their explorations of health as defined, diagnosed, and dealt with in different societies and cultures.

Importantly, pathographies explore how experiences of health, illness, and disability are socially embedded and culturally shaped. As such, comics use individual embodied experiences to encourage readers to think more broadly about the discourses of health and ability that shape the experiences of these young protagonists as they move with and against currents of power. The visualization of sickness and health is accomplished in many of these texts through inventive textual and visual practice, encouraging readers to rethink the dominant tropes of unspeakability, invisibility, and inaudibility that have characterized medical narratives in the past. Such comics continue to affirm the agentic vision of the young person through their representation of characters who take an active role in response to the medical events that shape them personally. As with previous texts that this study has examined, comics narrativize the lived experiences of young people, not necessarily in relation to a narrative of rescue or self-rescue.

Evoking the style of cartoonist Lynn Johnston, creator of the comic strip *For Better or For Worse*, Raina Telgemeier's graphic oeuvre foregrounds the experiences of young people as they grow and develop against a backdrop of everyday interpersonal conflicts and the self-consciousness that is part of going through middle school. One of the most successful comics ever to be published, spending 175 weeks on the *New York Times*' "Paperback Graphic Books" bestseller list, *Smile* (2010) is a graphic memoir about Telgemeier's extensive experiences with dental reconstruction after severely damaging her two front teeth in an accident in sixth grade. From the perspective of her eponymous avatar Raina, readers endure her pain and discomfort, her experience of novocaine and codeine, and her recovery period after the first of what will turn out to be many dental surgeries throughout her childhood and adolescence. (Raina's accident is prolonged over twenty-four cringeworthy panels.) Telgemeier's comic visualizes in graphic detail the medical procedures that Raina endures, the plaster casts made of her teeth, the X-rays of her mouth that show how far the two front teeth have been driven deep into the jaw bone from the impact with the curb. The text also represents root canals (along with syringes and drills), and there is an extended discussion of braces, brackets, headgear, and mouth molds. Informative and explicit at times, *Smile* provides for young readers a perspective with which they can empathize, the viscerality of the experience (strengthened by the text's visual and tactile qualities) enhancing a connection with the protagonist. Fascinatingly, the comic juxtaposes sequences set in the dentist's or orthodontist's office with equally uncomfortable sequences that feature Raina and her peer group, members of which belittle her, making her feel self-conscious about her changed physical appearance. A friend's uncharitable statement at her birthday party—"Cool, so you'll look normal soon?"—is immediately juxtaposed with the contortions and violent straightening and aligning of her teeth that the orthodontist inflicts (43–44). In this way, Telgemeier makes clear that the dental crisis is just part of the narrative's larger concern with the interpersonal challenges that Raina experiences as part of growing older. The "subtle pressure" exerted by the braces, the "slight discomfort" and outright pain that she feels in the dentist's chair are akin to the torment she experiences with her peer group (44).

Enmeshed with the grim details about this dental predicament is an analysis of the societal expectations that govern a young girl's growth process, as the get-well card from her teacher Mr. Cruz dramatizes. The card features a happy face with the caption "smile" under it. As previously argued, this yellow emoji that appears on three of Telgemeier's comics (*Smile*, *Sisters*, and *Guts*) invites young readers to see themselves and their anxieties, insecurities, and compulsions reflected in these narratives. This emoji becomes suggestive of many of *Smile*'s overarching themes: the pressure put on girls to be fun, happy, and smiling at all times, which in turn "depoliticizes girls and positions them as compliant in their own subjugation" (Coulter); the need for a "perfect" smile and, by extension, a flawless appearance; the pressure to "smile" and be positive even when undergoing an awful experience. This dental crisis shapes Raina's day-to-day experience dramatically: After the accident and recovery from the surgeries, she returns to school feeling trepidation, dread, self-consciousness, and worry that everyone is staring at her. Worse, her peer group revels in learning more about the experience, peppering her with questions about the grisly details. Raina's intensifying feelings of insecurity over her physical appearance push her to confide in her mother, who responds dismissively with, "Lots of kids wear funny stuff to help fix their bodies . . . You probably just don't realize it because no one talks about it" (56). Her mother's statement unfortunately reinforces Western society's implicit assumptions about bodily norms and beauty ideals. "Well, maybe someone should start talking about it!!" Raina responds indignantly. "Maybe it would make us feel less like freaks" (56). Just as Liu and Takeda interrogate the alignment of discussions of "freakery" with bodily abnormality, Telgemeier looks to "normalize" life experiences that young people undergo, like puberty, zits, peer pressure, bodily changes, romance, and so forth in an effort to counteract feelings of isolation and alienation that youngsters endure when they feel different from the norm. Perhaps more importantly, Telgemeier encourages young readers to stand up for themselves, to refuse to submit passively to bullying or aggression. In reading *Smile, Sisters,* and *Guts,* white, middle-class young readers are invited to see their own experiences represented by means of inventive visual practice. Recognizable feelings and ordeals in turn validate their own lived experiences (with bullying, anxiety, or perhaps even dental problems). Raina turns to art to cope with the bullying of her peers, making use of "the power of visual rhetoric to offer advice in a format that lacks distance or condescension" (Tarbox 139). As a pathography, *Smile* effectively connects with young readers, fostering empathy in the process.

Telgemeier's most recent graphic narrative, *Guts* (2019), again seeks to expand the parameters of lived and felt experiences and validate experiences of anxiety, panic attacks, and phobias, which are increasingly common among young people. (According to the WHO, mental health conditions account for 16 percent of the global burden of disease and injury in people aged ten to sixteen years ["Adolescents"].) With its tongue sticking out and worry lines around the eyes, the emoji on the text's cover again introduces the text's conceit. A graphic text intended "for anyone who feels afraid," as the dedication clarifies, the title alludes at once to Raina's stomach troubles, as well as to the energy, verve, and courage she develops over the course of the narrative to combat playground bullies and paralyzing anxiety attacks. An early experience with the stomach flu provokes a profound fear of vomiting; Raina's extreme panic attack (prolonged over eleven panels) provides an embodied representation of youthful anxiety. Readers see as though from her perspective, and the visualization of her as holding onto the edge of a precipice only to lose her grip and plunge into the void conveys the particularly intangible nature of fear and worry, in turn evoking empathy among many readers who might see aspects of themselves in Raina. *Kirkus Reviews* alludes to this mimetic tendency in its assessment of the text: "With young readers diagnosed with anxiety in ever increasing numbers, this book offers a necessary mirror to many" ("Guts"). *Guts* attempts to represent the visceral nature of fear for readers: Emanata, pictorial symbols emanating from a character to suggest anxiety or confusion, communicate that something is wrong with Raina, even though there are no distinct physical symptoms that point to a specific physiological cause. Over two panels, Raina asks herself, "Can you be sick even if you're not sick?" and "Can you be healthy even if you hurt?" (69). The thermometer affirming her lack of fever is juxtaposed with the actual pain that she genuinely registers in her body, visualized as lightning bolts emanating from her stomach. Both are equally "real," the narrative asserts, if motivated by different causes.

*Guts* proves effective at tackling a topic that is frequently underdiscussed in contemporary children's literary culture: health and wellness (physical, spiritual, emotional, and mental) and the mind/body connection (the thoughts, feelings, beliefs, and attitudes that can affect a body's biological functioning). *Guts* avoids the biomedical focus on symptom, cause, and treatment, concerned as it is with Raina's more subjective experience of her physical and mental health. In an effort to help her daughter learn how to cope with this anxiety that is in turn affecting the health of her body, Mrs. Telgemeier takes her daughter to see a therapist, Lauren, whose open-ended questions provoke a significant panic attack in Raina. A green hue fills the three panels that cannot contain all of the worries that preoccupy her; the impact of Raina's fears is emphasized by their size in comparison to her small stature on the page. Size, perspective, and color are especially effective tools to communicate this idea. Interestingly, the panels are predominantly wordless, calling attention to Raina's inability to articulate what is wrong: "Thoughts can exist . . . Feelings can exist . . . But words do not always exist" (76–77), she admits in frustration. In an interview with the *New York Times*, Telgemeier affirms the use of the visual over the strictly literary when representing anxiety. "Comics are great because you don't always have to talk with words. [. . .] You can talk with pictures and symbols, you can use color, you can use lines, you can use the medium to push ideas without having to fully explain them" (Alter). *Guts* is arguably Telgemeier's most visual text, addressing a very common occurrence through image rather than word, making use of inventive visual practice to speak directly about a young person's mind/body connection and mental health.

Part of the purpose of *Guts* is to vividly present common experiences of anxiety and equip young readers with tools with which to respond effectively. Later in the text, Telgemeier offers an intimate representation of a panic attack, prolonged over the course of eighteen panels, during which Raina is invited to identify ten separate and individually realized levels of anxiety to codify how anxious the bullying in the school yard leaves her (149–53; see figure 5.1). A useful table for readers (and for Raina), it visualizes the gradual intensification of a "typical" panic attack, the physical symptoms intensifying at each level. Lauren talks her through the attack, gently encouraging Raina to breathe deeply and to concentrate on the floor beneath her feet, in this way modeling a calmness in the mind that might translate to the body. For many young people, interpersonal conflicts and

FIGURE 5.1. Raina and her therapist discuss anxiety. Raina Telgemeier, *Guts*. Graphix, 2009, p. 149.

worries about peer groups and friends moving away are all-important and as such can have an inordinate effect on one's mind and body, as they do with Raina. With the help of her therapist, Raina gradually learns that articulating her thoughts and concerns lessens that anxiety—that deep breathing and a calm clearing of the mind help dispel those fears. The authenticity of Telgemeier's narratives is often in this way enhanced by the direct associations made by the creator with her avatar. "I want to make sure my readers know that this is my personal story," Telgemeier comments in her postscript to *Guts*. "I want to encourage you to talk about how you feel. You can write it down, draw pictures or comics, make music or plays, or simply share with your friends. It takes guts to admit how you feel on the inside, but chances are, others will be able to relate." In this regard, Telgemeier engages directly with the still relatively taboo topic of mental well-being, encouraging readers to take an active role in the health (physical and mental) concerns that affect them directly. In the process, she emphasizes that these challenges are felt by many as opposed to few.

## Graphic Narratives of Disability and Medical Trauma: *Mirror Mind*, *El Deafo*, and *Stitches*

The power of graphic works like *Smile* and *Guts* is that they "bring into public lived realities that often tend to be stigmatized, excluded, or disavowed by societies like our own that cherish efficiency, health, and success" (Squier and Krüger-Fürhoff 3). They visualize a need (especially among young people) to regain control over one's body, to reclaim it from the hands of healthcare professionals and from ableist assumptions everywhere in society. In a postscript appended to *El Deafo*, her graphic memoir about hearing impairment, Cece Bell observes: "But the way I *felt* as a kid—that feeling is all true. I was a deaf kid surrounded by kids who could hear. I felt different, and in my mind, being different was *not* a good thing. I secretly, *and* openly, believed that my deafness, in making me so different, was a disability. And I was ashamed." As this section examines, Tory Woollcott, Cece Bell, and David Small share a desire to refute normative conceptions of health and illness and employ inventive visual and textual practices to do so. Just as importantly, these aesthetically complex texts visualize the young person's agentic response to their particular medical challenge, in the process valuing and validating their perspectives.

In the careful balance it strikes between word and image, comics provides a distinctive opportunity for representing the experiences of people with conditions that affect the acquisition, retention, understanding, and processing of information. People with developmental disorders (like autism) or learning disabilities, resulting from impairments in psychological processes in combination with abilities for thinking and reasoning, "often find the traditional linear narrative of the autonomous subject difficult, if not impossible, to construct and communicate" (Birge). Tory Woollcott's *Mirror Mind: Growing Up Dyslexic* (2009), a comic published by the International Dyslexic Association as an informational guide for young readers, persuasively represents the difficulties that people with dyslexia, and other learning disorders, can experience in acquiring oral and written language abilities, as well as math skills. Black-and-white graphics capture the starkness of life that protagonist Victoria experiences at school because of the problems she encounters with spelling and forming words correctly, such as reversing sounds in words or confusing words that sound alike. Early on, the text visualizes the confused and mixed-up input that Victoria takes in when looking at the blackboard. The panels are split down the middle, suggesting the "mirror mind" of a dyslexic, who can write letters backward or upside down, and for whom words on the board can seem completely incomprehensible. This type of comic is especially persuasive at raising awareness of the signs and symptoms of this learning condition and, even more importantly, at providing information about how this different learning style (and society's preconceptions about learning challenges) can marginalize young people, however inadvertently. Woollcott personifies dyslexia, for example, as a shameful, serpent-like creature that threatens to overcome her and as an octopus that encircles and entraps her, overwhelming her in real life just as it does on the page: "Now it was real . . . now it had a name, and it stopped being little," Victoria narrates, acknowledging the significant weight that the disorder exerted over her everyday life, the corners of her existence that its long tentacles have reached into and transformed. Made painfully aware of her "difference," she repeatedly depicts herself sitting quietly, alone, while her peers around her respond with apparent ease to the lessons. The smallness of Victoria within the panels—especially when taken out of the classroom by a counselor for extra help with reading and writing—emphasizes her feelings of isolation and difference even more. "Tikkie [the counselor] tried hard and was very nice, but she didn't help me as much as bring attention to the fact I couldn't read," Woollcott observes.

*Mirror Mind* depicts the microaggressions and outright prejudice that people living with dyslexia experience with frequency. Well-meaning attempts made by family and friends to "normalize" the "disorder" (a word that, already, implicitly suggests impairment) are not helpful to the young person who is learning to live with it. For Woollcott, in fact, such attempts at normalizing her experience separate her further from her peers and from expected indicators of learning and development. Victoria resists playing with the kids in her "special" education class because of the negative connotations that such a class inspire in her (as it does among the other children in her school). "I didn't want to admit I was one of them," Victoria admits. Shame and embarrassment are feelings that she registers for herself as much as for her peers in class. She represents them as black silhouettes that are completely unremarkable, as though they are not worthy of being remembered or even visualized.

And yet, this comic is especially persuasive at representing Victoria's eventual success at learning to decode the world around her, the gradual process by which indistinguishable letters become abstract designs and eventually words that she can read, in large part thanks to a trio of specialists and teachers, whom she credits with "giving her words," as the dedication clarifies. This transformation is visualized as a momentous event in which Victoria's experience of marginalization comes to an end once she learns the tools needed to fit into a literate society. "I felt like I had discovered myself. I felt new. I felt like I was a person all of a sudden," she proclaims. "Now I had a connection to all these writers. People who left shapes behind for me." Produced by a young person, *Mirror Mind* foregrounds the child's voice in the narration of their own lived experience of a learning disability and is an important tool then in fostering empathy among young readers. Victoria's upsetting claim that reading allowed her to feel like "a person all of a sudden," however, highlights the powerful pressure people feel to align themselves with typical cognitive behaviors and patterns. In this way, although *Mirror Mind* provides useful, first-person insight into the feeling of isolation that a young person struggling with a learning disability often feels, it follows the time-worn, rhetorical pattern of overcoming upon which narratives of disability often rely (as will be discussed later in the chapter). Victoria becomes "normal"—the narrative argues—through the act of reading. And yet very little interrogation is made in *Mirror Mind* of the pedagogical and social structures that exacerbated the protagonist's isolation in the first place.

Many of the texts about young people and/in graphic medicine name and interrogate the social and cultural constructions of disability that shape the experiences of their young protagonists. Discussions informed by a disability studies or disability rights perspective (one that points out the constructed nature of the condition) have the potential to help readers develop more informed views of impairment, ones that rely less frequently on rhetorical patterns of triumph or overcompensation over one's bodily or mental variation. As we have seen already in *Smile*, *Guts*, and *Mirror Mind*, characters draw attention to the social and cultural barriers that people with disabilities experience on a daily basis, providing direct verbal and visual challenges to myths and stereotypes, especially in terms of making decisions and acting in ways that counter pervasive narratives that depict them as pitiable victims needing rescue or heroes that save the day. In essence, comics about bodily variation are persuasive tools for knowledge building, narratives that can educate young readers about their own assumptions about normality and in turn inspire them to become more aware of their own experiences moving through an able-bodied and able-minded world.

Winner of the Newbery Award in 2015, Cece Bell's graphic memoir *El Deafo*, a text aimed at elementary school–aged readers, is particularly noteworthy here, as it depicts the loss of the protagonist's hearing due to her experience of spinal meningitis at four years old. This comic explores the physical and environmental challenges with which a suddenly impaired young person must contend. As Telgemeier does in *Smile* and *Guts*, and as Woollcott attempts in *Mirror Mind*, Bell is determined to foster a connection with her young readers, encouraging them to empathize with her abrupt experience of hearing impairment by means of her rabbit avatar. "I wanted to show what it felt like to be the only deaf kid in my elementary school. I needed a good visual metaphor, and rabbits, with their big ears and amazing hearing, were perfect for that," Cece Bell comments in an interview with the *Guardian* ("Cece Bell"). Typically, in comics and cartoons, rabbits are identified by their exaggerated ears, which in this case visually draw a reader's attention to Cece's hearing (or, more accurately, her hearing loss) and the importance placed on an ability to hear as a norm that governs her everyday experience, pre- and postimpairment. By depicting herself as a rabbit, then, with wires leading all the way up to the tops of her long, floppy ears, Bell calls attention to the detectable nature of disability that abruptly sets her apart from the communities around her, who struggle to accommodate this impairment.

The first part of the comic outlines Cece's transformation into a hearing-impaired person and the immediate attendant challenges that that entails. Words in the dialogue balloons appear in gray scale but quickly fade into nothingness as Bell visualizes the hearing loss that occurred overnight in the hospital, a loss that left her unable to communicate with the doctors and nurses who came to see her. "Everything is so—*quiet*," she notices, the comic in turn capturing that silence visually through the blank dialogue balloons (C. Bell 6). At home, she loses her mother temporarily because, once out of sight, she cannot hear her movements. Bell presents the paradoxical absence of perceptible speech by the blankness of Cece's speech bubbles and those of her mother. Their great mutual distress at being unable to communicate with one another is represented by squiggly red emanata, emotion lines radiating from each. Cece, relieved, finally realizes: "I can't hear" (12; see figure 5.2). Their joint recognition that something is wrong propels them to seek help from the doctor, and Bell in turn depicts the gradual process of diagnosis:

FIGURE 5.2. Cece searches for her mother. Cece Bell, *El Deafo*. Amulet Books, 2014, p. 12.

She shows the tests that Cece experiences at the audiologist's office—Bell's own audiogram is inserted as an intertext to enhance the text's verisimilitude—and then her transformative experience when she first inserts her new hearing aids.

Speech is the social practice that Cece must work to develop once again. Not only must she work hard to decipher the speech to which she is now regaining access through her hearing aids (sounds that she struggles to understand; Bell represents words that are all jumbled up and unintelligible),

FIGURE 5.3. Cece's experience of speech using hearing aids. Cece Bell, *El Deafo*. Amulet Books, 2014, p. 24.

but she must also learn new strategies to use when interacting and communicating with family and friends. One panel depicts Cece's struggle to converse with her best friend, Emma, by visualizing them as though they are swimming underwater and speaking through snorkels (see figure 5.3). This panel is especially persuasive at conveying the mix-ups that occur when a hearing-impaired person is trying to communicate, especially when they cannot read another's lips. Bell uses this moment to summarize many of the pitfalls that hearing people make when they are trying to talk to someone who is deaf: Relying on exaggerated mouth movements and/or shouting to communicate, they can also block their mouths with their hands, which presents a significant challenge for lip reading. Group discussions are especially taxing because there are too many lips to observe, Cece learns very quickly (31–32). The visualization of these early days of learning to live with a hearing impairment conveys to young readers how easily it is for able-bodied people to marginalize people, even inadvertently. And, yet, Bell's text values and validates the invaluable personal insights that Cece, who *becomes* impaired and who must learn to navigate her environments anew, can provide.

Disability theorists challenge the assumptions underlying the concept of "normal," arguing that what we think of as normal is socially and culturally constructed. When a creator uses the medium to represent their personal experiences of impairment, they "potentially deliver a new way of thinking about, expressing, and sharing that experience" (Walters 176). As *El Deafo* argues, the institutions of home, school, doctor's office, playground, and speech class are all spaces in which Cece is continually misinterpreted and not heard. Cece inhabits a "bubble of loneliness" (46) because she sees herself as unlike everyone else and because those around her continually remind her of this difference. At school and in the playground, Cece experiences the same quests for friendship, the loneliness, and casual bullying typical of young people her age, only made worse by this difficulty in communication. Bell's comic demonstrates the limitations of the people around her who cannot value Cece as a person because of her impairment, suggesting that it is they who are in fact disabled. Insensitive instructors (like her gym teacher, Mr. Potts) who are reluctant to wear the microphone that connects to Cece's Phonic Ear are clearly disabled because they bully the children (including Cece) in their class who do not conform to their rigid expectations of bodily normalcy. *El Deafo* consistently depicts the majority of characters with whom Cece interacts as impaired because of this inability to respond helpfully to a deaf person (Smith-D'Arezzo and Holc 73). Bell's memoir and the visual medium, in this case, are extremely persuasive at drawing a young reader's attention to the social and cultural constructions of disability.

In December 2006, the United Nations General Assembly formally adopted the Convention on the Rights of Persons with Disabilities in order to promote, defend, and reinforce the human rights of all persons with disabilities. Since the American Individuals with Disabilities Education Act (1990) and this UN Convention mandated equal access to education for children with physical and mental disabilities, more children's literature authors have begun to include characters and their experiences of impairment or bodily and/or mental variation in their texts. This inclusion of protagonists with particular health conditions and disabilities in children's literature is similar to other initiatives that have looked at introducing diversity (cultural, racial, ethnic, sexual, gender, bodily, etc.) into literature and the curriculum. While this trend has certainly brought welcome representational multiplicity, there is always a "risk of over-signifying the disability dimension of a person's identity" and falling back into traditional narrative patterns of overcoming or victimization (Smith-D'Arezzo and Holc 74). Importantly, however, *El Deafo* "moves away from a medical view of disability, wherein disability is broadly depicted as a defect within the person that needs to be 'cured or eliminated,'" by focusing on Bell's "singular lived experiences" (Kersten 283). In this way, readers are invited to understand the point of view of one deaf person. Although Bell's graphic text depicts her protagonist as hearing-impaired, the text does not emphasize her efforts to find acceptance as an impaired person, nor does it advocate for Cece's need to transform her impairment into a superpower. In fact, Cece's rich interior life "is part of who she is as a girl and her hearing aid is part of her expressive embodiment" (Smith-D'Arezzo and Holc 73). The physical diagram of the Phonic Ear that she wears on her body enshrines it as part of Cece's everyday experience, an appliance that she relies on to hear and that in turn becomes part of her identity, inseparable from her social self. Although she must wear an undershirt under the Phonic Ear to make it comfortable and bear its not insignificant weight, Cece is quite impressed by the device, as the splash page and the recurrent use of exclamation points emphasize: "The Phonic Ear is enormous! It is heavy! And I am totally keeping it hidden!" (39). Her exuberance at the novelty of the device and her ambivalence about it emerge through Bell's visuals. In turn, Cece imagines this hearing device as something that gives her intriguing special powers, since the Phonic Ear provides her with an ability to hear her teachers wherever they are in the school, an ability that becomes a source of fun for her peers.

El Deafo becomes the alter ego that Cece increasingly relies on to escape from and respond to the isolation that people's normative views about hearing and impairment force upon deaf people. One particular page visualizes Cece's transformation of the slur "deafo" into an empowering descriptor that she adopts to reclaim her sense of power (C. Bell 84). As El Deafo, Cece wears her hearing aid proudly. Occupying the space on her chest where the "S" would sit on Superman, the Phonic Ear is shown to be central to Cece's alter ego. This power transports her with excitement and a sense of possibility, which is in turn mirrored by the dynamic visuals. The cloud-shaped panels in which Cece becomes a superhero in her flights of imagination use the expressive function of the frame (Groensteen) to give voice to the frustrations she feels as she educates her friends about deafness and deals with her insecurities (as a girl and as a hearing-impaired person). And yet, importantly, Bell resists the rhetorical pattern of overcompensation in that she never allows this superhero avatar to take over. El Deafo can do all kinds of things that Cece cannot, thanks to the power of the imagination: She can fly, and she can speak her mind and stand up for herself in front of her friends. It is Cece, however, who struggles with her hearing loss as well as with her everyday problems with friends, boys, and her mother. No one "saves" her from the prejudice (direct and inadvertent) that she experiences on a daily basis; she must learn to live with it and educate those around her in the process. *El Deafo* argues that Cece's youthful power resides in her embodiment of difference and her acceptance of those experiences shaping who she is as a person. Cece's first-person perspective enhances the subjective and affective abilities of the comic in emphasizing to young readers how one young person's particular experience of impairment is socially embedded and culturally shaped.

Similar to *Smile*, *Guts*, and *El Deafo*, David Small's *Stitches: A Memoir* (2009) investigates a young person's agency (or lack thereof) in relation to illness, disability, and medical treatment. *Stitches* visualizes David's childhood and youth in 1950s Detroit, living with an abusive family that hid from him the fact that he had cancer, a cancer that his father likely caused because of the X-ray treatments he administered to David as a child to "cure" him of his sinus and digestive problems. The title of Small's comic is especially pertinent with regards to the issue of a young person's agency in relation to medical diagnosis and treatment. Referring to the literal wound on David's throat, a physical reminder of the impact that his abusive parents had on his body, the title can also allude to the movement of a needle through the edges of a wound that is being sutured up, referencing metaphorically the long process of healing from this medical abuse that takes place for years afterward with the assistance of David's therapist. David's voice is quite literally lost in the medical procedures that are performed on him as a young person. His memoir uses the tropes of unspeakability, invisibility, and inaudibility that characterize traumatic narratives. In effect, *Stitches* visualizes David's (and Small's) attempts to reclaim control over his body (and his experience of health trauma) from the health-care professional who was a part of his own family. A doctor who misused his position of power by treating his son for vague illnesses, David's father administered innumerable shots and enemas, treatments that continually violated David's dignity as a young boy. His father's faith in medical interventions is the source of this trauma: Close-up images of David's eyes and their terror/agony contrast with his father's opaque glasses, frequently positioned above him in the panel or at a distance. The hostile eye of the X-ray machine is juxtaposed with David's eyes as he looks up, vulnerably, into the device. His young, anxious face—simplified to eyes, nose, and mouth, in turn forming a radiation sign—offers a silent commentary on the profound harm that this medical treatment has on his body (Koch 35). The penetrating eye of the X-ray is similar to his father's eyeless, blank lenses "signaling a cruel or at least impenetrably incomprehensible human being who intentionally, mindlessly, or unwittingly mistreats the child protagonist in his or her care" (Orbán 176). In David's case, the medical imaging becomes a destructive tool and more widely signals the "intrusive and depersonalizing medical gaze" (Koch 39) that harms as opposed to heals. David's lack of input into his diagnosis and treatment is emblematic of the lack of agency that he experiences throughout his childhood and youth.

Small's ironic representation of the team of radiologists, whose weapons are "miraculous wonder rays that would cure anything," presents, with macabre flourish, the face of medicine becoming inhuman(e). The biomedical model of medicine is depicted by Small as being woefully inadequate when practiced by doctors with less interest in the patient and more investment in the progress that they were supposed to represent. His father—and, by implication, the other "soldiers of science" featured in the ads of *Life* magazine—is flawed by arrogance and stalled by a lack of urgency. When a family friend observes a growth on David's neck, his parents do not get him the diagnostic help that he needs, choosing instead to ask another friend informally at a work function to examine it. While on his yacht, the doctor friend immediately (and informally) diagnoses a "cebaceous cyst" (Small 129), a common noncancerous skin growth, and invites David's parents to bring him in for an appointment. Parental inefficiency gives way to total ineptitude, and somehow three and a half years elapse before David finds himself in a hospital before his first surgery, reflecting on the safety that he feels in the hospital in comparison to the threat he endures at home. "No one can love a hospital," he thought calmly while waiting for the anesthesia to take effect, "but those bland, functional spaces and fixtures were a part of my life. There, I felt safe" (160). Hospital doctors and medical personnel, whom he considered a part of his "extended family," he describes as his "protectors" (160). His parents, in contrast, are his antagonists, who lie to him repeatedly about what is discovered during the first and then second surgeries. David (and readers) learns afterward that the surgeon removed his thyroid gland and one of his vocal cords without his consent or even informing him of that intention, ultimately leaving him voiceless—physiologically and metaphorically. Small's depiction of David's eventual discovery of the truth—he finds the letter his Mama wrote to his grandmother in which she admits that David did not know that thyroid cancer was the reason for the operation—speaks to the extreme protectionism and infantilization that his parents employed with him, their disrespect for his basic human right to know about and to consent to the surgery, and their desire to conceal their own complicity in his medical condition in the first place.

Not surprisingly, these surgeries leave him deeply traumatized. David's depiction of himself afterward as specter, a silhouette, a "pictorial lacuna" (El Refaie, "Monsters" 64) with no remarkable features, highlights his feelings of disempowerment and invisibility brought about by his parents' choices (and malpractices). "When you have no voice, you don't exist," he observes resignedly (212). David's newly developed impairment cannot be contained strictly within the biomedical sphere, however; it is also socially constructed. "David has a speech *impairment* that can mostly be explained by medical causes, but it is his social environment that *disables* his ability to express himself," Christina Koch observes (32).

Small's graphic memoir of familial abuse and the voicelessness of the young person in relation to medical diagnosis and treatment provoked an outcry from critics and reviewers after its publication in 2009. The controversy that surrounded *Stitches* highlights assumptions about the limits of youthful knowledge, agency, and witness that play out in the publishing industry, especially with regard to representations of young people and medical interventions. A *New York Times* bestseller, *Stitches* won an Alex award for books written by adults with special appeal for teen readers. (Memoirs that consistently appear on the American Library Association Alex list include adventure tales, stories of survival and overcoming, rise and redemption narratives, narratives of "foreign" childhoods, and medical/illness stories [Gilmore and Marshall 19]). *Stitches'* status as a nonfictional trauma narrative, however, caused many to challenge its nomination for this book award in large part due to, as Gilmore and Marshall argue, its "refusal to represent trauma in the service of ameliorative or neoliberal agendas" (17–18). Specifically, Small's memoir resists providing an ending that is inspiring. Instead, his text disrupts assumptions about youthful innocence safeguarded by the adults in his life who "did the best they knew how" (Gilmore and Marshall 33). Echoing earlier panics about youth and comics in the 1950s, Small's graphic text about cancer and familial abuse belongs to a larger discussion about constructions of childhood and adolescence in North America. In its visualization of parental mistreatment, *Stitches* avoids the rhetoric of emotional uplift and the personal redemption narrative, and in this regard deviates widely in approach and content from previous Alex award nominees and recipients. As *Growing Up Graphic* has argued, reading material for young readers has occasioned many debates among adults, educators, parents, and librarians and is often governed by precautionary strategies enacted by adults over content deemed "suitable" or "appropriate" for young readers. As the reception history of *Stitches* reminds us, even though Small's graphic text foregrounds the young person's voice and agency in relation to medical experience, the messages that that voice communicates proved to be particularly distressing for adult reviewers.

Susan Honeyman notes a similar protectionist tendency among writers of children's literature about terminal illness: the inclination to withhold the truth from dying child patients and readers, thus perpetuating a rights-suppressive perspective. Such books as Virginia Hamilton's *Bluish* (1999) and Cynthia Kadohata's *Kira-Kira* (2004) bypass open awareness about the disease in favor of denial or dishonesty, "demonstrating the pervasiveness of a protectionism that in fact impinges upon [young people's] participatory rights to full knowledge and self-determination of their bodies" (Honeyman 180). In actuality, these precautionary tendencies protect parents and adults rather than the affected children and disrespect young people by not allowing them to be informed and participate in their own experience as knowing medical subjects. "The pretense of 'getting better' and 'thinking positively,' though sensible in the abstract, simply imposes a greater emotional and social burden on a suffering child," Honeyman observes (180). Dishonesty frequently comes to dominate family dynamics, hospital conversations, social media, and public ritual when a child experiences a life-threatening illness (180). Consequently, as studies confirm, young people internalize these taboos about illness and death and keep up the "expected pretense" with their parents in an effort to protect them, while silently coping (or not) with their own medical diagnosis by themselves (184). In actuality, this silencing contradicts the child-rights discourse of the UNCRC, according to Article 12, which specifically acknowledges a young person as being capable "of forming his or her own views" and as having the legal right to express those views freely.

As *El Deafo* and *Stitches* prove, comics about young people and/in graphic medicine undoubtedly serve an informational and activist purpose, employing the graphic form's visual and tactile qualities to communicate important information about medicine and consent. They also emphasize—perhaps more pertinently—how experiences of health, illness, and bodily variation are socially embedded and culturally shaped. Giving a voice to the frequently voiceless, these comics foreground a child's agency (or lack thereof) in relation to medical procedures as the text's central conceit.

## Disability in Literature and Ableist Assumptions of "Normalcy"

"Disability is everywhere in literature," Clare Barker and Stuart Murray assert in their introduction to *The Cambridge Companion to Literature and Disability* (1). And yet, as Richard III's deformity, Ahab's missing leg in *Moby Dick*, Tiny Tim's crutch in *A Christmas Carol*, and Captain Hook's prosthetic hand in *Peter and Wendy* suggest, impairment was and still is often figured more as a metaphorical indicator of character than as a commentary on the everyday realities of people living with various types of impairment. Comics also have a long history of employing bodily variation for the purpose of social criticism. British caricaturist and illustrator George Cruikshank (1792–1878) depicted the unpopular George IV as obese, seated with crutches at his sides, for example, to suggest his particular powerlessness, while the British weekly *Punch* regularly codified the Irish as ugly and racially distinct, with "physical marks of visible difference" that became indicators of their "moral, political, and socioeconomic" inferiority (Whalen et al. 3). More recently, superhero comics employ bodily variation and even disability as part of the narrative structure of the stories, whether disability is treated as an inherent character flaw (as in the case of the Joker and Dr. Doom) or something to be overcome through the acquisition of abilities not otherwise given to mortals. For example, Daredevil becomes blind after a radiation accident but develops enhanced reflexes known as "radar sense"; *X-Men*'s Professor X (Charles Xavier) is "wheelchair-bound," but his powerful mental abilities mean that "he can transcend his physical body"; Hawkeye is hearing impaired but has "incredible visual acuity" (Chute, *Why* 245). The list goes on.

In *Narrative Prosthesis* (2000), David Mitchell and Sharon Snyder demonstrate how disability frequently figures as both a "prompt and prop for narrative," often conflating narrative and character (Couser, "Disability" 603). Disability life writing, for example, can employ particular rhetorical formulae that in turn reinforce common disability myths that do little to enlighten readers to the lived realities of people living with bodily or mental variations (Couser, *Signifying* 33). Five such patterns predominate: triumph, horror, spiritual compensation, nostalgia, and emancipation. Most frequent is the rhetoric of triumph that demands that people with disabilities overcome or compensate for their disability; common in such narratives are plots that recount their protagonists' mastery over adversity, with the required happy endings (Jacobs and Dolmage, "Difficult" 76). (This is the paradigm that David Small's *Stitches* specifically refuted and that critics consequently found so objectionable.) Such narratives that feature "supercrips" who overcome adversity were often referred to by late disability activist Stella Young as "inspiration porn," inspirational because they feature disabled people who "overcompensate for their supposed deficiencies," a triumph that is in truth "the exception rather than the rule" (Couser, "Disability" 203). Narratives like these are especially valued in the literary marketplace yet are doubly offensive because they suggest that disability can be overcome through hard work and a positive attitude. In contrast, the rhetoric of horror represents disability as a terrifying condition, as any number of examples from literature and comics testify (the Joker is one of many). At its worst, this rhetoric encourages revulsion from disability; at its best, pity for the "afflicted." Tropes of spiritual compensation in turn suggest that disability is a punishment for a moral failing; part of the implicit purpose of such a text is to make the subject a better Christian (Couser, *Signifying* 37). Texts dominated by nostalgia (as in Jean-Dominique Bauby's *The Diving Bell and the Butterfly*) reflect about a period of time before the protagonist became disabled—in the case of Bauby, by a massive stroke to his brain stem (Couser, *Signifying* 38–39). Finally, the rhetoric of emancipation, reminiscent of a slave narrative, traces a movement from "virtual imprisonment to relative freedom" in the sense that emancipation is part of a movement to "deinstitutionalize disabled people" (44–45). As David Mitchell and Sharon Snyder remind readers, it appears that "we rarely represent disability without making automatic connections to the various stories we feel it might, as the consequence of its very existence, tell" (2). Graphic pathographies, then, offer personal experiences of bodily or mental variation that, crucially, seek to counter such established rhetorical patterns through inventive textual and visual means.

In response to inaccurate and misleading representations of people with impairments, a new mode of social realism in disability literature has emerged, one that continues now with the graphic medicine movement. Lennard J. Davis's *Enforcing Normalcy* (1995) and Rosemarie Garland-Thomson's *Extraordinary Bodies* (1997) are foundational texts that expose the confining power of the so-called normal. Both Davis and Garland-Thomson argue that "normalcy" and the "normate" are "ideological and bureaucratic constructions" (Barker and Murray 3). The biomedical model of disability, along with its implicit valuing of the "normal" body, developed and institutionalized through methods of measurement, testing, and bureaucratization, established the expectation that the majority of the population must conform. Gradually, in contrast, the social model of disability began to gain prominence by identifying systemic barriers, attitudes, and methods of exclusion, which make it difficult for people who live with impairments. As a social and cultural construction—in everyday life as much as in literature—bodily variation is not so much an inherent "property of bodies as a product of cultural rules" that dictate what a body should be or can do (Barker and Murray 4).

The field of disability studies has responded directly to this "medically enforced reign of normal." A new approach distinguishes between *impairment* (an "individual limitation linked to a medically based problem that impairs one or more basic life functions") and *disability* ("the individual limitation produced by society's failure to accommodate to the impairment";

Squier 73). This new emphasis productively draws attention to people's political and social rights to access, mobility, and independence and in turn highlights the ways that legal, educational, social, medical, and physical environments can be and often are disabling. This social model approaches disability (as this study does, with the concept of childhood) as a socially constructed form of exclusion that "takes its shape through social relations, cultural representations, and modes of production and reproduction" (Ansell 187). Disability and impairment, then, cannot be separated from considerations of age, race, class, sexuality, gender, citizenship, nation, religion, health status, and other categories of difference. Although this approach has been extremely useful in producing change in legislation and pedagogical understandings of literature, critics are concerned that it offers little to no focus on the body and on biomedical understandings of disability (Barker and Murray 6). Insisting that disability is a "construct" can risk effacing the body's materiality, denying the pain and suffering caused by impairment (Couser, *Signifying* 30). Alison Kafer responds to these concerns in the "hybrid political/relational model of disability" (4) that she offers, one that rethinks the social and biomedical frameworks from within queer and feminist critiques of identity. In response to this particular worry about effacing the materiality of the body, a new focus in literature (and in comics culture) attends to "complex embodiment," how the body and its (re)presentations are mutually dependent and transformative, and how personal experiences of impairment manifest in the young person's body.

As the growing number of comics by people with bodily or mental variations suggests, disabled people have much to gain through the use of literary and visual representation. Pathographies, specifically, can narrativize complex information about the embodiment of illness and impairment from the perspective of diverse speaking subjects, offering engaging visual representations of bodily or mental variation. Most importantly, by means of these first-person perspectives, pathographies resist the dominant tropes of invisibility and inaudibility that have rendered such speaking subjects marginal. As the Cooperative Children's Book Center's 2019 study reports, only 3.4 percent of all children's literature has a disabled main character ("The Numbers"). It is even more challenging to find disabled protagonists at the intersection of multiple marginalized identities, such as disabled people of color, disabled LGBTQ+ characters, disabled cultural or religious minorities, or disabled fat characters. Graphic pathographies of bodily or mental variation, then, respond to a particular need in the market for such narratives. In all instances analyzed here, these comics value the everyday lived realities of young people, refuting the rhetorical tendency to frame these stories into narratives of rescue or self-rescue. One of the particular affordances of these pathographies about mental illness, specifically, is that they help to visualize the invisible nature of disability.

## Visualizing the Invisible Nature of Mental Illness: *Marbles, Fun Home,* and *Swallow Me Whole*

With their innovative form and content, comics offer a particularly multimodal opportunity for representing understandings of bodily variation, health, illness, and diagnosis. There is a broad spectrum of disabilities (both visible and invisible) already represented in comics for readers of all ages: Texts feature, for example, amputation, autism, blindness, deafness, depression, Huntington's, multiple sclerosis (MS), obsessive-compulsive disorder (OCD), speech impairment, spinal injury, and so on (Whalen et al. 8). Graphic pathographies are effective at representing the consciousness of someone suffering from a mental disorder and/or depression, offering in the process powerful antidotes to stigmatizing beliefs. They specifically respond to the silence, shame, and denial people with such mental disorders may feel.

By no means a graphic narrative written for young readers, Ellen Forney's *Marbles: Mania, Depression, Michelangelo & Me* (2012) is a powerful example of the possibilities that comics can provide for representing a creator's embodied representation of bipolar disorder in art. Forney captures in her drawings and in the very aesthetic of the text the heightened intensity of her manic states, visualizing the multistage process of thought as one idea builds on another at a frantic pace as her mania escalates into a full-blown psychotic episode. In particular, the sketch-journal format allows her to visualize herself in various and varied states of mania, in turn giving "agency to the individual experiencing the illness" by working against the biomedical model of illness where the medical practitioner observes the patient and draws a conclusion based on numerical and literal data (Velentzas). Forney is particularly interested in the approach to her disorder taken by the medical establishment. Her subjective experience of diagnosis is presented alongside the *Diagnostic and Statistical Manual of Mental Disorders* (*DSM*), juxtaposing the supposed authority that the *DSM* attempts to claim over her body and mind against the importance she places on her own creativity as a stabilizing authority. Employing "subjective intrapersonal dialogue," Forney "invites the reader into the mind of a person dealing with mental illness" and inspires empathy in the process (Eugene 238). Emanata (special effects lettering, motion lines, particular panel shapes, etc.) visualize the affective facets of Forney's experiences. More specifically, she captures her euphoric mental state by a freedom from structure, fluid lines and images representing a distinct (and manic) contrast to traditional, regularized, and more controlled comics paneling emblematic of her mental state between full-blown episodes of mania. Fascinatingly, Forney's specific deployment of panel lines distinguishes between her renderings of manic episodes and objective reality: Her depressive bouts are in this way boxed in by panels that capture the oppression that she feels, whereas her manic episodes visually overwhelm or exceed the borders of the pages. The dizzying aesthetic of *Marbles* captures the all-powerful intensity of Forney's wild periods and her particularly subjective experience of mania. Informative about symptoms of bipolar disorder, as well as medications and their side effects, *Marbles* provides a complex representation of bipolar disorder, refuting the invisible nature of mental illness by cataloguing, through this arrestingly visual mode, the extreme feelings and experiences brought on by this disorder that might not otherwise be represented.

The comics form is also very effective at representing the "compulsive spatial focus and arranging" that is so typical of OCD (Chute, *Why* 253). First Justin Green's *Binky Brown Meets the Holy Virgin Mary* (1972) and then Alison Bechdel's *Fun Home: A Family Tragicomic* (2006) laid the groundwork for comics' representations of disorders in which people have recurring, unwanted thoughts, ideas, or sensations that make them feel driven to do something repetitively. Bechdel's OCD operates both thematically and formally within her graphic memoir. Ascribing an "aspect of compulsion" (134) to her creativity, Bechdel visualizes the compulsive behaviors she began to display at age ten: An obsession with numbers and a focus on routines and incantations to ward off bad luck deepen into a fixation with acknowledging her epistemological lack of certainty about everything around her. In her journal, for example, her worry about mimetic accuracy surfaces in minutely scrawled statements, "I think," between and over each written statement, emphasizing this uncertainty graphically. Alison's compulsive desire to exert control is in this way visualized in the graphic memoir. Diary entries, meticulously reproduced, become visually and literally occluded by this visual shorthand: "Soon I began drawing it right over names and pronouns. It became a sort of amulet, warding off evil from my subjects," she confesses (142). The obsessiveness demonstrated in her journal entries extends to Bechdel's laborious drawing techniques (she digitally photographs herself in every single pose that she depicts in her memoir and then reproduces it on paper) and to her obsessive ruminations about her father's death/suicide within the memoir itself. Thus, in its self-conscious return to the same questions over and over again, "*Fun Home* performs the very compulsions that it thematizes" (Barounis 146).

The power of comics' visual approaches to mental disorders lies in this ability to approximate a personal (and frequently invisible) experience that might not otherwise be possible to articulate. The "haptic charge" of drawing in this case is even more able to capture the subjective and affective qualities of the comic's content about mental disorder, awakening readers to an affective reality beyond the page itself.

Nate Powell's YA graphic narrative, *Swallow Me Whole* (2008), is especially topical because of its focus on the experiences of two adolescents living with schizophrenia and obsessive-compulsive disorder. Importantly, the text resists distinguishing between hallucination and objective reality, recognizing that for people living with recurrent psychotic episodes there is no such difference. From the beginning, for example, there is a notable lack of traditional panel lines, a method that blurs the temporal distinction between past and present, objective reality and fantasy. Page numbers are also missing, which leaves a reader feeling unmoored within the text. Without any such conventional directional and temporal markers, a reader is propelled along with siblings Ruth and Perry, as everyday lived realities become increasingly characterized by psychotic episodes (Ruth's of visions of giant cicadas flying around her; Perry's of a small wizard who appears on the end of his pen to give him orders). The title page provides a pertinent insight into this text about schizophrenia: Across a densely packed page that depicts a hospital's parking lot and a street in a neighborhood, winding tentacles seem to reach out toward Ruth and Perry. Inset across these images are three separate narrative boxes that read: "This has been happening all my life," "It's the only way I know our world," and "Makes sense to me" (Powell). Declarative and fragmented statements that could apply to Ruth and Perry equally in this way describe (and affirm) their subjective experiences of reality. Their hallucinatory episodes—periods in which they feel strangely disassociated from the people around them and when they lose track of time—define their respective everyday experiences, having lived like this for as long as they can remember. As *Swallow Me Whole* clarifies, Ruth and Perry (and, by implication, many people who live with schizophrenia) come to know the world around them by means of and in relation to these hallucinatory episodes. As young readers discover, these experiences make more sense to the siblings than the disorienting everyday world through which they must navigate.

Over the course of the narrative, readers watch and accompany Ruth and Perry as their lives unravel around them, as they are consumed, "swallowed" even, by their respective visions. By means of their subjective perspectives, readers come to appreciate how the institutions of home and school misinterpret and/or misdiagnose individuals who might not necessarily conform to expected behaviors and learning patterns. Ruth and Perry attempt to fit in, but with minimal success, especially in Ruth's case. The obsessive order that she uses to hold off an episode (her impeccably organized bookshelves full of specimen jars with carefully preserved cicadas) serves as an impressive testament of her determination to exert control over her mental health. As *Swallow Me Whole* visualizes, however, that control is precarious. Gradually, the white negative space between and among the panels becomes black, suggesting the increasingly tenuous grasp that Ruth and Perry have on their daily routines of home and school and the approaching onset of their respective episodes. Sarah Thaller argues that the cicadas emphasize schizophrenia's "chronic nature," the fluctuation of its intensity, its ebb and flow (55). Onomatopoeic ribbons of sound conveying the buzzing of the cicadas that Ruth hears eventually swarm over entire pages as her daily routine is wholly disrupted by hallucinations. The size of the lettering in these ribbon lines in turn evokes the mounting intensity of her schizophrenic episode. On one splash page, Powell presents Ruth as covered in cicadas, finally "swallowed whole" by her visions (see figure 5.4). At the same time, Perry experiences a hallucinatory episode of his own, although of a wholly different nature. While completing his homework, he speaks to a small wizard figure who orders him around, promising to enlighten him about a mysterious "mission" that he is expected to fulfill. A reader's empathy is provoked by Powell's visualization of the particular delusions suffered by these two young siblings. His many aesthetic decisions minimize the distance between reader, Ruth, and Perry, producing a reading experience that approximates the disorientation and panic that these young people might feel at the approach of a hallucinatory event.

This graphic pathography's criticism of medical diagnostic procedures highlights the failure of biomedicine to validate patients' respective experiences and, ultimately, leaves them to cope—alone—with their hallucinations. Powell juxtaposes two separate experiences of medical diagnosis, both of which fail the young patients. Worried about her daughter's increasingly violent outbursts and confusing behavior, Ruth's mother takes her to see a psychiatrist, Dr. Newell, for help. Newell ignores Ruth, addressing her mother instead. He speaks of Ruth's condition in the third person, confirming that there are "signs of obsessive-compulsive disorder" and some "schizophrenic and dissociative patterns," and prescribes some pills, all the while failing to engage with Ruth. Ruth is, in this way, the subject of Newell's analysis, but as Powell's text visualizes, the doctor fails to provide any tangible means of support for her. "There is in truth no explanation for

FIGURE 5.4. Ruth experiences a hallucinatory episode. Nate Powell, *Swallow Me Whole*. Top Shelf, 2008.

the doctor's failure to engage with the patient save that, in having made up his mind as to her condition, he has already written her off as an agent in her own recovery, turning all of his attention instead to the mother," Jared Gardner observes (150). In contrast, Perry's pediatrician (Dr. Connoly) addresses the young man directly, asks questions, makes eye contact during the appointment, yet also fails to take Perry's concerns seriously. In trying to alleviate any anxieties Perry might have in confiding in him, Connoly, with his breezy commentary, leaves little emotional space for Perry to occupy. In spite of this, Perry openly confides in him about the hallucinatory visions of the wizard that he has been experiencing for years; Connoly, sadly, misinterprets this revelation, dismissing it as evidence of "stress" and even describes Perry as a "wizard" of drawing to his step-father, thus misconstruing all of the information his patient has provided for him. Both doctors in their respective processes of diagnosis miss an important opportunity to provide support. Jacobs and Dolmage note how many disability narratives begin in a doctor's office, "where the disability can be explained or sanctioned or diagnosed by a medical professional" ("Accessible" 357). In this instance, by juxtaposing Ruth and Perry's respective experiences of schizophrenia and their interactions with medical personnel, Powell visualizes two distinct approaches to diagnosis, both of which fail to validate the patients' experiences.

Powell's pathography of schizophrenia privileges the perspectives of Ruth and Perry in an attempt to show different experiences of mental illness and also to emphasize the need for community, especially between and among young people who might feel afraid and ashamed of their symptoms. Throughout their adolescence, Ruth and Perry offer each other support while coping with their hallucinations. Perry's ability to offer assistance, however, becomes increasingly compromised as Ruth's descent into a particularly powerful episode begins. He does not know how to respond to his sister's calm assertion that she knows "a supreme order. When I give into it, I channel it" or when she defends her violent outbursts toward her teacher and principal as being completely reasonable. Powerless when faced with his sister's intensifying mania, Perry can only respond, "Just be careful" and reassert that he is there for her. As previously discussed, medical professionals have failed these youngsters and left them to cope with their respective conditions by themselves. It is Perry who intuits the beginning of Ruth's most powerful episode. Returning home after school, he is immediately overcome by his own vision of the cicadas that are in the process of "swallowing" his sister whole. Black pages depict the devouring of Ruth: As readers turn the pages, more and more of Ruth is engulfed by the black, negative space of the page (see figure 5.5). Three fully black blank pages immediately after this frightening sequence separate Ruth's story from that of Perry, confirming Ruth's actual disappearance. Her disappearance is also emphasized by the missing persons report that her mother fills out afterward with a local police officer. Alone now, without his sister, Perry is left

FIGURE 5.5. Ruth is swallowed by cicadas. Nate Powell, *Swallow Me Whole*. Top Shelf, 2008.

to process Ruth's disappearance. As the text emphasizes, however, Perry's mental health is as precarious as his sister's: That he is beginning to interact with the subjects of his sister's hallucinations (the cicadas and a giant frog with whom Ruth used to communicate) does not provide an optimistic closure to the narrative. Indeed, his dead grandmother's warning—"Watch out . . . it'll swallow you whole"—also foreshadows Perry's seemingly inevitable disappearance into his own illness.

As *Marbles*, *Fun Home*, and *Swallow Me Whole* prove, creative graphic formats effectively visualize the invisible nature of mental illness. Comics creators strategically deploy elements such as size, color, layout, paneling, and repetition to "depict the intricacies and abstract ambits of the mental health experience" (Venkatesan and Saji 39). They also represent subjective time sequences that move away from chronological/objective time, in turn enhancing the affective abilities of the text. Not all of these graphic pathographies end optimistically, as *Stitches* and *Swallow Me Whole* make clear. But in their refusal of optimism lies their particular acknowledgment of the disorder that can often characterize medical experiences.

## Acts of (Re)Creation: *My Body in Pieces*, *Tyranny*, and *Lighter Than My Shadow*

Frequently in comics, creators make use of the "curative utility of drawing" (Venkatesan and Peter, "Drawing" 104) as a form of therapy or meditation in response to medical events. In Small's *Stitches*, for example, imagination and art are instrumental for David in the reclamation of his control over his own body, as well as for his recovery from his cancer surgeries and his family's continued emotional abuse. As a child, he sought refuge in a fantasy world in which he played Alice from *Alice's Adventures in Wonderland*. Alice—like David—inhabited an "incongruous adult world" (Mallan 171); however, in contrast to Alice, who eventually grows to display her agency in Carroll's Wonderland, David has limited knowledge and control in his own world.

Art—the drawing of comics—provides a temporary respite from his suffering and allows David to visualize his particularly embodied experiences of illness, trauma, and abuse. The visual epigraph to Small's comic introduces this conceit: Three consecutive images depict a youthful David diving into his work, in effect becoming his art. The parameters distinguishing inside and outside are in this way breached from the text's opening page, as David later visualizes himself sliding down his own esophagus into his stomach to bear witness to the damage that his parents have enacted on his body. In doing so, Small invites readers to align body and text by means of art that he uses to create an imagined space for himself in which he can find comparative safety. By diving into the page and exploring his body, Small insists on his embodied experience of trauma and abuse, refusing to interpret his eventual voicelessness as an abstract metaphor and insisting instead on his speech impairment as the direct result of unnecessary medical interventions. When David awakens from the two surgeries that were supposed to remove the cyst on his neck, he invites the reader to "step inside" their own mouths (Small 182). Together, David encourages us to imagine our vocal cords, "which make the sounds of your voice, your curses and your prayers" (183). He then encourages the reader to visualize how different his own vocal cords now look after the removal of one, which has in turn left him voiceless. David frames his shock and trauma at seeing the "crusted black track of stitches" down his neck as a dialogue between his mind and his body. "Surely this is not me," his mind insists. "No, friend, it surely is," his body replies (191). In this moment, David struggles to align his sense of self with a new body awareness and image, given his new (and sudden) experience of impairment, brought on by the medical choices made by his parents without his consent.

For David Small, artistic renderings of bodily cavities and architectural interiors offer a safe haven from an environment that did not care to safeguard his best interests as a young person. Immediately after the surgeries, David represents himself as a mise en abyme, a silently shouting cavernous mouth inside another silently shouting mouth reproduced endlessly. In this powerful image, David calls attention to his anguish and anger. And yet David (and, by extension, Small) eventually finds his voice in art. "Art became my home," Small asserts. "Not only did it give me back my voice, but art has given me everything I have wanted or needed since" (302). His subjectivity is represented visually as interior spaces that he explores in an effort to escape the outside world, spaces that he must also claim for himself. With help from therapy, David eventually comes to accept his weak voice and scar, the physical markers of his trauma and disability, as a part of himself. Drawing, in this way, becomes an act of (re)creation as much as a mode of therapy.

The range of narratives, visual styles, and approaches to graphic medicine that *Smile, El Deafo, Swallow Me Whole,* and *Stitches* represent only scratch at the surface of the complex representations of health, illness, and disability that emerge in comics for young people. As this chapter has already demonstrated, pathographies are an effective and affective popular form for readers, young and old, and speak to an apparent "need and desire in our current moment for narrative *and* visual chronicles of struggles with sickness" (Chute, "Cancer" 421). A corresponding focus in comics is one that examines eating disorders—anorexia nervosa, bulimia nervosa, binge eating disorder, and accompanying symptoms of obsessive-compulsive disorder, as well as a concurrent fixation with thinness and control—again engaging with the materiality of the body and its impacts on a young person's identity. Eating disorders are most often reported among adolescents and young women. Up to 13 percent of youth may experience at least one eating disorder by the age of twenty (Petre). The visuality of the medium permits a confrontation with the body's materiality in a way that text-based pathographies do not (Wegner 66). Frequently, these texts foreground the ways in which art and the act of creation are central to a young protagonist's quest for bodily self-acceptance. As this final section argues, comics like *My Body in Pieces*, *Tyranny*, and *Lighter Than My Shadow* offer representations of young people's individual struggles with eating disorders, the graphic medium allowing the creator greater control over their self-image and their ability to approximate, visually, the accompanying loss of objectivity in perceptions and representations of their body. In these narratives, especially, "the body cannot be omitted, and it cannot be ignored" (Couser, "Body" 350). Visual representations of eating disorders offer a particularly affective approach to these complex mental and physical health conditions.

No text is more applicable to this section's concern with art and embodiment than Marie-Noëlle Hébert's *My Body in Pieces* (2019 in French; 2021 in English), a graphic memoir aimed at readers aged 14 to 18 that visualizes her lifelong struggle with weight and bodily perception. Entirely drawn in graphite pencil, the text's shadowy, blurry lines capture Hébert's deeply difficult memories of her youth. The title calls attention to her recollections of individual body parts, the fragmentation of that body thanks to societal pressures about thinness and beauty, and the long and involved process (personal and artistic) needed to reassemble those pieces into a whole. The predominant shade of black conveys Hébert's sense of deep depression, isolation, and alienation from her body. Pressured by her parents throughout her childhood and youth to conform to sizeist expectations of bodily "normalcy," Marie-Noëlle's profound frustration with her sense of self is represented by a page that breaks up her face into twenty extreme-close-up panels, each of which represents particular attributes of her face that she does not like. Not surprisingly, this close visual analysis of her face and body erodes her self-esteem even further: "Each day I focus on finding fault with my body, one piece at a time," she confesses (Hébert 28). Gradually these panels begin to include scissors that she imagines using to trim the fat off various parts of her body or to shape it so as to conform to the beauty standards that barrage her on all sides. By depicting herself as a marionette, whose body parts are seemingly manipulated by those around her, Hébert emphasizes her loss of control. "The secret to being beautiful—never try to look like a fat girl who thinks she's thin. Cover up your body. It's embarrassing," she repeats to herself. "Use fashion tricks to hide your flaws. Forget about what you want and do what you're told" (36). Profoundly negative self-perception, and her embodied experience of shame and dismay, in turn shape Hébert's exchanges with the people around her, especially her parents. She isolates herself from everyone, shutting them out and spending "as much energy as I want hating myself, my body" (67).

As in *Stitches*, Hébert's graphic text imagines a self-empowerment that only begins to emerge once she starts therapy and uses her art (and the creation of this graphic memoir) to face the pressures imposed by her family and society to be thin and beautiful. Her eventual epiphany relies on an acceptance of her body as it is: "I will flaunt my femininity if I want. The way I want, when I want. Fat included," she asserts (87). Eventually assembling the visual "pieces" of her body into a full and complete sense of self in this text, one that she looks after, cherishes, and is proud of, Hébert makes use of the creative process to reconstruct her sense of self by providing a sheltered space from which she can reflect on her experiences. Confronting her parents about their negative messaging and finally looking at and accepting her body as a whole, Marie-Noëlle comes to a realization, "This is my body, and it's beautiful. Maybe I'll actually believe that someday" (98). Hébert's text allows her to revisit and re-create past traumatic experiences by organizing those singular experiences into a whole narrative, one that in turn allows her to reflect on the larger prevalence of "thinspiration" as a social and cultural pressure. The aesthetic of *Body in Pieces*—in particular, Hébert's use of graphite pencil—certainly conveys the trace of the creator's presence in the text. Drawing readers into the narrative and awakening them to an affective reality beyond the page, a text like Hébert's communicates the deeply personal experience of an eating disorder and the distorted body image occasioned by pressures imposed by her social and cultural environments.

As has previously been discussed, assumptions about any types of "normalcy" (racial and ethnic, ableist, gender and sexual, developmental and bodily, etc.) are dangerous because they disregard or marginalize the experiences of entire groups of people. The qualities, states, abilities, and actions of our bodies are partly determined by the values and assumptions that our culture imposes on us. In truth, no one experiences physicality in a way that is straightforward and stable throughout life. In her theorization of dynamic embodiment, Elisabeth El Refaie develops one central idea: that the experience of illness and/or disease unsettles our usual relationship with our bodies and in the process changes our thought patterns. El Refaie adapts Maurice Merleau-Ponty's idea that bodies are normally characterized by "disappearance" to describe how, when our bodies seize our attention in the experience of illness or sudden disability, our physicality actually forces itself *back into* our consciousness. In this way, bodies—in the process of capturing our attention—begin to "dys-appear," as El Refaie puts it (*Metaphor* 56). This representation of bodily "dys-appearance," the preoccupation with body weight and body image, is nowhere more visually apparent than in these comics about young people struggling with eating disorders. Texts like Marie D'Abreo's *Beautiful: A Girl's Trip through the Looking Glass*, Lesley Fairfield's *Tyranny*, and Katie Green's *Lighter Than My Shadow* are useful for visualizing bodily distortion that many of the young protagonists experience. Bodies—especially the bodies of young women—are clearly the territory over which biomedicine and biocultural construction wage war. Doctors and psychotherapists work intently with the young people in these texts to reprogram the neurotic, perfectionist, and impulsive behaviors (often linked to a higher risk of developing an eating disorder [Petre]) that govern their everyday ways of being. Cultural factors like family influence, peers and pressures, and body shaming also influence these young people. Media and their endorsement of "thinspiration" in turn promote cultural expectations and ideals of bodily perfection that are unattainable (Venkatesan and Peter, "Famishment" 528).

Frequently, creators of such texts find creative methods to represent their respective experiences of an eating disorder. They personify the negative body messaging, illusory ideals of beauty, and perfectionism as monstrous figures who assault the protagonists with hateful and insidious thoughts. In Lesley Fairfield's comic (2009), for example, Tyranny is the personification of protagonist Anna's eating disorder, who holds her in a death grip from the very first page. Tyranny is the most powerful element in the text: An abstract rendering of a female body, Tyranny's threatening aspects come from the damaging messages she communicates to Anna ("I told you not to eat. You are too fat!!" [1]) and the squiggly emanata that represent her dangerous vitality, which eventually exceed the panels' frames and visually overwhelm Anna. Intended for readers eleven or older, *Tyranny* is an indictment of contemporary cultures of beauty and the ever-elusive pursuit of thinness, intensified by the media and fashion industries. Fairfield visualizes the precarious barometer of "normalcy" that very quickly erodes in her protagonist when her objective perception of herself and her physique begin to diverge. To emphasize the extreme importance that her eating disorder begins to exert over Anna, Tyranny gradually begins to exceed the parameters of each panel. By means of these snaky emanata, Tyranny seems so much more oppressive, controlling, and ultimately impossible to withstand. Readers are invited to understand how Anna arrived at the experience of body distortion by means of

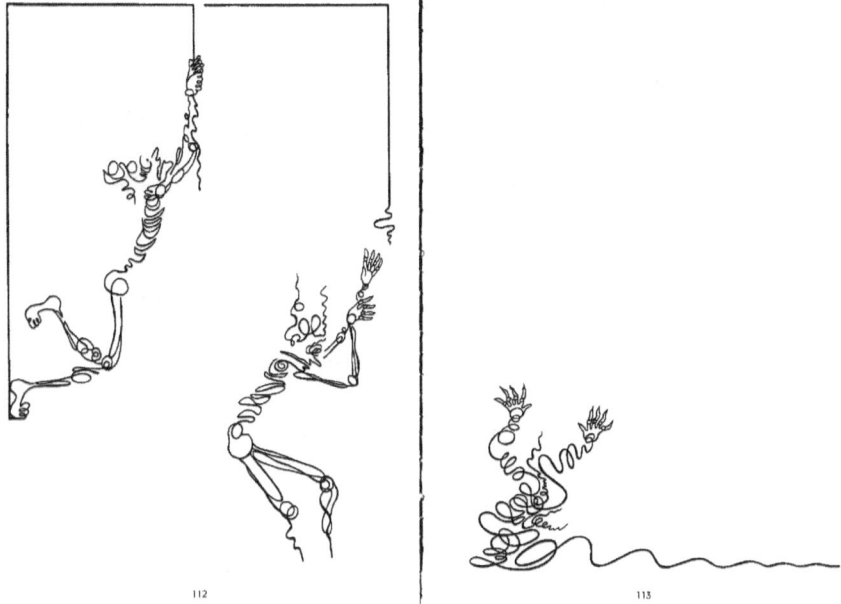

FIGURE 5.6. Tyranny loses its grip on Anna's story. Lesley Fairfield, *Tyranny*. Tundra Books, 2009, pp. 112–13.

the negative bodily messaging that she consumed from childhood. Indeed, this messaging becomes all-encompassing: Defending her size to her loved ones who express concern, Anna herself grows to resemble Tyranny more and more, coming to conflate the disease with her very identity: "There's nothing wrong with me!" she insists desperately. "Why can't you accept me the way I am?" (29).

As is the case with so many of these graphic pathographies, art becomes an important mode of therapy and healing for the young protagonists. With the help of a psychiatrist, Anna learns to calm her thoughts and to value them as true indicators of what she wants. Fairfield emphasizes Anna's writing and art as crucial in her struggle to regain control over these impulses. By means of these modes, Anna refuses to accept Tyranny's powerful hold over her anymore. Through force of will, Anna forces Tyranny out of her mind, a process that Fairfield represents in a very innovative way. Tyranny tries desperately to hold onto the comic's panel line, but eventually loses hold and, in turn, all distinctiveness, finally dissolving into a mess of unthreatening squiggles (see figure 5.6). Fascinatingly, Anna overpowers Tyranny by means of her art, choosing logical narrative patterns over the random ebullience of Tyranny's damaging energy.

The useful combination of words and images in these graphic texts about eating disorders approximates the lived experiences of these young people affectively, capturing the slippery slope down which they travel in terms of bodily distortion as they undergo a crisis that is both physical and mental.

Comics have frequently been dismissed as immature and uncomplicated. McCloud's linking of comics with inadequate cognitive development in *Understanding Comics*—as seen in the epigraph to this chapter—shows how widespread and dismissive that assumption continues to be. As comics about young people and/in graphic medicine prove, however, comics can make use of personal narratives about health, illness, and bodily variation to encourage readers to think more broadly about the discourses of health and ability that shape their everyday experiences. Typically, children are viewed as apolitical: "Their worlds [are] seen as social and cultural spaces, not political arenas. Children are understood to belong to the private sphere, whereas politics is confined to the public sphere" (Ansell 205). Comics such as the absorbing ones I have analyzed erase this disassociation of children from politics, reinforcing yet again that the bodies of young people speak volumes about their agency and human rights as they are safeguarded (or not) by the environments in which they grow. Susan Honeyman argues that literature can "provide liberatory ideals that press for the recognition of children's medical rights" (190). These texts bring to the foreground matters of health and wellbeing for readers. In so doing, they move beyond policing negative portrayals of illness or disability to recognizing disability as an engine of innovation.

CONCLUSION

# Comics and the COVID Crisis

> The coronavirus pandemic affects all countries and people, and the need for stories about how we survive and live on in this time is huge.
> —Björn Sundmark, "Children's Covid-19 Literature"

COVID-19, a highly infectious disease caused by the novel coronavirus SARS-CoV-2, was first identified in the Chinese city of Wuhan in December 2019. Lockdown measures there initially failed, however, and the disease spread rapidly to other parts of mainland China and the rest of the world. Worried by its "alarming levels of spread and severity" and by "the alarming levels of inaction" across the world (Saji et al. 137), the World Health Organization declared a Public Health Emergency of International Concern on 30 January 2020, finally labeling it a pandemic on 11 March 2020. For the next couple of years, while the world waited anxiously for the development and distribution of vaccines, medical experts recommended quarantine, isolation, masking, and social distancing to curb the spread of the disease. Even so, as of 7 January 2023, more than 663 million cases have been reported and 6.71 million COVID-related deaths have been confirmed. The end of this catastrophe is still not in sight.

This public health crisis has highlighted racial and geographic discrimination that is all too systemic across the globe, worsened by the devastating impact that the pandemic has reaped on the international economy. Financial woes and job precarity have affected citizens on a global and individual level. Largely confined to their homes, citizens were forced to transform these homes into work spaces, often shared by a number of people, and impromptu schoolrooms, as parents' and caregivers' attention was divided between work and the duties of educating young people once the schools and daycares were closed. Over the past three years, the pandemic has exposed the home as a "space in which power is unevenly distributed according to gender, sexual orientation, ethnicity, and other registers of identity" (Snell 1). The many incidents of gendered, racial, and ethnic violence attest to the unequal distribution of safety and power within the home and the nation state. The people most intimately affected by this pandemic are those whom society has frequently marginalized, the victims of capitalism: BIPOC people; people living with disabilities; people living in poverty; refugees, asylum seekers, and undocumented immigrants; older people residing in long-term care homes; people in carceral institutions; women; and young people (Snell 1). The impacts of the COVID pandemic are still too early to determine fully; there is no doubt, however, that its reach will be felt for years to come. The recommended risk-mitigation strategies of social distancing and isolation, and the concomitant scarcity of touch and physical contact between people, have had serious consequences on the mental health of people around the world.

The COVID pandemic has caused significant disruption to the lives of billions of people, the lives of children and adolescents, in particular. In April 2020, UNICEF reported that 2.34 billion young people live in one of the 186 countries worldwide that imposed some form of movement restrictions because of COVID; 60 percent of these children reside in one of the eighty-two countries that experienced a full or partial lockdown (Graber et al. 143). Even into 2023, young people's everyday experiences continue to be embedded in and shaped by the COVID crisis. They are affected by similar axes of difference (economic, geographic, classist, ethnic, ableist, gendered, racialized, etc.) that shape the lives of adults. Overnight, their everyday pleasures, habits, and schedules were disrupted; extracurricular activities were abruptly cancelled; and interruptions in information flow and communication patterns across social media and online platforms transformed their everyday interactions with peers, family, and teachers. Over the first two and a half years of the pandemic, schools (locations in which young people once spent a significant portion of their daily lives) moved back and forth between in-person teaching and online learning platforms in response to the spread of the virus, and children (and all people, for that matter) had to combine home, school, and social interaction within one environment that in turn included a new set of physical and mental distractions in their daily experiences. In spring 2020, the very spaces through which young people once moved so freely were quickly restricted, demarcated, or cohorted, such that even playgrounds became off-limits for fear of potential exposure to the virus. Over the course of the pandemic, a lack of access to technology and/or Internet resources also highlighted the inequities that affect young people's learning abilities in a virtual classroom. Poorly functioning or limited access to computer devices in the education sector and bad connectivity led to a "digital divide" that continues to separate young people of varied socioeconomic and racial backgrounds. Frequently, multiple devices were shared among several members of a single household, or parents who had to work outside the home were not present to monitor whether the young people logged on for homeschooling. For those two and a half years especially, school was, at best, inconsistent and, at worst, ineffective. Many family members and caregivers had to relearn early school subjects to assist young people with their studies. The impact of the COVID crisis on individuals and families has been significant; the breadth of that experience in the education sector will only be determined in the coming years.

Young people around the globe continue to be affected differently by the pandemic based on their particular life experiences and geographic locations. At the same time, many are contending with other major and minor life events (ranging from parental divorce, changing family structures, and death, to the loss of socially significant occasions like proms and graduation ceremonies), parental or personal employment, loss of recreational activities, and the like (Vest Ettekal and Agans 14). Even though researchers and health-care professionals suggested that young people are generally less clinically affected by all strains of the virus, they are nonetheless troubled by "reduced access to food, nutrition, essential social and health services, preventative care measures and the detrimental possible effects of prolonged school closures such as a widening learning gap and socio-economic disparity" (Graber et al. 144). Fear and anxiety are common emotions that adults and young people share: We learned to live with the fear of catching COVID, fear of losing a loved one, fear of becoming close with other people after months and months spent apart, and so forth. Evidence suggests that prolonged school closures, social isolation, and the restrictions on socialization will have significant impacts on young people's well-being and growth (Vest Ettekal and Agans 2).

Over the course of the pandemic, the world waited breathlessly for the invention and delivery of vaccines that could offer some protection against the virus. Since December 2020, a number of vaccines have been approved and distributed around the world, which resulted in mass vaccination campaigns. The issue of vaccine delivery for young people once again ignited a controversy over children's rights and, more specifically, the controls that adults, parents, and caregivers exert over the medical and human rights of young people. Similar to mid-twentieth-century controversies over the allegedly negative impacts of comics on young readers and over the "appropriateness" of certain subject matter in YA reading material, recent firestorms across North America blew up over whether primary and secondary schools should or would issue a mandate requiring vaccines in all school-aged young people. Many parents and caregivers disagreed vociferously about the best way to protect the medical well-being of children and youth, worried about the potential side effects of the vaccines, and debated how best to safeguard their (meaning, adults') rights and individual choices.

Not surprisingly, given these multiple uncertainties and fears about COVID, comics became instrumental for readers in information gathering and beginning to process the sociopolitical and emotional implications of this global crisis in visual form.

## COVID Comics: Illness and Pedagogy

As *Growing Up Graphic* has argued, comics about particular predicaments and challenges experienced by young people have become a potent vehicle for the wide dissemination of information about young people's lived experiences. They are also effective at encouraging empathetic identification among their readers and advancing human rights' claims and campaigns. Comics can represent and narrativize complex information about marginalization and suffering, from the varied perspectives of the undocumented migrant lost at sea to that of the young person confined within the walls of their residence during a global pandemic. Importantly, they narrate the experiences of young people, not necessarily in relation to a story of rescue or self-rescue. Indeed, the youngsters at the heart of these texts take an active role in the events that shape them personally, whether that takes the form of creative self-reflection or the act of becoming individual agents of rights' activism. Finally, their voices contribute vital perspectives about narratives of nation, belonging, identity, health, and wellness. In many respects, these stories use the local to encourage readers to think more broadly about individual experiences of history and how one's personal experiences are *not* universally shared.

The COVID comics that this conclusion surveys specifically link the local with the global, evoking embodied experiences of illness and precarity and relying on deeply personal memories, family stories, and sources such as letters, journals, photographs, and conversations that make abstract statistics about the spread of the virus, case numbers, and death statistics come alive on the page. Over the course of this pandemic, images that range from epidemiological maps or infographics to photographs or comics about masking and social distancing served "to inform, provide meaning, and illustrate the outbreak narrative in ways that help us process, reflect on, and understand our experiences" (Callender et al. 1061) as well as to "validate the deeply personal experiences of a pandemic that have been abstractly defined by case numbers and death statistics" (1062). Not surprisingly, the comics form (especially digital comics or comics circulated on social media) was especially well-suited to communicate across cultures and around the world, ironically mirroring the viral nature of the coronavirus itself. Early on, for example, the National University of Singapore assembled a number of individual digital COVID-related comics into *The COVID-19 Chronicles*, a series of one hundred artifacts of comics art that juxtapose humor and scientific guidance while reflecting on the social challenges that the global community faced during the first wave of the pandemic. Collected and shared very quickly thanks to the digital medium, these comics catalogue a range of emotional responses, recording widespread anxiety about the risk of becoming infected. *This Quarantine Life: A Covid-19 Era Comics Anthology* is another collection (a free digital download) that was assembled by the Art Students League in New York City in response to the early days of the virus, anthologizing contributions by seventy-six artists-in-quarantine from the United States, Australia, China, Bahrain, Czech Republic, Italy, and Japan that visualize how each country responded to this important time in contemporary history.

As the rapid proliferation of COVID comics attests, the digital comics medium has allowed global communication and convergence in a way that was simply not employed before now.

As chapter 5 argued, comics offer a powerful contribution to understandings of illness and health. They are quick to read, and because they are emotionally resonant, they can reach a variety of audiences, evoking empathic responses in the process. They often feature the perspective of the young person, whose voice is frequently lost in the noise of adult responses. Comics are inviting to many readers, as Scott McCloud argues. The simple lines of the comic or cartoon provoke reader identification (*Understanding* 36). In terms of their visual rhetoric, and by means of the principle of amplification through simplification, comics about COVID can convey particular risk-mitigation strategies in a quick and effective fashion. "Comics have been used successfully in science communication during the current Covid-19 pandemic," Ciléin Kearns and Nethmi Kearns argue. "Many terms such as 'social distancing' and 'flattening the curve' went from textbook jargon to household conversation in a matter of days to weeks around the world" (139).

The distinctly pedagogical use of COVID comics depends, in part, on the power of the visual. Throughout the pandemic, governments and international and national agencies drew on comics' visual rhetoric to educate people around the world about mask-wearing, social distancing, and handwashing strategies. Sharon Logan, along with a group of migrant returnees, produced comic strips that provided accurate and clear information about COVID protection measures to people at risk during the act of migration, as well as to those at risk of exploitation and abuse by human traffickers and smugglers in West Africa. When the virus spread to West Africa in 2020, for example, volunteers for the Migrants as Messengers program (MaM)—approximately 250 returnees from seven countries in West Africa, including Côte d'Ivoire, Gambia, Guinea, Liberia, Nigeria, Senegal, and Sierra Leone—collaborated to provide information in comics formats to communicate protective messages to communities who were facing language, technology, and literacy barriers ("Liberia"). These comics point to the pragmatic and ethical affordances that comics offer for readers. Just as they can effectively communicate the latest precautionary health measures, they have also proven to be particularly adept at addressing ethical issues that this period of history has inadvertently highlighted, such as "disability access, racial and economic health disparities" throughout various areas of the world, the rights of health-care and other essential workers, and the "vulnerabilities of low-wage immigrants" (Saji et al. 141).

Although many of these COVID comics understandably feature predominantly adult characters, as well as the perspectives of first responders and health-care professionals, the voices of young people are increasingly becoming a focus. The *COVID Chronicles*, published by the Graphic Mundi imprint of Penn State University Press (the initial site for the graphic medicine movement), collected more than sixty short comics that document how individuals, societies, governments, and markets responded to the early days of the global crisis. Some strips feature young people's experiences of this global health event. Sage Stossel's strip, "PAW Patrol to the Coronavirus Rescue," for example, juxtaposes the frantic attempts that two parents make during the first lockdown in the United States to protect their young son from learning the frightening news. They register the pandemic through his eyes as he struggles to process the headlines about the virus that he sees while still at school and apply it to his own life, worrying about things that are especially pertinent to a young person (will Santa Claus catch the coronavirus in the North Pole?) and other more poignant fears that he shares with his parents (will his grandmother fall ill?). The young person's faith in superpowers and the comfort he takes in watching PAW Patrol cartoons is one with which the parents empathize (especially given the irresponsible approach that their then president took toward the spread of the virus across the US). Stossel's strip makes use of the superhero metaphor to visualize the polarization of human and virus, positioning the virus as a concern that needs to be eradicated and focusing on imaginative heroes that can offer hope and, in the process, function as "a heuristic tool to relay the collective force of humanity" (Saji et al. 145). It also addresses the powerlessness that children and adults both feel in response to the sudden changes made to their everyday lives by a force that seemed to defy even the world's most powerful leaders.

Similarly, Justin Larocca Hansen's comic "If I Was" makes use of fantasy wish-fulfillment to empower a young person. A young Black boy—frustrated at being forced to isolate as a protective measure against the disease, to see his friends only on screens, to see his mom leaving for work wearing a mask—imagines himself as a superhero who would "smash COVID-19 right in the kisser!" (Boileau and Johnson 125), "blast COVID out of the skies!" (126), and "suck up all the coronavirus so nobody would get sick!" (127). Fantasies of action (as opposed to inaction) are visualized as entire splash pages: Colorful and dynamic, they call attention to the imaginative possibilities of the young person depicted in stark contrast to the life of stasis that he endures at home in isolation. Too quickly, the little boy returns to reality and realizes that as a young person he does not have the power to produce substantial change, other than to safeguard himself and the people around him by relying on strategies that minimize risk, such as washing his hands, wearing a mask, and trusting "in the real heroes that keep us safe . . . like my mom" (128). Interestingly, these two comic strips rely on a convention that is omnipresent in COVID comics: Readers and creators look to superhero narratives, positioning the virus as a supervillain, and health-care workers (and members of the general populace) as "inspirational exemplars who save humanity from infection and death" (Saji et al. 146). The superheroic mode—for the young people visualized in these two comics—allows them to feel less helpless and scared. Their youthful perspective in turn links the private and familial experiences of this pandemic to the public upheaval that still affects the whole world.

Thanks to the affordances of social media and digital platforms, individual comics responses to COVID-19 almost immediately began to interact digitally and communicate with a larger, more global audience of readers. The accessibility of comics also allowed unfamiliar and complex ideas to be built up over a sequence of panels, while the "use of simplification, schematic representation, and metaphor" helped to make abstract health concepts and the real impact of statistics more tangible (Kearns and Kearns 139). In turn, as McCloud reminds us, simplification invites relatability, such that the more symbolic the comics characters are, the more people (and readers) they could be considered to represent. As *Growing Up Graphic* has argued, the act of reading often encourages knowledge gathering, producing understanding and empathy. Rebecca Scherr has described the "visceral engagement with the pain of others" that comics allow as a reader becomes involved in a world that is represented on the page or on the screen (20). In keeping with the previous texts that this study has explored, COVID comics invite an engrossing, emotional engagement "experienced as bodily feeling" (20): The line separating creator from reader is increasingly breached as both live through the pandemic concurrently and in their own capacities. The "haptic charge" of drawing itself (24) draws readers into the page and is used, in so many examples of these COVID comics, to awaken readers to an affective reality beyond the page itself.

Recently, the Allegheny Health Network, which serves Pennsylvania and New York, collaborated with Marvel Comics to tell the stories of first responders, brought to life in a comic book, *The Vitals: True Nurse Stories*, which debuted to national and international acclaim in December 2020. This issue was followed up with a second issue, *The Vitals: True EMS Stories*, introducing to readers the particularly challenging experiences of healthcare practitioners. These two comic books humanize abstract statistics in a way that is quite similar to many of the comics that this project examines, specifically the texts about child soldiers, immigrants, displaced people, and Indigenous communities in Canada. Medical personnel and patients alike assume centrality in the COVID outbreak narrative, in turn humanizing the concept of the hero that is so ubiquitous in comics ("Marvel").

The impressive number of visual texts that this pandemic continues to provoke speaks to the viral nature of comics in responding to a global crisis and in inspiring connection among people even in a time of social isolation and quarantine. COVID, of course, is an illness without borders, and the storytelling that this medium produces can communicate information while also, and perhaps more importantly, generating an informed empathy among readers that has therapeutic, coping, and healing benefits.

## COVID Comics for Young Readers

Although COVID comics by young people for young readers have not yet been published by mainstream presses, I have no doubt that they will be in time. In general, the comics currently circulating introduce pragmatic, informational material about the virus, produced by adult creators for youthful audiences. A notable exception includes a collection of drawings, sketches, and mixed-media artefacts made by youths during the pandemic and assembled by Nikki Martyn, program head of early childhood studies at the University of Guelph-Humber, that proves the psychological impact the pandemic is having on adolescents ("How Art"). In all cases, the visual medium is extremely effective at capturing youthful perspectives, the emotional charge of the drawings communicating the emotional toll that this time has had on young people in a way that is possibly more resonant than words could be.

Shannon Hale and LeUyen Pham, creators of the award-winning chapter book series for young readers *The Princess in Black* (2014–), produced a free, downloadable comic in 2020 titled *The Princess in Black and the Case of the Coronavirus*. Packaged just as the popular chapter books are, it tackles a topic that is very pertinent for young readers from the perspectives of the well-loved characters of the series, demonstrating again the effective use of the comics form. As Hale wrote on Twitter: "We thought it might help if kids had a book friend who gets what they're going through" (@haleshannon 2020). In contrast to the absurd monsters that the Princess in Black generally tackles, the eponymous character alludes to a new "problem that she can't defeat by herself [. . .] a germ so tiny, we can't even see it." The community that the Princess in Black establishes so easily with her readers provides reassurance that they are not alone and that this virus is something that can only be defeated if everyone works together. She proceeds to reassure readers: "The way we can help fight this problem is as easy as 1-2-3!" (3). In this informational comic, the Princess in Black, along with her friends Frimplepants and the Goat Avenger, invites young readers to wash their hands (or paws, hooves, or tentacles, as the case may be) thoroughly and completely. Another peer, Princess Sneezewort, models social distancing and self-isolating: "I've canceled all of my play-dates until the germ is defeated," Sneezewort declares happily (5). Princess Magnolia (the alter ego of the Princess in Black) encourages her reading friends to self-isolate from people and to wear face masks: "When you're around people who don't live with you . . . wear a face mask and keep at least one Frimplepants [her magic steed] away" (6). On the concluding page of the short comic, the Princess in Black, again dressed as a hero, invites her readers to see themselves in her: "Working together we can solve this problem. See you soon, friends!" (7). Hale and Pham use their widely popular characters to provide knowledge about this new health concern to their audience of young readers and, in the process, model an agentic response to combatting the disease as they encourage youngsters to learn to protect themselves and each other.

As Hale and Pham's digital booklet proves, COVID comics *for* kids have emerged to alleviate fears about the disease and its rapid spread by providing scientific information for young readers in accessible formats that balance word and image. Children's books, videos, infographics, and comics have emerged as the principal tools used to communicate accurate information about mask-wearing, social distancing, and hand-washing with creative flair and appealing design. Young readers and their importance in the struggle against the coronavirus have been recognized the world over, as has been gradually reflected in the comics mode. For example, comic strips promoted by the South African health department, featuring a well-known literary character named Wazi, answer questions about the coronavirus. *Oaky and the Virus* (written by South African author, poet, and academic Athol Williams) helps children understand why they must stay home, wash their hands thoroughly, wear a mask, and socially isolate. Such texts have a wide audience. *Oaky and the Virus* is widely available in South Africa and has been translated into a number of languages. Similarly, the Ministry of Health and Family Welfare of the Government of India published a comic called *Kids, Vaayu & Corona: Who Wins the Fight?* in which Indian superhero Vaayu educates young readers about health precautions.

Directed at a slightly older reading demographic, *Priya's Mask* presents a more inventive—and less explicitly didactic—comics approach to the coronavirus. In this text, India's first comic book superhero, Priya, a hero who usually fights rapists and drug and sex traffickers, is redeployed to fight a new, more abstract enemy: the coronavirus. A rape survivor who flies around on a tigress, Priya befriends a little girl, Meena, to show her the personal sacrifices that health-care workers like her mother have made as well as to battle particular COVID myths that circulate, specifically the idea that children are not at risk of contracting the virus. At the same time, Priya also acknowledges—validates—the fear and anxiety that young people can face. Creator Ram Devineni explains that he produced the series to respond to the general misinformation that was being spread about the disease and to convey the "need for compassion and humanity in such times" (Banerji). "Those are the voices of people who are more afraid than they are aware. Kindness shows us the way while fear makes us weak," Priya tells her new friend, acknowledging the popular misinformation about COVID that circulates while teaching Meena about the importance of personal protection (Prakash). *Priya's Mask* also reaches a substantial audience, as it has been translated into Tamil, Kannada, and Malayalam. Although starkly different in terms of subject matter, both *Priya's Mask* and *Kids, Vaayu & Corona* honor the role that young people play in curbing the spread of the coronavirus.

The comics form has traditionally been employed by nongovernmental organizations (NGOs) and governmental organizations as a way of communicating information to as wide an audience as possible. *Priya's Mask*, for example, was a collaboration between the US Consulate General in Chennai with support from South Indian social media influencers. *Stay Safe Stay Strong* by NGO Ek Tara, in collaboration with artist Falguni Gokhale, was created to educate children living in the Topsia and Tiljala slums of West Bengal about the coronavirus. In the comic, protagonist Tara balances talk about employment being impacted by the pandemic ("my father has no job now") and school closures with a plea to young readers to "behave in a responsible way" by adhering to COVID restrictions (Mazumdar). Executive program manager of Ek Tara, Anupriya Bhattacharya, describes the narrator as an "urban slum girl who the children would relate to" and clarifies that the comic book specifically addresses "issues from the daily lives of these children who are growing up amidst deprivation worsened by the pandemic" (Mazumdar). For Bhattacharya, one of the principal motives for creating this comic book was that, even in the face of serious challenges like losing a job, no access to disposable income, and no food, the problem of COVID must be addressed first (Mazumdar). Published in four languages (Hindi, Bengali, Marathi, and English) and distributed to 40,000 children across West Bengal, *Stay Safe Stay Strong* advises young readers to employ the safety precautions that would help protect themselves and their families against risk, as well as encourage the habit of reading. All of these comics are examples that further prove Mark Heimermann and Brittany Tullis's claim: "Complex and sensitive national and sociocultural issues can also be expressed and explored in comics through the use of child characters" (8), an argument that has been proved by the varied comics approaches to challenges and predicaments endured by young people the world over, as this book has explored.

The primary purpose of COVID comics for kids is pedagogical and protective, at present. In Singapore, artist Sonny Liew and Hsu Li Yang, an infectious disease expert, created comics that featured anthropomorphic characters Baffled Bunny and Curious Cat, who sought medical clarification from Doctor Duck about precautionary measures that they were being asked to take against the virus. In New York City, in an effort to increase vaccinations among young people ahead of a return to school in fall 2021, then mayor Bill de Blasio announced a new incentive: Children ages twelve and over who received their first COVID vaccine at one of three city-run sites cosponsored by SOMOS Community Care and Marvel Entertainment would receive an exclusive limited edition comic book, *Avengers: We Are Resilient*, for their trouble (Wong). More important than the collector's edition, it seems to me, is the particular choice of characters in the issue. *We Are Resilient* tells the story of the Avengers, in this case frontline health-care workers and members of a Latinx family, who unite to convey information about vaccines and to build trust of vaccines among the Black, Brown, and Latinx communities. By means of this comic book, doctors (in partnership with Marvel comics) looked to overcome mistrust and hesitancy as vaccination rates plateaued in these communities in the United States. As these initiatives suggest, collaborations among NGOs, governmental organizations, public health groups, and entertainment affiliates are especially useful at reaching all types of audiences with scientific knowledge about COVID while educating them about vaccine availability.

Comics and graphic narratives have a remarkable ability to humanize particular challenges and predicaments experienced by young people, whether it is the reality of a young man living in a displacement camp in Beirut or a small girl registering her first moments of hearing loss. All of the graphic narratives that *Growing Up Graphic: The Comics of Children in Crisis* has examined foreground experiences of personal and/or political conflict, but—importantly—focus on the young subject's complex responses to crises. As this conclusion has discussed, the primary purpose of COVID comics is to disseminate information about the virus and process the sociopolitical and emotional fallout of this time in history. Just as important is the focus that these visual texts place on stories of survival in the face of global uncertainty. This is what these comics share with many of the other graphic narratives for young readers that this project has examined. They are a testament to young readers' "need for stories about how we survive and live on in this time" (Sundmark 84). They offer important stories of hope in the face of serious adversity.

# WORKS CITED

"12 Canadian Books That Have Been Challenged." *CBC Books*, 28 February 2020, https://www.cbc.ca/books/12-canadian-books-that-have-been-challenged-1.4311368.

Abate, Michelle Ann. "'Springtime in the South is Like a Song in My Heart': Raina Telgemeier's *Drama*, the Romanticization of the Plantation South, and the Romance Plot." *Children's Literature in Education*, vol. 48, 2017, pp. 355–77.

Abate, Michelle Ann, and Gwen Athene Tarbox. Introduction. *Graphic Novels for Children and Young Adults*, edited by Abate and Tarbox, UP of Mississippi, 2017, pp. 3–16.

Abdelrazaq, Leila. *Baddawi*. Just World Books, 2015.

Acosta, Angela Moreno. "The 'Japaneseness' of OEL Manga: On Japanese American Comics Artists and Manga Style." *Drawing New Color Lines: Transnational Asian American Graphic Narratives*, edited by Chiu, Hong Kong UP, 2015, pp. 227–44.

Adams, Jeff. *Documentary Graphic Novels and Social Realism*. Peter Lang, 2008.

African Charter on the Rights and Welfare of the Child (ACRWC), 1999, http://www.achpr.org/instruments/child/.

Agamben, Giorgio. *Homo Sacer: Sovereign Power and Bare Life*. Translated by Daniel Heller-Roazen, Stanford UP, 1998.

Ahmed, Sara. "Orientations: Toward a Queer Phenomenology." *GLQ: A Journal of Lesbian and Gay Studies*, vol. 12, no. 4, 2006, pp. 543–74.

———. *Queer Phenomenology: Orientations, Objects, Others*. Duke UP, 2006.

Aldama, Frederick Luis. "Multicultural Comics Today: A Brief Introduction." *Multicultural Comics: From Zap to Blue Beetle*, edited by Aldama, U of Texas P, 2010, pp. 1–26.

———. "Putting Childhood Back into World Comics: A Foreword." *Picturing Childhood: Youth in Transnational Comics*, edited by Heimermann and Tullis, U of Texas P, 2017, pp. vii–xiii.

Alfarhan, Haya Saud. "Visual Detention: Reclaiming Human Rights through Memory in Leila Abdelrazaq's *Baddawi*." *Documenting Trauma in Comics*, edited by Davies and Rifkind, Palgrave Macmillan, 2020, pp. 153–71.

Alter, Alexandra. "How Raina Telgemeier Faces Her Fear." *New York Times*, 21 October 2019, https://www.nytimes.com/interactive/2019/10/21/books/raina-telgemeier-guts-anxiety.html.

Anker, Elizabeth. *Fictions of Dignity: Embodying Human Rights in World Literature*. Cornell UP, 2012.

Ansell, Nicola. *Children, Youth and Development*. 2nd ed., Routledge, 2017.

Arizpe, Evelyn, et al. *Visual Journeys through Wordless Narratives: An International Inquiry with Immigrant Children and* The Arrival. Bloomsbury, 2014.

Arseneault, Jesse. "On Canicide and Concern: Species Sovereignty in Western Accounts of Rwanda's Genocide." *ESC: English Studies in Canada*, vol. 39, no. 1, 2013, pp. 125–47.

Austen, Ian. "How Thousands of Indigenous Children Vanished in Canada." *New York Times*, 7 June 2021, https://www.nytimes.com/2021/06/07/world/canada/mass-graves-residential-schools.html.

Baetens, Jan, and Hugo Frey. *The Graphic Novel: An Introduction*. Cambridge UP, 2015.

Banerji, Annie. "India's 'Badass' Female Comic Superhero Fights a New Enemy—COVID-19." *National Post*, 2 December 2020, https://www.reuters.com/article/us-health-coronavirus-india-comic-trfn-idUSKBN28C1Z5.

Barker, Clare, and Stuart Murray. "Introduction: On Reading Disability in Literature." *The Cambridge Companion to Literature and Disability*, edited by Barker and Murray, Cambridge UP, 2018, pp. 1–13.

Barounis, Cynthia. "Alison Bechdel and Crip-Feminist Autobiography." *Journal of Modern Literature*, vol. 39, no. 4, 2016, pp. 139–61.

Barrie, J. M. *The Collected Peter Pan*. Oxford UP, 2019.

Batty, Nancy Ellen. "'We Are the World, We Are the Children': The Semiotics of Seduction in International Children's Relief Efforts." *Voices of the Other: Children's Literature and the Postcolonial Context*, edited by McGillis, Garland Publishing, 1999, pp. 17–38.

Beaty, Bart. "The Fighting Civil Servant: Making Sense of the Canadian Superhero." *American Review of Canadian Studies*, vol. 36, no. 3, 2006, pp. 427–39.

Beaty, Bart, and Stephen Weiner, editors. *Critical Survey of Graphic Novels, History, Theme, and Technique*. Salem Press, 2013.

Bechdel, Alison. *Fun Home: A Family Tragicomic*. Mariner Books, 2006.

Bell, Cece. *El Deafo*. Amulet Books, 2014.

Bell, John. *Invaders from the North: How Canada Conquered the Comic Book Universe*. Dundurn Group, 2006.

Bialeschki, M. Deborah, et al. "Camp Experiences and Developmental Outcomes for Youth." *Child and Adolescent Psychiatric Clinics of North America*, vol. 16, 2007, pp. 769–88.

Bigelow, Benjamin, and Rüdiger Singer. "Introduction: Migration in Twenty-First-Century Documentary Comics." *INKS: The Journal of the Comics Studies Society*, vol. 5, no. 1, 2021, pp. 1–17.

Birge, Sarah. "No Life Lessons Here: Comics, Autism, and Empathetic Scholarship." *Disability Studies Quarterly*, vol. 30, no. 1, 2010, n. pag.

Boileau, Kendra, and Rich Johnson, editors. *COVID Chronicles: A Comics Anthology*. Graphic Mundi, 2021.

Borkent, Mike. "Seeing Histories, Building Futurities: Multimodal Decolonization and Conciliation in Indigenous Comics from Canada." *Graphic Indigeneity*, edited by Aldama, UP of Mississippi, 2020, pp. 273–98.

Bradford, Clare. "Race, Ethnicity and Colonialism." *The Routledge Companion to Children's Literature*, edited by Rudd, Routledge, 2010, pp. 39–50.

———. "'To Hold Up Prisms': Australian and Canadian Indigenous Publishing for Children." *Bookbird: A Journal of International Children's Literature*, vol. 42, no. 2, 2004, pp. 30–37.

———. *Unsettling Narratives: Postcolonial Readings of Children's Literature*. Wilfrid Laurier Press, 2007.

Brown, Chester. *Louis Riel: A Comic Strip Biography*. Drawn & Quarterly, 2003.

Bruhm, Steven, and Natasha Hurley. Introduction. *Curiouser: On the Queerness of Children*, edited by Bruhm and Hurley, U of Minnesota P, 2004, pp. ix–xxxviii.

Bui, Thi. *The Best We Could Do*. Abrams ComicArts, 2018.

Bulson, Eric. "Wiping the Windshield of Your Mind." *Times Literary Supplement*, 27 April 2018.

Bumatay, Michelle, and Hannah Warman. "Illustrating *Genocidaires*, Orphans, and Child Soldiers in Central Africa." *Peace Review: A Journal of Social Justice*, vol. 24, no. 3, 2012, pp. 332–39.

Burger, Alissa. Introduction. *Teaching Graphic Novels in the English Classroom*, edited by Burger, Palgrave Macmillan, 2018, pp. 1–8.

Burroughs, John. "Camping with President Theodore Roosevelt." *The Atlantic*, May 1906, https://www.theatlantic.com/magazine/archive/1906/05/camping-with-president-theodore-roosevelt/307260.

Callender, Brian, et al. "The Art of Medicine: COVID-19, Comics, and the Visual Culture of Contagion." *The Lancet*, vol. 396, 2020, pp. 1061–63.

Camlot, Heather. "Comic Craze." *Quill & Quire*, May 2020, pp. 7–8.

"Case Study: *Drama*." *Comic Book Legal Defense Fund*, 6 May 2021, http://cbldf.org/banned-challenged-comics/case-study-drama/.

Castricum, Simona. "Public Bathrooms Are Gender Identity Battlefields. What If We Just Do It Right?" *The Guardian*, 3 October 2018, https://www.theguardian.com/commentisfree/2018/oct/03/public-bathrooms-are-gender-identity-battlefields-what-if-we-just-do-it-right.

Cavna, Michael. "George Takei Has Talked about His Family's Internment Before. But Never Quite Like This." *Washington Post*, 12 July 2019, https://www.washingtonpost.com/entertainment/books/george-takei-has-talked-about-his-familys-internment-before-but-never-quite-like-this/2019/07/11/f3320c6e-a3fd-11e9-b732-41a79c2551bf_story.html.

"Cece Bell: I Wanted to Show What It Felt Like to Be the Only Deaf Kid at My School." *The Guardian*, 27 April 2015, https://www.theguardian.com/childrens-books-site/2015/apr/27/cece-bell-el-deafo-newbery-medal-deafness-childrens-books.

Chabon, Michael. "Keynote Speech." *Comics Cube*, 26 September 2011, http://www.comicscube.com/2011/09/michael-chabon-2004-keynote-speech.html.

Chaney, Michael A. Introduction. *Graphic Subjects: Critical Essays on Autobiography and Graphic Novels*, edited by Chaney, Wisconsin UP, 2011, pp. 3–9.

Cheurfa, Hiyem. "Testifying Graphically: Bearing Witness to a Palestinian Childhood in Leila Abdelrazaq's *Baddawi*." *Auto/Biography Studies*, vol. 35, no. 2, 2020, pp. 359–82.

Chikuma-Reyns, Chris, and Gail de Vos. Introduction. *Canadian Review of Comparative Literature*, vol. 43, no. 1, 2016, pp. 5–22.

Chouliaraki, Lilie. *The Spectatorship of Suffering*. Sage Publications, 2006.

Chun, Christian. "Critical Literacies and Graphic Novels for English-Language Learners: Teaching *Maus*." *Journal of Adolescent & Adult Literacy*, vol. 53, no. 2, 2009, pp. 144–53.

Chute, Hillary. "Comics as Literature? Reading Graphic Narrative." *PMLA: Publications of the Modern Language Association of America*, vol. 123, no. 2, 2008, pp. 452–65.

———. *Disaster Drawn: Visual Witness, Comics, and Documentary Form*. Belknap Press, 2016.

———. "*Our Cancer Year*, and: *Janet and Me: An Illustrated Story of Love and Loss*, and: *Cancer Vixen: A True Story* (review)." *Literature and Medicine*, vol. 26, no. 2, 2007, pp. 413–29.

———. "The Texture of Retracing in Marjane Satrapi's *Persepolis*." *Women's Studies Quarterly*, vol. 36, nos. 1–2, 2008, pp. 92–110.

———. *Why Comics? From Underground to Everywhere*. HarperCollins, 2017.

Chute, Hillary, and Marianne DeKoven. "Comic Books and Graphic Novels." *The Cambridge Companion to Popular Fiction*, edited by Glover and McCracken, Cambridge UP, 2012, pp. 175–95.

Collins, Lauren. "Europe's Child-Refugee Crisis." *New Yorker*, 27 February 2017, http://www.newyorker.com/magazine/2017/02/27/europes-child-refugee-crisis.

Cook, Daniel Thomas, and John Wall, editors. *Children and Armed Conflict: Cross-Disciplinary Investigations*. Palgrave Macmillan, 2011.

Coulter, Natalie. "Stop Telling Girls to Smile—It Pressures Them to Accept the Unjust Status Quo." *The Conversation*, 7 March 2021, https://theconversation.com/stop-telling-girls-to-smile-it-pressures-them-to-accept-the-unjust-status-quo-156092.

Couser, G. Thomas. "Is There a Body in This Text? Embodiment in Graphic Somatography." *Auto/Biography Studies*, vol. 33, no. 2, 2018, pp. 347–73.

———. *Signifying Bodies: Disability in Contemporary Life Writing*. U of Michigan P, 2009.

———. "Signifying Selves: Disability and Life Writing." *The Cambridge Companion to Literature and Disability*, edited by Barker and Murray, Cambridge UP, 2018, pp. 199–211.

Cregan, Kate, and Denise Cuthbert. *Global Childhoods: Issues and Debates*. Sage Publications, 2014.

Cressman, Jodi. "The Embodied Witness of Graphic Pathology." *Graphic Embodiments: Perspectives on Health and Embodiment in Graphic Narratives*, edited by DeTora and Cressman, Leuven, 2021, pp. 23–30.

Cromer, Michael, and Penney Clark. "Getting Graphic with the Past: Graphic Novels and the Teaching of History." *Theory and Research in Social Education*, vol. 35, no. 4, 2007, pp. 474–91.

Czerwiec, MK. "Medical Narrative: Representing AIDS in Comics." *AMA Journal of Ethics*, vol. 20, no. 2, 2018, pp. 199–205.

———. *Taking Turns: Stories from HIV/AIDS Care Unit 371*. Penn State UP, 2017.

Czerwiec, MK, et al. *Graphic Medicine Manifesto*. Penn State UP, 2015.

"David Alexander Robertson Calls Graphic Novels the Perfect Teaching Tool." *CBC Radio*, 12 November 2015, http://www.cbc.ca/radio/unreserved/comics-graphic-novels-art-and-their-power-to-tell-stories-1.3316281/david-alexander-robertson-calls-graphic-novels-the-perfect-teaching-tool-1.3316294.

Davies, Dominic. "Crossing Borders, Bridging Boundaries: Reconstructing the Rights of the Refugee in Comics." *Refuge in a Moving World: Tracing Refugee and Migrant Journeys Across Disciplines*, edited by Fiddian-Qasmiyeh, UCL Press, 2020, pp. 177–92.

———. "Dreamlands, Border Zones, and Spaces of Exception: Comics and Graphic Narratives on the US-Mexico Border." *Auto/Biography Studies*, vol. 35, no. 2, 2020, pp. 383–403.

———. "Introduction: Documenting Trauma in Comics." *Documenting Trauma in Comics: Traumatic Pasts, Embodied Histories, and Graphic Reportage*, edited by Davies and Rifkind, Palgrave Macmillan, 2020, pp. 1–26.

Davies, Dominic, and Candida Rifkind, editors. *Documenting Trauma in Comics: Traumatic Pasts, Embodied Histories, and Graphic Reportage*. Palgrave Macmillan, 2020.

Davis, Rocío. "National and Ethnic Affiliation in Internment Autobiographies of Childhood by Jeanne Wakatsuki Houston and George Takei." *American Studies*, vol. 51, no. 3, 2006, pp. 355–68.

Dawes, James. "Human Rights, Literature, and Empathy." *The Routledge Companion to Literature and Human Rights*, edited by McClennen and Moore, Routledge, 2016, pp. 427–32.

Dean-Ruzicka, Rachel. "'What the Junk?' Defeating the Velociraptor in the Outhouse with the Lumberjanes." *Graphic Novels for Children and Young Adults*, edited by Abate and Tarbox, UP of Mississippi, 2017, pp. 218–32.

de Finney, Sandrina. "Playing Indian and Other Settler Stories: Disrupting Western Narratives of Indigenous Girlhood." *Continuum: Journal of Media & Cultural Studies*, vol. 29, no. 2, 2015, pp. 169–81.

Denson, Abby. *Tough Love: High School Confidential*. Manic D Press, 2006.

Denson, Shane, et al. "Introducing Transnational Perspectives on Graphic Narratives: Comics at the Crossroads." *Transnational Perspectives on Graphic Narratives*, edited by Denson et al., Bloomsbury, 2013, pp. 1–12.

Dickson-Gilmore, Jane, and Brandon Mitchell. *Making It Right: A Community Justice Story*. Illustrated by Tara Audibert, The Healthy Aboriginal Network, 2016.

Doughty, Terri, and Dawn Thompson. Introduction. *Knowing Their Place? Identity and Space in Children's Literature*, edited by Doughty and Thompson, Cambridge Scholars Publishing, 2011, pp. 1–5.

Dudek, Debra. "'Good Relationships Mean Good Lives': Warrior-Survivor Identity/ies in David Alexander Robertson's *7 Generations*." *Canadian Review of Comparative Literature*, vol. 43, no. 1, 2016, pp. 39–50.

Dürr, Morten. *Zenobia*. Illustrated by Lars Horneman, Seven Stories, 2018.

Edelman, Lee. *No Future: Queer Theory and the Death Drive*. Duke UP, 2004.

"Edmonton Woman Pens Graphic Novel about Aboriginal Gang Violence and Healing." *CBC News*, 28 April 2015, http://www.cbc.ca/m/touch/aboriginal/story/1.3052758.

Edwards, Dylan. *Transposes*. Foreword by Alison Bechdel, Northwest, 2012.

El Refaie, Elisabeth. "Of Men, Mice, and Monsters: Body Images in David Small's *Stitches: A Memoir*." *Journal of Graphic Novels and Comics*, vol. 3, no. 1, 2012, pp. 55–67.

———. *Visual Metaphor and Embodiment in Graphic Illness Narratives*. Oxford UP, 2019.

Episkenew, Jo-Ann. *Taking Back Our Spirits: Indigenous Literature, Public Policy, and Healing*. U of Manitoba P, 2009.

Eugene, Nicole. "Graphic Narratives: Bechdel's *Fun Home* and Forney's *Marbles*." *Mental Illness in Popular Culture*, edited by Packer, ABC-Clio, 2017, pp. 233–42.

Eveleth, Kyle. "Striking Camp: Empowerment and Re-Presentation in *Lumberjanes*." *Queer as Camp: Essays on Summer, Style, and Sexuality*, edited by Kidd and Mason, Fordham UP, 2019, pp. 188–210.

"Every G20 Nation Wants to Be Canada, Insists PM." *Reuters*, 26 September 2009, https://www.reuters.com/article/columns-us-g20-canada-advantages/every-g20-nation-wants-to-be-canada-insists-pm-idUSTRE58P05Z20090926.

Fairfield, Lesley. *Tyranny*. Tundra Books, 2009.

Fast, Elizabeth, and Delphine Collin-Vezina. "Historical Trauma, Race-based Trauma and Resilience of Indigenous Peoples: A Literature Review." *First Peoples Child & Family Review*, vol. 5, no. 1, 2010, pp. 126–36.

Fawaz, Ramzi, and Shanté Paradigm Smalls. "Queers Read This!: LGBTQ Literature Now." *GLQ: A Journal of Lesbian and Gay Studies*, vol. 24, nos. 2–3, 2018, pp. 169–87.

Foley, Pam, and Stephen Leverett. Introduction. *Children and Young People's Spaces: Developing Practice*, edited by Foley and Leverett, Palgrave Macmillan, 2011, pp. 1–8.

Forney, Ellen. *Marbles: Mania, Depression, Michelangelo, & Me*. Avery, 2012.

Galchinsky, Michael. "Framing a Rights Ethos: Artistic Media and the Dream of a Culture without Borders." *Media, Mobilization, and Human Rights: Mediating Suffering*, edited by Borer, Zed, 2012, pp. 67–95.

Gardner, Jared. "Ethics Case: How Should a Stigmatized Diagnosis Be Conveyed? How What Went Wrong Is Represented in *Swallow Me Whole*." *AMA Journal of Ethics*, vol. 20, no. 2, 2018, pp. 148–53.

Garland, Sarah. *Azzi in Between*. Frances Lincoln, 2012.

Garland-Thomson, Rosemarie. *Staring: How We Look*. Oxford UP, 2009.

Gillard, Ann, et al. "Supporting Transgender and Gender Nonconforming Youth at Summer Camp." *Journal of Parks and Recreation Administration*, vol. 32, no. 3, 2014, pp. 92–105.

Gillman, Melanie. *As the Crow Flies*. Iron Circus Comics, 2017.

Gilmore, Leigh. "Witnessing *Persepolis*: Comics, Trauma, and Childhood Testimony." *Graphic Subjects: Critical Essays on Autobiography and Graphic Novels*, edited by Chaney, U Wisconsin P, 2011, pp. 157–63.

Gilmore, Leigh, and Elizabeth Marshall. "Trauma and Young Adult Literature: Representing Adolescence and Knowledge in David Small's *Stitches: A Memoir*." *Prose Studies*, vol. 35, no. 1, 2013, pp. 16–38.

Gloeckner, Phoebe. *A Child's Life and Other Stories*. Frog Books, 2000.

Goellnicht, Donald C. "'Ethnic Literature's Hot': Asian American Literature, Refugee Cosmopolitanism, and Nam Le's *The Boat*." *Journal of Asian American Studies*, vol. 15, no. 2, 2012, pp. 197–224.

Goldberg, Elizabeth Swanson. *Beyond Terror: Gender, Narrative, Human Rights.* Rutgers UP, 2007.

Goodenough, Elizabeth, editor. *Secret Spaces of Childhood.* U of Michigan P, 2003.

Graber, Kelsey, et al. "A Rapid Review of the Impact of Quarantine and Restricted Environments on Children's Play and the Role of Play in Children's Health." *Child Care Health Development*, vol. 47, no. 2, 2021, pp. 143–53.

Gravett, Paul. *Graphic Novels: Everything You Need to Know.* Collins Design, 2005.

Groensteen, Thierry. *The System of Comics.* Translated by Bart Beaty and Nick Nguyen, UP of Mississippi, 2007.

Gubar, Marah. "The Hermeneutics of Recuperation: What a Kinship-Model Approach to Children's Agency Could Do for Children's Literature and Childhood Studies." *Jeunesse: Young People, Texts, Cultures*, vol. 8, no. 1, 2016, pp. 291–310.

Gutman, Marta, and Ning de Coninck-Smith, editors. *Designing Modern Childhoods: History, Space and the Material Culture of Children.* Rutgers UP, 2008.

"Guts." *Kirkus Reviews*, 12 May 2019, https://www.kirkusreviews.com/book-reviews/raina-telgemeier/guts-telgemeier/.

Hackett, Abigail, et al. Introduction. *Children's Spatialities: Embodiment, Emotion and Agency,* edited by Hackett et al., Palgrave Macmillan, 2015, pp. 1–17.

Halberstam, J. Jack. *In a Queer Time & Place: Transgender Bodies, Subcultural Lives.* NYU Press, 2005.

Halberstam, Judith [Jack]. *Female Masculinity.* Duke UP, 1998.

Hale, Shannon. "We thought it might help if kids had a book friend who gets what they're going through." *Twitter*, 21 April 2020, https://twitter.com/haleshannon/status/1252744661073977344?lang=en.

Hale, Shannon, and LeUyen Pham. *The Princess in Black and the Case of the Coronavirus.* Candlewick, 2020.

Hall, Justin, editor. *No Straight Lines: Four Decades of Queer Comics.* Fantagraphics, 2015.

Halperin, David. *How to Be Gay.* Belknap Press, 2012.

Halsall, Alison, and Jonathan Warren. "Global Crossings and Intersections." *The LGBTQ+ Comics Studies Reader,* edited by Halsall and Warren, UP of Mississippi, 2022, pp. 107–13.

Harris, Elizabeth A., and Alexandra Alter. "With Rising Book Bans, Librarians Have Come Under Attack." *New York Times*, 6 July 2022, https://www.nytimes.com/2022/07/06/books/book-ban-librarians.html?referringSource=articleShare.

Hatfield, Charles. *Alternative Comics: An Emerging Literature.* UP of Mississippi, 2005.

———. "Charles Hatfield's Kindercomics." *The INKS & The Comics Studies,* 3 July 2018, http://extra-inks.comicssociety.org/2018/07/03/charles-hatfields-kindercomics/.

———. "Comic Art, Children's Literature, and the New Comics Studies." *Lion and the Unicorn,* vol. 30, no. 3, 2006, pp. 360–82.

———. "Introduction: Comics & Childhood." *ImageTexT: Interdisciplinary Comics Studies,* vol. 3, no. 3, 2007, n. pag.

Hébert, Marie-Noëlle. *My Body in Pieces.* Translated by Shelley Tanaka, Groundwood Books, 2021.

Heimermann, Mark, and Brittany Tullis. "Introduction: Bridging Comics Studies and Childhood Studies." *Picturing Childhood: Youth in Transnational Comics,* edited by Heimermann and Tullis, U of Texas P, 2017, pp. 1–12.

Henzi, Sarah. "'A Necessary Antidote': Graphic Novels, Comics, and Indigenous Writing." *Canadian Review of Comparative Literature*, vol. 43, no. 1, 2016, pp. 23–38.

Hesford, Wendy. "Contingent Vulnerabilities: Child Soldiers as Human Rights Subjects." *The Routledge Companion to Literature and Human Rights*, edited by McClennen and Moore, Routledge, 2016, pp. 69–77.

———. *Violent Exceptions: Children's Human Rights & Humanitarian Rhetorics*. The Ohio State UP, 2021.

"Highlights from the Report of the Royal Commission on Aboriginal Peoples." *Indigenous and Northern Affairs Canada*, August 1991, http://www.aadnc-aandc.gc.ca/eng/1100100014597/1100100014637.

Honeyman, Susan E. "Lies We Tell Sick Children: Mutual Pretense and Uninformed Consent in Cancer Narratives." *Lion and the Unicorn*, vol. 40, no. 2, 2016, pp. 179–95.

Hong, Christine. "The World-Form of Human Rights Comics." *The Routledge Companion to Literature and Human Rights*, edited by McClennen and Moore, Routledge, 2016, pp. 193–205.

Hopkins, Peter. "Young People's Spaces." *Children and Young People's Spaces: Developing Practice*, edited by Foley and Leverett, Palgrave Macmillan, 2011, pp. 25–39.

Hopkins, Zoe. *It Takes a Village*. Illustrated by Amancay Nahuelpan, Healthy Aboriginal Network, 2012.

Howard, Yetta. "Unsuitable for Children? Adult-erated Age in Underground Graphic Narratives." *American Literature*, vol. 90, no. 2, 2018, pp. 283–313.

"How Art Reflects Children's Struggles during Pandemic." *CBC News*, 15 January 2021, https://www.cbc.ca/news/health/art-children-covid-19-1.5875082.

Hubert, and Marie Caillou. *Adrian and the Tree of Secrets*. Arsenal Pulp, 2013.

Humphreys, Jessica Dee, and Michel Chikwanine. *Child Soldier: When Boys and Girls Are Used in War*. Illustrated by Claudia Dávila, Kids Can, 2015.

"Indigenous Story Studio." https://istorystudio.com/.

Jacobs, Dale. *Graphic Encounters: Comics and the Sponsorship of Multimodal Literacy*. Bloomsbury, 2013.

Jacobs, Dale, and Jay Dolmage. "Accessible Articulations: Comics and Disability Rhetorics in *Hawkeye* #19. *INKS: The Journal of the Comics Studies Society*, vol. 2, no. 3, 2018, pp. 353–68.

———. "Difficult Articulations: Comics Autobiography, Trauma, and Disability." *The Future of Text and Image: Collected Essays on Literary and Visual Conjunctures*, edited by Amihay and Walsh, Cambridge Scholars Publishing, 2012, pp. 69–89.

Jenkins, Christine, and Michael Cart. *Representing the Rainbow in Young Adult Literature: LGBTQ+ Content since 1969*. Rowman & Littlefield, 2018.

Jones, Alexandra. "The Story of Her Life." *Michigan Daily*, 2 December 2004, https://www.michigandaily.com/content/story-her-life.

Kafer, Alison. *Feminist, Queer, Crip*. Indiana UP, 2013.

Kane, Peter-Astrid. "After Years of Progress on Gay Rights, How Did the US Become So Anti-LGBTQ+?" *Guardian*, 28 April 2022, https://www.theguardian.com/us-news/2022/apr/28/lgbtq-rights-us-dont-say-gay.

Kearns, Ciléin, and Nethmi Kearns. "The Role of Comics in Public Health Communication during the COVID-19 Pandemic." *Journal of Visual Communication in Medicine*, vol. 43, no. 3, 2020, pp. 139–49.

Keen, Suzanne. "Fast Tracks to Narrative Empathy: Anthropomorphism and Dehumanization in Graphic Narratives." *SubStance*, vol. 40, no. 1, 2011, pp. 135–55.

Kehily, Mary Jane, editor. *Understanding Childhood: A Cross-Disciplinary Approach.* Policy, 2013.

Kelley, James. "Unseen Scars: Recalling Traumatic Moments in Individuals with PTSD in *War Brothers.*" *Cultures of War in Graphic Novels: Violence, Trauma, and Memory*, edited by Prorokova and Tal, Rutgers UP, 2019, pp. 91–104.

Kersten, Sara. "'We Are Just as Confused and Lost as She Is': The Primacy of the Graphic Novel Form in Exploring Conversations around Deafness." *Children's Literature in Education*, vol. 49, no. 3, 2018, pp. 282–301.

Kersulov, Michael L., et al. "When Young Writers Draw Their Voices: Creating Hybrid Comic Memoirs with *The Absolutely True Diary of a Part-Time Indian.*" *Graphic Novels for Children and Young Adults*, edited by Abate and Tarbox, UP of Mississippi, 2017, pp. 171–88.

Kertzer, Adrienne. *My Mother's Voice: Children, Literature, and the Holocaust.* Broadview, 2002.

———. "'What Good Are the Words?': Child Memoirs and Holocaust Fiction." *Children and Armed Conflict: Cross-Disciplinary Investigations*, edited by Cook and Wall, Palgrave Macmillan, 2011, pp. 22–38.

Khaiwal, Ravindra, and Suman Mor. *Kids, Vaayu & Corona: Who Wins the Fight?* Government of India, 2020, https://countercurrents.org/2020/03/a-comic-strip-on-coronavirus-for-kids-kids-vaayu-corona-who-wins-the-fight/.

Kidd, Kenneth B. "'A' is for Auschwitz: Psychoanalysis, Trauma Theory, and the 'Children's Literature of Atrocity.'" *Children's Literature*, vol. 33, 2005, pp. 120–49.

———. *Freud in Oz: At the Intersections of Psychoanalysis and Children's Literature.* U of Minnesota P, 2011.

———. "Introduction: Lesbian/Gay Literature for Children and Young Adults." *Children's Literature Association Quarterly*, vol. 23, no. 3, 1998, pp. 114–19.

Kidd, Kenneth, and Derritt Mason. "Camping Out: An Introduction." *Queer as Camp: Essays on Summer, Style, and Sexuality*, edited by Kidd and Mason, Fordham UP, 2019, pp. 1–24.

King, Thomas. *The Inconvenient Indian.* Anchor Canada, 2013.

Kirsch, Adam. *The Global Novel: Writing the World in the 21st Century.* Columbia Global Reports, 2016.

Kleist, Reinhard. *An Olympic Dream: The Story of Samia Yusuf Omar.* SelfMadeHero, 2016.

Koch, Christina Maria. "'When You Have No Voice, You Don't Exist'?: Envisioning Disability in David Small's *Stitches.*" *Disability in Comic Books and Graphic Narratives*, edited by Foss et al., Palgrave Macmillan, 2016, pp. 29–43.

Køhlert, Frederik Byrn. *Serial Selves: Identity and Representation in Autobiographical Comics.* Rutgers UP, 2019.

Kvaran, Kara. "SuperGay: Depictions of Homosexuality in Mainstream Superhero Comics." *Comics as History, Comics as Literature*, edited by Babic, Fairleigh Dickinson, 2014, pp. 141–56.

LaBoucane-Benson, Patti. *The Outside Circle: A Graphic Novel.* Art by Kelly Mellings, Anansi, 2015.

Le, Nam. *The Boat*. Adapted by Matt Huynh, Kylie Boltin, and Matt Smith, 29 April 2015, https://www.sbs.com.au/theboat.

———. "The Boat." *The Boat*. Anchor Canada, 2008, pp. 230–72.

Leavitt, Sarah. *Tangles: A Story about Alzheimer's, My Mother and Me*. Jonathan Cape, 2011.

Lehoczky, Etelka. "Life, Love and Hockey (Oooh, And Pie) In 'Check Please!'" *NPR*, 30 September 2018, https://www.npr.org/2018/09/30/639601217/life-love-and-hockey-oooh-and-pie-in-check-please.

Levell, Nicola. *Michael Nicoll Yahgulanaas: The Seriousness of Play*. Black Dog Publishing, 2016.

Leverett, Stephen. "Children's Spaces." *Children and Young People's Spaces: Developing Practice*, edited by Foley and Leverett, Palgrave Macmillan, 2011, pp. 9–24.

Lewis, N. "Human Rights, Law and Democracy in an Unfree World." *Human Rights, Fifty Years On: A Reappraisal*, edited by Evans, Manchester UP, 1998, pp. 77–103.

"Liberia: Comic Strips Provide Preventative Information to Protect People from Virus." *IOM—UN Migration*, 8 July 2020, https://medium.com/@UNmigration/liberia-comic-strips-provide-preventative-information-to-protect-people-from-virus-8cd465812669.

Liu, Marjorie, and Sana Takeda. *Monstress*. Vol. 1, Image Comics, 2019.

MacDonald, Heidi. "How Graphic Novels Became the Hottest Section in the Library." *Publishers Weekly*, vol. 260, no. 18, 2013, pp. 20–25.

Malkki, Liisa. "Refugees and Exile: From 'Refugee Studies' to the National Order of Things." *Annual Review of Anthropology*, vol. 24, no. 1, 1995, pp. 495–523.

Mallan, Kerry. *Gender Dilemmas in Children's Fiction*. Palgrave Macmillan, 2009.

Manderson, Desmond. "From Hunger to Love: Myths of the Source, Interpretation, and Constitution of Law in Children's Literature." *Law and Literature*, vol. 15, no. 1, 2003, pp. 87–141.

Maroh, Jul. *Blue Is the Warmest Color*. Arsenal Pulp, 2013.

Marshall, Elizabeth, and Leigh Gilmore. "Girlhood in the Gutter: Feminist Graphic Knowledge and the Visualization of Sexual Precarity." *Women's Studies Quarterly*, vol. 43, nos. 1–2, 2015, pp. 95–114.

Martins, Catarina. "The Dangers of the Single Story: Child-Soldiers in Literary Fiction and Film." *Childhood*, vol. 18, no. 4, 2011, pp. 434–46.

"Marvel and AHN Team Up to Celebrate Nurses." *Marvel*, 3 December 2020, https://www.marvel.com/articles/comics/marvel-and-ahn-team-up-to-celebrate-nurses.

Mazumdar, Jhinuk. "NGO Raises Covid Awareness among Slum Kids through Comics." *Telegraph India*, 9 September 2021, https://www.telegraphindia.com/west-bengal/calcutta/covid-safety-through-comics-ngo-effort-to-raise-awareness-among-slum-kids/cid/1825281.

McLeod, Neal. "Coming Home through Stories." *(Ad)dressing Our Words: Aboriginal Perspectives on Aboriginal Literatures*, edited by Ruffo, Theytus Books, 2001, pp. 17–36.

McCloud, Scott. *Reinventing Comics*. Perennial, 2000.

———. *Understanding Comics: The Invisible Art*. HarperPerennial, 1993.

McKay, Sharon E., and Daniel Lafrance. *War Brothers, The Graphic Novel*. Annick, 2013.

"Meet Snowguard: Marvel Comics' New Inuk Teen Superhero." *CBC Books,* 25 April 2018, http://www.cbc.ca/books/meet-snowguard-marvel-comics-new-inuk-teen-superhero-1.4634479.

Mickwitz, Nina. "Comics Telling Refugee Stories." *Documenting Trauma in Comics,* edited by Davies and Rifkind, Palgrave Macmillan, 2020, pp. 277–96.

———. "Introduction: Discursive Contexts, 'Voice,' and Empathy in Graphic Life Narratives of Migration and Exile." *Auto/Biography Studies,* vol. 35, no. 2, 2020, pp. 459–65.

Mitchell, Brandon. *Lost Innocence.* Illustrated by Tara Audibert, Healthy Aboriginal Network, 2013.

Mitchell, David T., and Sharon L. Snyder. *Narrative Prosthesis: Disability and the Dependence of Discourse.* U of Michigan P, 2001.

Moore, Alan, and Melinda Gebbie. *Lost Girls.* Top Shelf, 2006.

Musinsky, Flavia. "Queer Pedagogy at Indian Brook Camp." *Queer as Camp: Essays on Summer, Style, and Sexuality,* edited by Kidd and Mason, Fordham UP, 2019, pp. 51–64.

Myers, Kimberly, and Michael Goldenberg. "Medical Education: Graphic Pathographies and the Ethical Practice of Person-Centered Medicine." *AMA Journal of Ethics,* vol. 20, no. 2, 2018, pp. 158–66.

Naghibi, Nima, et al. "Migration, Exile, and Diaspora in Graphic Life Narratives." *Auto/Biography Studies,* vol. 35, no. 2, 2020, pp. 295–304.

Nel, Philip. "Migration, Refugees, and Diaspora in Children's Literature." *Children's Literature Association Quarterly,* vol. 43, no. 4, 2018, pp. 357–62.

Nichols, L. *Flocks.* Secret Acres, 2018.

Nikolajeva, Maria, and Carole Scott. *How Picturebooks Work.* Garland Publishing, 2001.

Nodelman, Perry. *The Hidden Adult: Defining Children's Literature.* Johns Hopkins UP, 2008.

———. *Words about Pictures: The Narrative Art of Children's Picture Books.* U of Georgia P, 1988.

North, Sterling. "A National Disgrace: And a Challenge to American Parents." *Chicago Daily News,* 8 May 1940.

"The Numbers are In: 2019 CCBC Diversity Statistics." *Cooperative Children's Book Center,* 16 June 2020, https://ccbc.education.wisc.edu/the-numbers-are-in-2019-ccbc-diversity-statistics/.

Orbán, Katalin. "A Language of Scratches and Stitches: The Graphic Novel between Hyperreading and Print." *Comics and Media,* edited by Chute and Jagoda, U of Chicago P, 2014, pp. 169–81.

Orr, Rachel. "'Laura Dean Keeps Breaking Up with Me,' Written by Mariko Tamaki and Illustrated by Rosemary Valero-O'Connell, Marries Two Forms of Storytelling." *The Lily,* 15 August 2019, https://www.thelily.com/our-lily-lit-club-pick-defies-traditional-storytelling-heres-how/.

Owen, Gabrielle. "Toward a Theory of Adolescence: Queer Disruptions in Representations of Adolescent Reading." *Jeunesse: Young People, Texts, Culture,* vol. 7, no. 1, 2015, pp. 110–34.

Pagliaro, Michael. "Is a Picture Worth a Thousand Words? Determining the Criteria for Graphic Novels with Merit." *English Journal,* vol. 103, no. 4, 2014, pp. 31–45.

Parker Royal, David. "Coloring America: Multi-Ethnic Engagements with Graphic Narrative." *MELUS*, vol. 32, no. 3, 2007, pp. 7–22.

———. "Foreword; or Reading Within the Gutter." *Multicultural Comics: From Zap to Blue Beetle*, edited by Aldama, Austin UP, 2010, pp. xi–xii.

Petre, Alina. "6 Common Types of Eating Disorders (and Their Symptoms)." *Healthline*, 30 October 2019, https://www.healthline.com/nutrition/common-eating-disorders.

Phillips, Jennifer. "Revising the Rhetoric of 'Boat People' through the Interactive Graphic Adaptation of Nam Le's 'The Boat.'" *Teaching Graphic Novels in the English Classroom*, edited by Burger, Palgrave Macmillan, 2018, pp. 149–66.

Polak, Kate. *Ethics in the Gutter: Empathy and Historical Fiction in Comics*. The Ohio State UP, 2017.

Postema, Barbara. "Following the Pictures: Wordless Comics for Children." *Journal of Graphic Novels and Comics*, vol. 5, no. 3, 2014, pp. 311–22.

———. *Narrative Structure in Comics: Making Sense of Fragments*. RIT, 2013.

Powell, Nate. *Swallow Me Whole*. Top Shelf, 2008.

Prakash, Shubhra. *Priya's Mask*. Art and coloring by Syd Fini and Neda Kazemifar, 2020, https://www.dropbox.com/s/vsd8pqiprna9onu/Priyas_Mask_Comic_English.pdf?dl=0.

Prince, Liz. *Tomboy: A Graphic Memoir*. Zest Books, 2014.

Pugh, Tison. *Innocence, Heterosexuality, and the Queerness of Children's Literature*. Routledge, 2011.

Pupavac, V. "Misanthropy without Borders: The International Children's Rights Regime." *Disasters*, vol. 25, no. 2, 2001, pp. 95–112.

Regan, Paulette. *Unsettling the Settler Within: Indian Residential Schools, Truth Telling and Reconciliation in Canada*. UBC Press, 2010.

Reynolds, Kimberly. *Radical Children's Literature: Future Visions and Aesthetic Transformations in Juvenile Fiction*. Palgrave Macmillan, 2007.

Rifkind, Candida. "Migrant Detention Comics and the Aesthetic Technologies of Compassion." *Documenting Trauma in Comics*, edited by Davies and Rifkind, Palgrave Macmillan, 2020, pp. 297–316.

———. "Refugee Comics and Migrant Topographies." *Auto/Biography Studies* 32, no. 3, 2017, pp. 648–54.

———. "Spotlight on Migrant and Refugee Comics." *INKS & The Comics Society Blog*, 8 July 2018, http://extra-inks.comicssociety.org/2018/07/08/spotlight-on-migrant-and-refugee-comics/.

Rifkind, Candida, and Jessica Fontaine. "Indigeneity, Intermediality, and the Haunted Present of *Will I See?*" *Graphic Indigeneity*, edited by Aldama, UP of Mississippi, 2020, pp. 340–60.

Rifkind, Candida, and Linda Warley. "Editors' Introduction." *Canadian Graphic: Picturing Life Narratives*, edited by Rifkind and Warley, Wilfrid Laurier UP, 2016, pp. 1–19.

Riggle, Ellen D. B. "Experiences of a Gender Non-Conforming Lesbian in the 'Ladies' (Rest)room." *Journal of Lesbian Studies*, vol. 22, no. 4, 2018, pp. 482–95.

Robertson, David Alexander. *7 Generations*. Illustrated by Scott B. Henderson, HighWater, 2012.

———. *The Ballad of Nancy April, Shawnadithit*. Illustrated by Henderson, HighWater, 2014.

———. *Betty: The Helen Betty Osborne Story*. Illustrated by Henderson, HighWater, 2015.

———. *The Life of Helen Betty Osborne: A Graphic Novel*. Illustrated by Madison Blackstone, In a Bind, 2008.

———. *Sugar Falls: A Residential School Story*. Illustrated by Henderson, HighWater, 2011.

Robertson, David Alexander, et al. *Will I See?* Art by GMB Chomichuk, HighWater, 2016.

Rose, Jacqueline. *The Case of Peter Pan: The Impossibility of Children's Fiction*. U of Pennsylvania P, 1984.

Rosen, David. *Armies of the Young: Child Soldiers in War and Terrorism*. Rutgers UP, 2005.

Sabin, Roger. *Comics, Comix and Graphic Novels: A History of Comic Art*. Phaidon, 1996.

Sacco, Joe. *Palestine*. Fantagraphics, 2015.

Saguisag, Lara. *Incorrigibles and Innocents: Constructing Childhood and Citizenship in Progressive Era Comics*. Rutgers UP, 2019.

Saguisag, Lara, and Matthew B. Prickett. "Introduction: Children's Rights and Children's Literature." *Lion and the Unicorn*, vol. 40, no. 2, 2016, pp. v–xii.

Saji, Sweetha, et al. "Comics in the Time of a Pan(dem)ic: COVID-19, Graphic Medicine, and Metaphors." *Perspectives in Biology and Medicine*, vol. 64, no. 1, 2021, pp. 136–54.

Sanders, Joe Sutliff. "Chaperoning Words: Meaning-Making in Comics and Picture Books." *Children's Literature*, vol. 41, 2013, pp. 57–90.

Sanderson, Steven Keewatin. *An Invited Threat*. Healthy Aboriginal Network, 2013.

———. *Just a Story*. Healthy Aboriginal Network, 2012.

Satrapi, Marjane. *The Complete Persepolis*. Translated by Anjali Singh, Pantheon, 2004.

Sattouf, Riad. *The Arab of the Future: A Childhood in the Middle East, 1978–1984*. Vol. 1. Translated by Sam Taylor, Metropolitan Books, 2015.

Schaffer, Kay, and Sidonie Smith. *Human Rights and Narrated Lives: The Ethics of Recognition*. Palgrave Macmillan, 2004.

Scherr, Rebecca. "Shaking Hands with Other People's Pain: Joe Sacco's *Palestine*." *Mosaic: An Interdisciplinary Journal*, vol. 46, no. 1, 2013, pp. 19–36.

Schneider, Edward. "A Survey of Graphic Novel Collection and Use in American Public Libraries." *Evidence Based Library and Information Practice*, vol. 9, no. 3, 2014, pp. 68–79.

Sedgwick, Eve Kosofsky. *Tendencies*. Duke UP, 1993.

Seltzer, Mark. "Wound Culture: Trauma in the Pathological Public Sphere." *October*, vol. 80, 1997, pp. 3–26.

Sendak, Maurice. *Caldecott & Co.: Notes on Books and Pictures*. Harper & Collins, 1988.

Sharpe, Christina. *In the Wake: On Blackness and Being*. Duke UP, 2016.

Sheyahshe, Michael A. *Native Americans in Comic Books: A Critical Study*. McFarland & Company, 2008.

Simpson, Leanne Betasamosake. *As We Have Always Done: Indigenous Freedom through Radical Resistance*. U of Minnesota P, 2013.

Sium, Aman, and Eric Ritskes. "Speaking Truth to Power: Indigenous Storytelling as an Act of Living Resistance." *Decolonization: Indigeneity, Education & Society*, vol. 2, no. 1, 2013, pp. i–x.

Small, David. *Stitches: A Memoir*. McClelland & Stewart, 2009.

Smith, Katharine Capshaw. "Forum: Trauma and Children's Literature." *Children's Literature*, vol. 33, 2005, pp. 115–19.

Smith, Michael. "'The Ego Ideal of the Good Camper' and the Nature of Summer Camp." *Environmental History*, vol. 11, no. 1, 2006, pp. 70–101.

Smith, Sidonie. "Human Rights and Comics: Autobiographical Avatars, Crisis Witnessing, and Transnational Rescue Networks." *Graphic Subjects: Critical Essays on Autobiography and Graphic Novels*, edited by Chaney, U of Wisconsin P, 2011, pp. 61–72.

Smith-D'Arezzo, Wendy, and Janine Holc. "Reframing Disability through Graphic Novels for Girls: Alternative Bodies in Cece Bell's *El Deafo*." *Girlhood Studies*, vol. 9, no. 1, 2016, pp. 72–87.

Snell, Heather. "Surviving a Pandemic." *Jeunesse: Young People, Texts, Cultures*, vol. 12, no. 2, 2020, pp. 1–14.

Sontag, Susan. "Notes on Camp." *Against Interpretation*. Farrar, Strauss and Giroux, 1966.

———. *Regarding the Pain of Others*. Picador, 2003.

Spillett, Tasha. *Surviving the City*. Illustrated by Natasha Donovan, HighWater, 2018.

Squier, Susan M. "So Long as They Grow Out of It: Comics, The Discourse of Developmental Normalcy, and Disability." *Journal of Medical Humanities*, vol. 29, no. 2, 2008, pp. 71–88.

Squier, Susan Merrill, and Irmela Krüger-Fürhoff. Introduction. *PathoGraphics: Narrative, Aesthetics, Contention, Community*, edited by Squier and Krüger-Fürhoff, Pennsylvania State UP, 2020, pp. 1–6.

Stamper, Christine. "'You Are My [Camp]fire': Tradition and Structure in Maggie Thrash's Graphic Memoir *Honor Girl*." *Children's Literature in Education*, vol. 50, no. 2, 2019, pp. 110–24.

Stassen, Jean-Philippe. *Deogratias: A Tale of Rwanda*. Translated by Alexis Siegel, First Second, 2006.

Stevenson, ND, et al. *Lumberjanes: Beware the Kitten Holy*. Vol. 1, Boom! Box, 2014.

Stockton, Kathryn Bond. *The Queer Child, or Growing Sideways in the Twentieth Century*. Duke UP, 2009.

Stonebridge, Lyndsey. *Placeless People: Writing, Rights, and Refugees*. Oxford UP, 2018.

———. *Writing and Righting: Literature in the Age of Human Rights*. Oxford UP, 2021.

Sundmark, Björn. "Children's Covid-19 Literature." *Bookbird: A Journal of International Children's Literature*, vol. 58, no. 3, 2020, pp. 84–85.

Takei, George, et al. *They Called Us Enemy*. Art by Harmony Becker, Top Shelf, 2019.

Tamaki, Mariko. *Laura Dean Keeps Breaking Up with Me*. Illustrated by Rosemary Valero-O'Connell, Groundwood Books, 2019.

Tamaki, Mariko, and Jillian Tamaki. *Skim*. Groundwood Books, 2010.

Tan, Shaun. "The Accidental Graphic Novelist." *Bookbird: A Journal of International Children's Literature*, vol. 49, no. 4, 2011, pp. 1–9.

———. *The Arrival*. Arthur A. Levine Books, 2006.

Tarbox, Gwen Athene. *Children's and Young Adult Comics*. Bloomsbury, 2020.

Telgemeier, Raina. *Drama*. Graphix, 2012.

———. *Guts*. Graphix, 2019.

———. *Smile*. Graphix, 2010.

Thaller, Sarah. "Comics, Adolescents, and the Language of Mental Illness: David Heatley's 'Overpeck' and Nate Powell's *Swallow Me Whole*." *Graphic Novels for Children and Young Adults*, edited by Abate and Tarbox, U of Mississippi P, 2017, pp. 45–58.

Thrash, Maggie. *Honor Girl: A Graphic Memoir*. Candlewick, 2015.

Thurber, Christopher, et al. "Youth Development Outcomes of the Camp Experience: Evidence for Multidimensional Growth." *Journal of Youth Adolescence*, vol. 36, no. 3, 2007, pp. 241–54.

Tilley, Carol L. "Seducing the Innocent: Fredric Wertham and the Falsifications That Helped Condemn Comics." *Information & Culture: A Journal of History*, vol. 47, no. 4, 2012, pp. 383–413.

Todres, Jonathan, and Sarah Higinbotham. *Human Rights in Children's Literature: Imagination and the Narrative of Law*. Oxford UP, 2016.

Tribunella, Eric. "Literature for Us 'Older Children': *Lost Girls*, Seduction Fantasies, and the Reeducation of Adults." *Journal of Popular Culture*, vol. 45, no. 3, 2012, pp. 628–48.

Trites, Roberta Seelinger. *Disturbing the Universe: Power and Repression in Adolescent Literature*. U of Iowa P, 2000.

———. "Queer Discourse and the Young Adult Novel: Repression and Power in Gay Male Adolescent Literature." *Children's Literature Association Quarterly*, vol. 23, no. 3, 1998, pp. 143–51.

———. *Twenty-First-Century Feminisms in Children's and Adolescent Literature*. UP of Mississippi, 2018.

"Truth, Dialogue & Storytelling: Patti LaBoucane-Benson on Art and Healing." *CBC Radio*, 23 October 2016, http://www.cbc.ca/radio/checkup/blog/truth-dialogue-storytelling-patti-laboucane-benson-on-art-and-healing-1.3816664.

"Truth and Reconciliation Commission of Canada: Interim Report." *TRC Website*, 2012, http://www.trc.ca/websites/trcinstitution/index.php?p=580.

"Truth and Reconciliation Commission Report Executive Summary." *TRC Report Online*, https://nevillepark.github.io/trc/#:~:text=The%20TRC%20report%20is%20a,%2C%20M%C3%A9tis%2C%20and%20Inuit%20people.

Tuck, Eve, and K. Wayne Yang. "Decolonization Is Not a Metaphor." *Decolonization: Indigeneity, Education & Society*, vol. 1, no. 1, 2012, pp. 1–40.

Ukazu, Ngozi. *Check Please! Book 1: #Hockey*. First Second, 2018.

United Nations. "Children and Armed Conflict," 2019, https://www.un.org/ga/search/view_doc.asp?symbol=S/2019/509&Lang=E&Area=UNDOC.

United Nations Convention on the Rights of the Child (UNCRC), 1989, http://www2.ohchr.org/english/law/crc.htm.

United Nations High Commissioner for Refugees (UNHCR), 2021, https://www.unhcr.org/figures-at-a-glance.html.

Usdin, Carly, et al. *The Avant-Guards*. Vols. 1 and 2, Boom! Box, 2019.

Van Camp, Richard. *A Blanket of Butterflies*. Illustrated by Scott Henderson, HighWater, 2015.

Velentzas, Irene. "Seeing the Sensation: Sketch-Journaling and the Embodiment of Mental Illness in Autographics." *Image TexT: Interdisciplinary Comics Studies*, vol. 9, no. 2, 2017, n. pag.

Venkatesan, Sathyaraj, and Anu Mary Peter. "Feminine Famishment: Graphic Medicine and Anorexia Nervosa." *Health*, vol. 24, no. 5, 2020, pp. 518–34.

———. "'I Want to Live, I Want to Draw': The Poetics of Drawing and Graphic Medicine." *Journal of Creative Communications*, vol. 13, no. 2, 2018, pp. 104–16.

Venkatesan, Sathyaraj, and Sweetha Saji. "Drawing the Mind: Aesthetics of Representing Mental Illness in Select Graphic Memoirs." *Health*, vol. 25, no. 1, 2021, pp. 37–50.

Vermette, Katherena. *A Girl Called Echo: Northwest Resistance*. Vol. 1, Illustrated by Scott B. Henderson, HighWater, 2017.

Vest Ettekal, Andrea, and Jennifer P. Agans. "Positive Youth Development through Leisure: Confronting the COVID-19 Pandemic." *Journal of Youth Development*, vol. 15, no. 2, 2020, pp. 1–20.

Vowel, Chelsea. *Indigenous Writes: A Guide to First Nations, Métis & Inuit Issues in Canada*. HighWater, 2016.

Wall, John. *Ethics in Light of Childhood*. Georgetown UP, 2010.

Wall, John, and Daniel Thomas Cook. "Conclusion: Crossing Disciplines." *Children and Armed Conflict*, edited by Wall and Cook, Palgrave Macmillan, 2011, pp. 209–11.

Walters, Shannon. "Graphic Disruptions: Comics, Disability and De-Canonizing Composition." *Composition Studies*, vol. 43, no. 1, 2015, pp. 174–77.

Wegner, Gesine. "Reflections on the Boom of Graphic Pathography: The Effects and Affects of Narrating Disability and Illness in Comics." *Journal of Literary & Cultural Disability Studies*, vol. 14, no. 1, 2020, pp. 57–74.

Whalen, Zach, et al. "Introduction: From Feats of Clay to Narrative Prose/thesis." *Disability in Comic Books and Graphic Narratives*, edited by Foss et al., Palgrave Macmillan, 2016, pp. 1–13.

Whitlock, Gillian. "Autographics: The Seeing 'I' of the Comics." *MFS: Modern Fiction Studies*, vol. 52, no. 4, 2006, pp. 965–79.

———. "Implicated Subjects." *Auto/Biography Studies*, vol. 35, no. 2, 2020, pp. 495–501.

"Why Comic-Style Information Is Better at Preparing Patients for Cardiac Catheterization." *EurekAlert!*, 16 April 2019, https://www.eurekalert.org/pub_releases/2019-04/c-ub-wci041619.php.

Williams, Athol. *Oaky and the Virus*. Illustrated by Taryn Lock, Theart Press, 2020.

Williams, Paul, and James Lyons. *The Rise of the American Comics Artist: Creators and Contexts*. UP of Mississippi, 2010.

Williams, Richard, and John Drury. "Personal and Collective Psychosocial Resilience: Implications for Children, Young People and Their Families Involved in War and Disasters." *Children and Armed Conflict*, edited by Cook and Wall, Palgrave Macmillan, 2011, pp. 57–75.

Winick, Judd. *Pedro & Me: Friendship, Loss, & What I Learned*. Square Fish, 2000.

Winner, Cherie. "Comics Aren't Just for Kids Anymore." *Penn State News*, 25 February 2021, https://news.psu.edu/story/632386/2021/02/16/research/comics-arent-just-kids-anymore.

Winter, Jessica. "What Should a Queer Children's Book Do?" *New Yorker*, 11 July 2022, https://www.newyorker.com/news/annals-of-education/lgbt-books-kids-ban.

Wochowski, Lana. Foreword. *No Straight Lines: Four Decades of Queer Comics*, edited by Hall, Fantagraphics, 2013, n. pag.

Wolf, Doris. "Confronting the Legacy of Canada's Indian Residential Schools: Cree Cultural Memory and the Warrior Spirit in David Alexander Robertson and Scott B.

Henderson's *7 Generations* Series." *Canadian Literature and Cultural Memory*, edited by Sugars and Ty, Oxford UP, 2014, pp. 337–53.

———. "The Seductions of Good and Evil: Competing Cultural Memories in Steven Keewatin Sanderson's Superhero Comics for Aboriginal Youth." *Children and Cultural Memory in Texts of Childhood*, edited by Snell and Hutchison, Routledge, 2014, pp. 179–96.

———. "Unsettling and Restorying Canadian Indigenous-Settler Histories in David Alexander Robertson's *The Life of Helen Betty Osborne* and *Sugar Falls*." *Canadian Graphic*, edited by Rifkind and Warley, Wilfrid Laurier UP, 2016, pp. 207–34.

Wolf, Doris, and Paul DePasquale. "Home and Native Land: A Study of Canadian Aboriginal Picture Books by Aboriginal Authors." *Home Words: Discourses of Children's Literature in Canada*, edited by Reimer, Wilfrid Laurier UP, 2008, pp. 87–106.

Wolk, Douglas. *Reading Comics: How Graphic Novels Work and What They Mean*. Da Cap, 2007.

Wong, Ashley. "Limited-Edition Comic Books for Children Getting Vaccinated." *New York Times*, 26 August 2021, https://www.nytimes.com/2021/08/26/nyregion/new-york-city-covid-19.html.

Woodhouse, Barbara Bennett. *Hidden in Plain Sight: The Tragedy of Children's Rights from Ben Franklin to Lionel Tate*. Princeton UP, 2008.

Woollcott, Tory. *Mirror Mind: Growing Up Dyslexic*. International Dyslexia Association, 2009.

World Health Organization. "Mental Health of Adolescents," 17 November 2021, https://www.who.int/news-room/fact-sheets/detail/adolescent-mental-health.

World Health Organization. "Preamble to the Constitution of the World Health Organization," 1946.

Yahgulanaas, Michael Nicoll. "Notes on Haida Manga." *Geist: Ideas and Culture, Made in Canada*, vol. 70, 2008, pp. 54–56.

———. *Red: A Haida Manga*. Douglas & McIntyre, 2009.

Young-Ing, Greg. "Aboriginal Text in Context." *(Ad)dressing Our Words: Aboriginal Perspectives on Aboriginal Literatures*, edited by Ruffo, Theytus Books, 2001, pp. 233–42.

# INDEX

Abate, Michelle Ann, 2, 14–15, 151
Abdelrazaq, Leila, 22, 75 fig. 2.3, 76–77, 78 fig. 2.4, 79 fig. 2.5, 80–81, 140. See also *Baddawi*
Acholi tribe. See *War Brothers, The Graphic Novel*
Acknowledging, 105–9, 118–19
active/activist reading, 8, 30–36, 43, 99, 191
activism, 4, 9, 29, 43, 134, 138, 164, 212
*Adrian and the Tree of Secrets* (Hubert and Caillou), 5, 128, 129, 141–43, 142 fig. 4.1
African Charter on the Rights and Welfare of the Child (ACRWC), 6
Agamben, Giorgio, 73
agency: overview, 6–7, 9–10, 13, 29–30, 55, 131, 135, 140, 147, 156, 170, 188; in *Baddawi*, 77; in *Child Soldier*, 30; in events that shape, 7, 127, 129, 135, 146, 195, 202; fantasies of, 215; as model, 32–33, 43; vs. powerlessness, 75, 169, 189, 208; in *7 Generations*, 117; in *Stitches*, 188–89, 190–91

Ahmed, Sara, 128, 138
al-Ali, Naji, 76
Al-Assad, Hafez, 77, 78 fig. 2.4
alienation, 65, 94, 169, 177, 204
Aliyak, Amka, 87n3
Allegheny Health Network, 216
Allen, Gus. See *Lumberjanes*
Al-Naksa, 79
*Alpha Flight*, 87n3, 125
Alzheimer's disease, 169, 171
ambiguity, 50, 52, 54
*American Born Chinese* (Yang), 15
American Civil War, 36n4
American Individuals with Disabilities Education Act, 186
American Revolution, 36n4
Amerimanga, 2
Amka Aliyak, 87n3
anime, 2–3
*Annie on My Mind* (Garden), 133
Ansell, Nicola, 1, 5, 35–37, 42, 58–59, 174, 194, 208

239

anticomics crusade, 16–17
anxiety: and child soldiers, 44; and children, overview, 26; and COVID, 211, 213, 218; and health, 170, 173, 177–80, 179 fig. 5.1; and representation, 57; and sexuality, 142, 148, 152, 161; and statelessness, 74, 78, 83
appropriation, 86n2, 87, 94, 155, 162
*Arab of the Future, The* (Sattouf), 31–32
Arendt, Hannah, 72–73
*Arrival, The* (Tan), 56, 58–59, 63–69, 66 fig. 2.2
artwork, 28, 50, 56, 173, 202–8
*As the Crow Flies* (Gillman), 128, 129, 155, 161–63
assimilation, 22, 90, 94, 105–6, 108–9, 116–18, 133, 144
asylum seekers. *See* migrant literature
Australia, 56, 64, 67–70, 213
autobiography, 5, 28, 87, 92
autonomy, 7, 31, 76–77, 170. *See also* agency
*Avant-Guards, The* (Usdin, Hayes, and Nalty), 128, 147, 153–54, 154 fig. 4.4
awards, 1, 15, 50, 68, 108, 130, 152, 158, 161, 183, 190, 217
*Azzi in Between* (Garland), 56, 59

*Backstagers, The* (Tynion and Sygh), 147–48
*Baddawi* (Abdelrazaq), 58, 75 fig. 2.3, 75–80, 78–79 figs. 2.4–2.5, 140
Baden-Powell, Robert Stephenson Smyth, 164
Baetens, Jan, 4–5, 28
*Ballad of Nancy April, The* (Robertson), 97–99, 98 fig. 3.2
Barrie, J. M., 132–33
basketball, 153–54, 154 fig. 4.4
bathrooms, 137–38
Beaty, Bart, 87n3
*Beautiful* (D'Abreo), 170, 206
Bechdel, Alison, 5, 125, 134, 196. *See also Fun Home*
*Beguiling, The*, 14
Bell, Cece, 180, 183–88, 184–85 figs. 5.2–5.3. *See also El Deafo*
Bell, John, 85–86

Bennett, Carolyn, 124
*Best We Could Do, The* (Bui), 64
*Binky Brown Meets the Holy Virgin Mary* (Green), 196
biomedical model, 174, 178, 189, 193, 194, 195, 198, 206
BIPOC people, 210, 220
bipolar disorder. *See Marbles*
*Blanket of Butterflies, A* (Van Camp), 96
*Blue Is the Warmest Color* (Maroh), 24, 135
*Bluish* (Hamilton), 191
Blume, Judy, 130
"Boat, The" (Huynh), 6, 58, 67–72
"Boat, The" (Le), 67–72
*Boat, The* (Le), 67
"boat people," 67
bodily "dys-appearance," 206
body image, 204–7
Boltin, Kylie. *See* "Boat, The" (Huynh)
*Bone* (Smith), 1
book bans, 24. *See also* censorship
book overview, 3–4, 5–6, 10–11, 12–13, 19, 212. *See also* chapter overviews
Boy Scouts, 163–64
Brazeau, Patrick, 87n3
Brown, Chester, 90n5
Bruhm, Steven, 132
Bui, Thi, 64
Bulson, Eric, 27
Byrne, John, 87n3

Caillou, Marie. *See Adrian and the Tree of Secrets*
*Cambridge Companion to Literature and Disability, The* (Barker and Murrary), 191
Camp Fire Girls, 164
*Camp Spirit* (Lenoir), 155
*Canadian Graphic* (Rifkind and Warley), 87–88
Canadian superheroes, 85–86, 87n3
cancer, 188–89
*Cancer Vixen* (Marchetto), 169, 171
Canuk, Johnny, 87n3
capitalism, 10, 121–22, 210
*Captain Canuck*, 87n3

INDEX • 241

Captain Zaz (*An Invited Threat*), 121, 122, 123 fig. 3.8, 124
Cart, Michael, 133
*Cartoons for Children's Rights* (UNICEF series), 8–9
*Case of Peter Pan, The* (Rose), 18
Catholicism, 107, 141–42
censorship, 16–17, 24, 126, 130–31
Chabon, Michael, 1, 25
chapter overviews, 21–25
*Check Please!* (Ngozi), 128, 147, 151–53
Chikwanine, Michel, 38–43, 40–41 figs. 1.1–1.2. See also *Child Soldier*
*Child Soldier* (Chikwanine and Humphreys), 5, 30, 38–43, 40–41 fig. 1.1–1.2, 54–55
child soldiers, 4, 30, 34–35, 36–39, 42–44, 47–49, 54–55, 60, 216. See also *Child Soldier; Deogratias, A Tale of Rwanda; War Brothers, The Graphic Novel*
child victim trope, 35n3. See also victimhood
childhood: and body image, 204, 207; in crisis, 11, 17; Global North perspectives on, 6, 37; innocence of, 5–6, 17–19, 33, 37, 42, 127, 130–31, 132–33, 156; medicine, 24, 190; protection of, 130; queer, 134, 138; Sendak's view of, 18–19; sexuality, 23–24, 131–32, 133; signaling catastrophe, 11–12; and war, 22, 32, 37, 59, 72, 80, 83 (*see also* child soldiers); as Western concept, 34–35, 36–37, 44, 59, 127, 194
children: comics abandoning, 1, 25–26, 174; and COVID lockdown, 210–11, 215, 218–20; exploitation of, 13, 23, 32, 58, 124 (*see also* child soldiers); growing sideways, 135–36; and health, 16, 121, 124, 174, 178, 186, 190–91, 192–94, 212; as political, 4–6, 13, 208, 219; and rights, 6, 8–9, 13, 25, 31, 136, 208, 212, 219; and sexuality, 24, 129–35; and trauma, 8, 18–20, 22, 25, 29, 31, 33–35, 35n3, 36–49, 58–72, 80, 81n3, 100, 105–7; and vaccines, 212; and war, 32, 36–49, 58–72, 77–80
"Children and Armed Conflict" (UN report), 32
*Children's and Young Adult Comics* (Tarbox), 21

children's literature: and the child, 18–21, 35; and comics, 1, 11, 19–21, 24; and diversity, 31, 33–35, 167, 186, 190, 194; industry, 1, 3–5, 9n4, 11, 13–14, 24, 35; and sexuality, 132–33; and trauma, 24–26, 33
*Child's Life and Other Stories, A* (Gloeckner), 130
Chinese Exclusion Act, 81n3
Chrétien, Jean, 106n8
Christianity, 107, 141–42, 162, 163
Chute, Hillary, 28, 31, 33, 57, 88, 125, 127, 171, 192, 196, 203
citizenship, 21, 72, 84, 124
Civil War, 151
Coalition against Trafficking in Women, 8
colonialism, 87, 90, 93–95, 96, 106, 108, 117
Comic Book Legal Defense Fund (CBLDF), 17n9
Comics Code Authority, 16, 125
comics/graphic narratives: and awards, 15; and Canada, 85–89, 90–93; and gender violence, 93, 100–105; as genre for young readers, 4–8, 10–11, 13–21, 25–26, 28–36, 57–58, 90–93, 109–10, 118–21, 127–34, 136, 138–41, 147–48, 153–57, 172–75, 191, 190–97, 202–8, 212, 215–19; global comics, 27–30, 31–36, 56–61, 63–65, 66 fig. 2.2, 67–72, 73–84, 219–20; graphic narrative terminology, 3n3, 88; industry overview, 1–11, 13–21, 89–90; and libraries, 14–15; negative press around, 15–17; presses, 4, 95–96, 119; and propaganda, 9; and regulation, 16–17, 125–26, 129–32. *See also* child soldiers; crisis comics overview; disabilities; graphic pathographies; health/health care; Indigenous peoples; LGBTQ+; migrant literature; Telgemeier, Raina; trauma
Comics Magazine Association of America (CMAA), 16
coming out, 129, 133, 141
commodification, 9n4, 11
Common Core State Standards Initiative, 14
compulsive behaviors, 195–99

concentration camps, 18, 73, 80–81, 158
*Contract with God, and Other Tenement Stories, A* (Eisner), 3n3
Convention on the Rights of Persons with Disabilities, 186
coronavirus (COVID-19), 209–20
*COVID Chronicles* (Penn State), 214–15
COVID comics, 212–20
crisis: "crisis temporality," 37–38, 43, 49; definition of, 11–12, 17, 22, 34, 92, 135, 173, 176, 209; refugee, 57, 61, 67, 71–72; of sexuality, 129, 135, 143, 145, 156, 164, 209–12, 216. *See also* crisis comics overview; COVID comics
crisis comics overview, 8–10, 12–13
Cruikshank, George, 191–92
culture of invisibility. *See* invisibility
Cuthbert, Denise, 31, 124
Czerwiec, MK, 24, 170, 172

D'Abreo, Marie. *See Beautiful*
Dallaire, Roméo, 38n5
Dark Horse Comics, 2–3
Dávila, Claudia, 39–41. See also *Child Soldier*
Davison, Al, 169
DC Comics, 2, 87, 125–26
de Blasio, Bill, 220
de Finney, Sandrina, 86n2
deafness. See *El Deafo*
decolonization, 92, 93
dehumanization, 65, 68, 71
Democratic Republic of Congo (DRC). See *Child Soldier*
Denson, Abby. See *Tough Love*
dental issues, 175–77
*Deogratias, A Tale of Rwanda* (Stassen), 5, 30, 49–55, 51 fig. 1.6
desensitization, 53, 173–74
detention facilities, 80–81. *See also* internment camps
diabetes, 121–23
*Diagnostic and Statistical Manual of Mental Disorders* (*DSM*), 195
diagrammatic representations, 171
Diamond Kids, 2, 14
*Diary of a Wimpy Kid, The* (Kinney), 1

difference, 168–69
digital divide, 211
Dingle, Adrian, 85–86
disabilities, 174, 185–86, 191–94, 210. See also *El Deafo*; *Mirror Mind*; *Stitches*
*Disaster Drawn* (Chute), 1, 13, 31, 33, 57, 127
disaster narratives, 9n4
disease, 8, 24, 100, 106, 134, 169–75, 177, 191, 205, 207, 209, 215, 218–20
disorientation, 138–39
Displaced Persons Branch, 73
displacement, 32, 56–57, 58, 59, 60 fig. 2.1, 61, 63–64, 66, 70, 72–73, 75, 80, 83, 127, 158, 220. See also *Azzi in Between*; *Baddawi*; *They Called Us Enemy*; *Zenobia*
diversity, 14, 29, 31, 45, 46–47, 95, 151, 165, 172, 186
drag kings, 159
Drag Queen Story Hour, 129n4
*Drama* (Telgemeier), 5, 15, 24, 128, 130, 147–48, 149 fig. 4.3, 150–51
drawing, 8, 202–8
Dürr, Morten, 5, 22, 57, 61–63. See also *Zenobia*
*Dykes to Watch Out For* (Bechdel), 125
"dys-appearance," 206
dyslexia. See *Mirror Mind*

eating disorders, 203–8
Edelman, Lee, 132
education, 6, 13, 56, 80, 106–7, 128–29, 139–41, 143, 157, 164, 181, 186, 211; comics and Indigeneity and, 85, 89, 92–95, 97, 109–10, 118, 121, 124; comics in, 13–14, 25, 32, 64, 100
Edward Stratemeyer Syndicate, 163
Edwards, Dylan, 5
Eisner, Will, 3n3
Eisner Awards, 15
*El Deafo* (Bell), 6, 173, 180, 183–88, 184–85 figs. 5.2–5.3, 191
El Refaie, Elisabeth, 173, 205–6
Ellis, Grace. See *Lumberjanes*
emancipation, 192, 193
emoticons, 172

empathy, 8–10, 35, 52, 54, 61, 66–68, 71, 154, 174, 177, 182, 195, 198, 216–17
empowerment, 35–36, 39, 43, 49, 121, 128–29, 147, 161–63, 189, 205
Episkenew, Jo-Ann, 109–10
escapism, 28–30
essentialism, 86–87, 88, 165
ethical engagement, 30–36
ethics of representation, 9, 57
Eurocentrism, 22, 94. *See also* Global North perspectives/Western lens
Eveleth, Kyle, 157–58
exploitation, 9, 32–33, 42, 58, 100, 122, 214. *See also* child soldiers

Fairfield, Lesley. See *Tyranny*
family values, 132
fantasy, 1, 5, 29, 88, 96, 102, 132, 142–43, 168, 197, 202, 215
Fawaz, Ramzi, 166–67
*Feminist, Queer, Crip* (Kafer), 138n7
*Firedancers* (Waboose), 92–93
First Second Books, 2, 14–15
*Flocks* (Nichols), 136
Florida, 129n4
*Flour Sack Flora* (Delaronde), 92–93
Forney, Ellen, 195–96
Frey, Hugo, 4–5, 28
*Fun Home* (Bechdel), 134, 173, 195–97, 202

gangs, 90, 139
Gardner, Jared, 199
Garland, Sarah. See *Azzi in Between*
Garland-Thomson, Rosemarie, 174, 193
gay assimilation, 133
Gebbie, Melinda, 131
gender, 89, 97, 100–104, 126–29, 131–41, 144, 150–60, 162–67, 186, 194, 205, 210. *See also* LGBTQ+; transgender
genocide, 22, 32, 34, 37, 49–54, 73, 105, 109. *See also* *Deogratias, A Tale of Rwanda*
Genocide Convention, 74
Gillman, Melanie. See *As the Crow Flies*
Gilmore, Leigh, 130, 190
*Girl Called Echo, A* (Vermette), 89, 94

Girl Scouts, 164
Global North perspectives/Western lens, 9, 22, 37, 40–41, 50, 94
Global South, 35n3, 37
globalization, 27–28
Gloeckner, Phoebe, 130
graphic medical comics. *See* graphic pathographies
*Graphic Medicine* (Czerwiec, Williams, and Squier), 172
Graphic Medicine movement, 24
graphic narratives. *See* comics/graphic narratives
graphic narratives, defined, 3n3, 88
graphic novels, defined, 3n3
*Graphic Novels for Children and Young Adults* (Abate and Tarbox), 2
graphic pathographies, 170–74, 175–77, 182, 195, 203. *See also Beautiful*; *El Deafo*; *Fun Home*; *Marbles*; *Mirror Mind*; *My Body in Pieces*; *Swallow Me Whole*; Telgemeier, Raina
graves, 23, 50, 105
Green, Justin, 196
Green, Katie. See *Lighter Than My Shadow*
Groensteen, Thierry, 44–45, 187
growing sideways, 135–36, 138
growing up, 135, 168
Gubar, Marah, 12–13
guilt, 49, 52, 114, 117
Gunn, Frederick William, 157
*Guts* (Telgemeier), 24, 173, 177–80, 179 fig. 51, 180

Haggard, H. Rider, 86
Haida Nation. See *Red: A Haida Manga*
Halberstam, J. Jack, 137, 156
Hale, Shannon, 217–18
Hall, Justin, 126
Hall, Lynn, 133
Halperin, David, 155–56, 159
Handala, 76–77
H&M, 86n2
Hansen, Justin Larocca, 215–16
*Harold and the Purple Crayon* (Johnson), 36
Harper, Stephen, 107–8

Hatfield, Charles, 3, 16, 19, 21, 30, 173
Hayes, Noah. See *Avant-Guards, The*
healing, 42, 49, 90, 92, 94, 105, 109–10, 118, 188, 207, 217
health: comics in, 13–14, 25, 32, 64, 100; general, 13, 16, 100, 105, 108, 110, 119–20, 139, 168, 174–78, 186, 188, 194–95, 202, 211, 214, 218; and illness, 24, 119–23, 139, 169–75, 178, 180, 198, 201, 208–10, 213, 218; and World Health Organization, 8
health/health care: and acts of creation, 202–8; biomedical model of, 174, 178, 189, 193, 194, 195, 198, 206; and control over body, 180, 188; defining health, 174–75; and disabilities (see disabilities); and dishonesty, 191 (see also *Stitches*); and history of graphic narratives, 169; mental health, 139n8, 177–80, 179 fig. 5.1, 195–202; and mind/body connection, 178; overview, 169–70; pathographies (see graphic pathographies); and political/relational model of disability, 194; and validating crises, 173, 177
Hébert, Marie-Noëlle, 170, 204–5
Heimermann, Mark, 21, 27, 219
Henderson, Scott B., 96–98, 111, 114, 117
Henzi, Sarah, 99, 109
Hesford, Wendy, 30, 35n3, 37, 61, 81n3
heteronormativity, 132–33, 139–41, 148, 150, 159. See also school
HighWater Press, 4, 95–96
Higinbotham, Sarah, 25, 36
Hilhorst, Dorothea, 60–61
HIV/AIDS care, 172
*HIV/AIDS: Stand Up for Human Rights* (UNHCR), 8
*HIV and AIDS: Human Rights for Everyone* (UNHCR), 8
hockey, 151–53
Holocaust, 18, 33, 34
home: as country, 12, 43, 56–57, 62–65, 68–69, 74, 76, 80, 106; and family, 117, 143–44, 152, 159, 164, 183, 200; as physical location, 53, 77, 80, 98, 102–3, 117, 128, 136, 138–39, 143–44, 155, 198, 203, 209–11, 215
homelessness, 17, 58, 93, 100, 106
homophobia, 125, 125n1, 129n4, 134, 141, 142–43, 161
homosexual visibility, 133

Honeyman, Susan, 190, 208
*Honor Girl* (Thrash), 6, 128, 155, 158–61, 160 fig. 4.5
hope: for comics, 28, 34, 44, 50, 54, 59, 62, 64, 71, 111, 215; for humanity, 10, 39, 44, 50, 60, 71, 89, 93, 118, 215, 220
Hopkins, Peter, 139
Hopkins, Zoe, 120
Horneman, Lars, 5, 22, 57, 61–63. See also *Zenobia*
hospitals, 69, 110–11, 117, 135, 169–70, 183, 189, 191
*How to Be Gay* (Halperin), 155–56
Hubert. See *Adrian and the Tree of Secrets*
human rights, 6, 8–10, 23, 25, 35, 39, 58–59, 72, 73–75, 186, 208, 212. See also United Nations Convention on the Rights of the Child
human traffickers, 58. See also people smugglers
humanization, 61, 67–68, 72, 74
Humphreys, Jessica Dee, 38, 39–40, 42. See also *Child Soldier*
Hurley, Natasha, 132
Hutus. See *Deogratias, A Tale of Rwanda*
Huynh, Matt. See "Boat, The" (Huynh)

identification, 5, 7, 9–10, 54, 119
identity: and ancestry, 110, 117–20; categories, 7, 22–23, 65, 67, 144–48, 152–53, 158–59, 169, 186–87, 194, 207, 210, 212; and power, 65, 67, 81, 99–100; and sexuality, 5, 127, 129, 131–40, 156, 161–63
"If I Was" (Hansen), 215–16
*I'll Get There* (Donovan), 133
immigrant, as term, 61
immigrants. See migrant literature
immorality, 16, 17
impairment vs. disability, 193–94
"In the Dumps" (Sendak and Spiegelman), 19–20 figs. 0.1–0.2
inclusivity, 156–57
Indian Removal Act, 81n3
Indian Residential School (IRS), 90, 105–9, 114
Indigenous Peoples: and Acknowledging, 105–9, 118, 119; apologies to, 107–8; and appropriation, 86n2, 94; and assimilation, 90, 94, 106, 116–17

(*see also* Indian Residential School); and Canadian publishing industry, 94–95; defined, 88; discourses and conquest, 93; and education, 85, 118–19; and essentialism, 86–87; healing, 90, 109–10; and importance of storytelling, 92; and increase in children's books, 92; and Indian Removal Act, 81n3; Inuit, 85, 86, 87n3; in *Justice League United*, 87n3; and "lost" generations, 105; Métis people, 90n5, 95; Nelvana of the Northern Lights, 85–86; and pop culture currency, 86n2; preserving languages of, 95; and reframing history, 96–105; and Relating, 119–24; and relocations, 105–7 (*see also* Indian Residential School); reserves, 119, 121–22; and Restoring, 119–24; sexualization of, 86; and "sixties scoop," 90; sovereignty, 92, 124; and storytelling, 93–94; and Touchstones of Hope, 89; and Truth Telling, 93–94, 108; women and double dispossession, 92–93. See also *Invited Threat, An*; *Outside Circle, The*; *Red: A Haida Manga*; *7 Generations*; *Tales from Big Spirit*; *Will I See?*

Indigenous Story Studio (ISS), 4, 23, 95, 119–24, 123 fig. 3.8

*Indigenous Writes* (Vowel), 85, 105–7, 109–10, 118

innocence, 4, 5, 6, 16–19, 22, 30, 33, 35, 37, 42, 54, 127, 130–33, 140, 156, 190

Innuksuk, Nyla, 87n3

International Criminal Court, 44n6

internet, 14, 36, 56, 211

internment camps, 73, 74, 80–81. See also *They Called Us Enemy*

intersectionality, 133, 151, 194

Inuit, 85, 86, 87n3

invisibility, 31, 33, 57, 127, 174, 189–90

*Invited Threat, An* (Sanderson), 121–24, 123 fig. 3.8

Iran, 7, 28n2

isolation, 133, 139n8, 182, 186. See also lockdowns

Israel, 76–77

*It Takes a Village* (Hopkins), 120

Jamieson, Victoria, 136
Japan, 2, 83, 89, 96, 213

Japanese anime, 2–3
Japanese internment camps, 73, 74, 80–81. See also *They Called Us Enemy*
Japanese manga, 2–3, 89
Johnny Canuck, 87n3
Johnston, Franz, 85
*Just a Story* (Sanderson), 120

Kafer, Alison, 138n7, 194
Kertzer, Adrienne, 34
Kidd, Kenneth, 24, 33, 34, 129, 156–57
*Kids, Vaayu & Corona* (Government of India), 218
Kids Can Press, 38
King, Thomas, 107–8
Kinney, Jeff, 1
*Kira-Kira* (Kadohata), 191
Kirsch, Adam, 27
*Kiss Me Deadly* (Van Camp), 120n10
Kleist, Reinhard. See *Olympic Dream, An*
Koch, Christina, 188, 190
Køhlert, Frederik Byrn, 174
Kony, Joseph. See *War Brothers, The Graphic Novel*
Kurdi, Alan, 61
Kyle, Richard, 3n3

LaBoucane-Benson, Patti, 90, 91 fig. 3.1, 92
Lafrance, Daniel. See *War Brothers, The Graphic Novel*
*Laura Dean Keeps Breaking Up with Me* (Tamaki), 5, 128, 143–47, 146 fig. 4.2
Le, Nam. See "Boat, The" (Le); *Boat, The* (Le)
Leavitt, Sarah, 169–71
Lebanon. See *Baddawi*
Leverett, Stephen, 136–37
LGBTQ+: and accurate reflections, 5; and assimilation, 133; comics overview, 125–28; coming out, 129, 133, 141; and death, 133, 134–35; discussions of, 129n4; as fastest growing category, 125; history of literature, 125–26, 129–35; homosexual visibility, 133; horizontal growing, 135–36; isolation, 133; normalizing, 128–29, 133–34, 148, 150–52; peer groups, 143; queer, as term, 126n2; and read-

ing, 165–66; space and orientation, 137–40, 145, 151–54 (*see also* school; summer camps); and "stable" identity, 127; suppression, 131; and Top Ten Most Challenged Books lists, 126n3. See also *Adrian and the Tree of Secrets*; *As the Crow Flies*; *Avant-Guards, The*; *Check Please!*; *Drama*; gender; *Honor Girl*; *Laura Dean Keeps Breaking Up with Me*; *Lumberjanes*; *Tough Love*; transgender

*Li Minoush* (Murray), 95

libraries, 14–15, 50, 126, 129n4, 130

*Life of Helen Betty Osborne, The* (Robertson), 88, 101, 105

*Lighter Than My Shadow* (Green), 169, 173, 202, 204, 206

literacy, 8, 13–14, 16–17, 64, 97, 99, 119, 170, 214

literary criticism, 20–21

*Little Duck, The* (Cuthand and Longman), 95

Liu, Marjorie. See *Monstress*

lockdowns, 209–11, 215

Logan, Sharon, 214

Lord's Resistance Army (LRA). See *War Brothers, The Graphic Novel*

*Lost Girls* (Moore and Gebbie), 131

*Lost Innocence* (Mitchell), 94, 99

*Louis Riel* (Brown), 90n5

*Lumberjanes* (Stevenson, Ellis, Watters, and Allen), 128, 155, 158, 163–66

*Making It Right* (Mitchell and Dickson-Gilmore), 121

Malkki, Liisa, 72–73

Mallan, Kerry, 165–66

manga, 2–3

*Manitou Raven*, 87

*Marbles* (Forney), 173, 195–96, 202

Marchetto, Marisa, 171

margins, 32, 44–45, 120, 127

Maroh, Jul, 24, 135

Marshall, Elizabeth, 7, 130, 190

Martins, Catarina, 37

Martyn, Nikki, 216

Marvel Comics, 87n3, 125–26, 216, 220

masculinity, 150–53, 158, 163, 164, 165

Mason, Derritt, 156–57

McCloud, Scott, 5, 30, 168, 172, 208, 213, 216

McKay, Sharon E. See *War Brothers, The Graphic Novel*

medical experiences. See health/health care

medical imaging, 188–89

Mellings, Kelly, 90, 91 fig. 3.1

mental health, 119, 139n8, 177–80, 179 fig. 5.1, 195–202, 210

Métis people, 88, 90n5, 95, 96, 100, 109, 118

Mickwitz, Nina, 34, 61

migrant, as term, 61

migrant literature, 34, 56–72, 214. See also *Arrival, The*; *Azzi in Between*; *Baddawi*; "Boat, The" (Huynh); "Boat, The" (Le); *Boat, The* (Le); displacement; *Olympic Dream, An*; *They Called Us Enemy*; *Zenobia*

migrants and COVID, 210, 214

Migrants as Messengers (MaM), 214

*Mirror Mind* (Woolcott), 173, 180–82

Mitchell, Brandon, 99, 121

Mitchell, David, 192, 193

"Mohican Syndrome," 86

*Monstress* (Liu and Takeda), 168–69

Moore, Alan, 131

moral panic, 16, 17, 126n3

morality, 16, 17, 37, 131. See also sexuality

*My Body in Pieces* (Hébert), 170, 204–5

Nahuelpan, Amancay, 120

Nalty, Rebecca. See *Avant-Guards, The*

*Narrative Prosthesis* (Mitchell and Snyder), 192

National Centre for Truth and Reconciliation, 108n9

Nel, Philip, 57

Nelvana Limited of Toronto, 85n1

Nelvana of the Northern Lights, 85–86, 87n3

Nichols, L., 136

Nikolajeva, Maria, 13

*No Straight Lines* (Hall), 125, 126

Nodelman, Perry, 13

nonbinary, 153, 164
nongovernmental organizations (NGOs), 29, 219–20
normal, as concept, 79, 135, 148, 150, 168, 176, 182, 183, 185–86, 192, 193, 204–5
normalization, 128–29, 133–34, 147–48, 150–52, 173, 176, 181
Northstar, 125
nostalgia, 17, 133, 140, 145, 151, 192, 193
"Notes on Camp" (Sontag), 155, 159

*Oaky and the Virus* (Williams), 218
Obama Administration, 137n6
OCD (obsessive-compulsive disorder), 195–99, 203
*Olympic Dream, An* (Kleist), 59–61, 60 fig. 2.1
Omar, Samia Yusuf, 59–61, 60 fig. 2.1
orientation, 23–24, 125, 128, 129n4, 136–40, 145, 147–48, 151, 158, 166, 171, 210. *See also* school
original English language (OEL), 2
*Our Cancer Year* (Pekar, Brabner, and Stack), 169
*Outside Circle, The* (LaBoucane-Benson), 90, 91 fig. 3.1, 92

pain, 8, 43, 69, 104, 111, 155, 169, 174–76, 178, 194, 216
*Palestine* (Sacco), 74
Palestinians, 74, 76, 77–78, 80. *See also* Baddawi
pandemics. *See* coronavirus
Parental Rights in Education, 129n4
parody, 156, 165
paternalism, 9, 35n3, 100, 107
*Path of the Warrior* (Van Camp), 120n10
pathographies. *See* graphic pathographies
Patriot Front, 129n4
"PAW Patrol to the Coronavirus Rescue" (Stossel), 214–16
*Pedro & Me* (Winick), 134
Pekar, Harvey, 169
Pemmican Publications, 95
people smugglers, 58, 63. *See also* human traffickers

*Persepolis* (Satrapi), 7, 11, 28n2, 29, 31
perspectives: of adults, 7; of health-care practitioners, 170, 198, 214; of marginalized peoples, 21, 32–35, 68, 77, 109, 170–71, 174, 180, 194, 212; of settler culture, 89; of young people, 7, 9n4, 22, 38, 46, 53, 56–57, 61, 63, 67, 72, 76, 101, 172, 175, 200, 213, 216–17
*Peter and Wendy* (Barrie), 132–33, 191
Pham, LeUyen, 217–18
Phonic Ears, 186–87
*Picturing Childhood* (Heimermann and Tullis), 21, 27
*Placeless People* (Stonebridge), 61
poverty, 29, 37–39, 56, 72, 100, 106, 121, 210, 219
Powell, Nate. *See Swallow Me Whole*
power: of comics to persuade, 3–6, 13, 21, 23, 25, 33, 35, 39, 88–90, 92–94, 100, 114, 118–21, 124, 177, 180, 197, 214; exploitation of, 31, 34, 73, 76, 96, 129–31, 174, 195; relations, 11, 22, 31, 80–81, 137, 139, 147, 163, 166, 169, 187–88, 210
powerlessness, 63, 75, 79, 81, 84, 192, 200, 215
prejudice, 7, 141, 143, 148, 181, 187, 192
preserving languages, 95, 106
*Princess in Black and the Case of the Coronavirus, The* (Hale and Pham), 217–18
*Priya's Mask* (Devineni), 219–20
*Prom, The* (film and theatre), 141n9
proms, 141, 146–47, 150
protectionism, 18, 189–90, 191
Proud Boys, 129n4
public restrooms, 137–38
publishers, 1–2, 4, 8, 11, 14, 16, 35
Pugh, Tison, 132–33

queer, as term, 125, 126n2
*Queer Child, The* (Stockton), 135–36
queer comics. *See* LGBTQ+
*Queer Phenomenology* (Ahmed), 128, 138

race, 6, 21, 23–24, 57, 62, 62n2, 74, 133, 135, 137, 139, 151, 194

racism, 62n2, 64, 80, 83, 94, 106n8, 107–9, 118–19, 210
rape, 36, 42, 50, 53, 130, 161, 218
reading, 4, 14, 93–94, 132, 136, 165–66, 173–74
reconciliation, 96, 106–7, 117–18. See also Acknowledging; Indigenous Peoples: and Restoring; Relating; Truth Telling
*Red: A Haida Manga* (Yahgulanaas), 89–90
reframing history, 96–105
refugees, 8, 12, 22, 28, 34, 55, 56–83, 140, 158, 210. See also *Azzi in Between*; *Baddawi*; "Boat, The" (Huynh); "Boat, The" (Le); *Boat, The* (Le); migrant literature; *Olympic Dream, An*; *They Called Us Enemy*; *Zenobia*
Relating, 119–24
relocations, 105–7
reserves, 106, 119, 121–22
residential schools, 23, 81, 90, 100, 105–9, 114, 127, 140
resilience, 19, 57, 60, 62, 71, 72, 76–78, 78 fig. 2.4, 81
Riel, Louis, 90n5
Rifkind, Candida, 28–29, 56–57, 87–88, 104
Right of Return (UN Resolution 194), 77
Robertson, David Alexander, 88–89, 92, 96–105, 110–18. See also *Ballad of Nancy April, The*; *7 Generations*; *Sugar Falls*; *Will I See?*
Roosevelt, Franklin Delano, 81
Roosevelt, Theodore, 164
Royal Commission on Aboriginal Peoples (RCAP), 105–6
Royal Hibernium Military School, 36n4
Royal Military Asylum, 36n4
Rwanda. See *Deogratias, A Tale of Rwanda*

Sacco, Joe, 74
Saguisag, Lara, 13, 21
*Sailor Moon*, 2
Sanderson, Steven Keewatin, 120–23
Satrapi, Marjane, 7, 28
Sattouf, Riad, 31–32
schizophrenia, 197–201
school: and book bans, 24, 126; and COVID, 139n8, 210–12, 219; and education, 96, 105–9, 117, 136, 181, 186, 198; as location, 14, 24, 36, 39, 46, 59, 78, 80, 81, 99, 114, 128, 139–51, 142 fig. 4.1, 155, 157, 178, 186, 198; school-age readers, 14, 39, 41–43, 81, 183. See also Indian Residential School
scouting, 163–64
Sedgwick, Eve Kosofsky, 126n2
*Seduction of the Innocent* (Wertham), 16–17
Senate Subcommittee to Investigate Juvenile Delinquency, 16, 130
Sendak, Maurice, 17–18, 19–20 figs. 0.1–0.2, 26
*7 Generations* (Robertson), 89, 110, 112–13 figs. 3.4–3.5, 114, 115–16 figs. 3.6–3.7, 116–18
*7 Miles a Second* (Wojnarowicz), 169
sexuality, 6, 23–24, 125–27, 129, 130–38, 140–41, 152, 154, 156, 158, 161, 163, 194. See also LGBTQ+
sexualization, 85, 86
shame, 44, 49, 74, 101, 131, 133, 180–81, 195, 200, 205
Sharpe, Christina, 57, 62n2
Shuster, Joe, 87n3
Sinclair, Murray, 105n7, 110
*Sisters* (Telgemeier), 177
"sixties scoop," 90, 91 fig. 3.1
*Skim* (Tamaki), 5, 126n3, 143–44
slavery, 58, 62n2, 81n3
Small, David, 5, 180, 188–90, 192, 202–3
*Smile* (Telgemeier), 169, 172, 175–77, 180, 182–83
Smith, Matt. See "Boat, The" (Huynh)
Smith, Sidonie, 8–10
Snowguard, 87n3
Sontag, Susan, 57, 155, 159, 174
sovereignty, 52, 61, 72, 84, 92, 124
spatial orientation, 128, 136–40, 151–53. See also school
Spiegelman, Art, 3n3, 17–18, 19–20 figs. 0.1–0.2
*Spiral Cage, The* (Davison), 169
sports, 139, 147, 151–53, 155
Squier, Susan, 170, 172, 180, 194
Stalin, Joseph, 67
Stassen, Jean-Philippe. See *Deogratias, A Tale of Rwanda*

*Stay Safe Stay Strong* (Ek Tara), 219
stereotypes, 9, 86, 93, 135, 148, 149 fig. 4.3, 150, 158, 163, 182–83
Stevenson, ND. See *Lumberjanes*
*Stitches* (Small), 5, 24, 173, 175, 188–90, 192, 202–4
Stockton, Kathryn Bond, 135–36
Stonebridge, Lyndsey, 56, 61, 72, 74–75, 77
storytelling, 3n3, 27–28, 57, 88–89, 92–94, 99, 111, 114, 118–20, 217
Stossel, Sage, 214–16
*Sugar Falls* (Robertson), 94, 95, 97, 105
suicide, 16, 100, 106, 110, 111, 114, 117, 120, 127, 134, 141–42, 196
suicide attacks, 32
summer camps, 12, 128, 138–40, 155–66, 160 fig. 4.5
superheroes, 85–86, 87n3, 125–26, 192, 215–16, 218
*Swallow Me Whole* (Powell), 173, 197–202, 199 fig. 5.4, 201 fig. 5.5
Syria, 31–32, 56–58, 61–62, 74. See also *Zenobia*

Takei, George, 75, 80–81, 82 fig. 2.6, 83–84
*Taking Turns* (Czerwiec), 172
*Tales from Big Spirit* (Robertson), 97–99
Tamaki, Jillian. See *Skim*
Tamaki, Mariko, 126n3. See also *Laura Dean Keeps Breaking Up with Me*; *Skim*
Tan, Shaun, 58, 63–64, 65, 84
*Tangles* (Leavitt), 170–71
Tarbox, Gwen Athene, 2, 14–15, 21, 177
Telgemeier, Raina, 15, 24, 130, 147–51, 169, 172, 173, 175–80. See also *Drama*; *Guts*; *Smile*
*They Called Us Enemy* (Takei), 58, 75, 80–81, 82 fig. 2.6, 83–84
Theytus Press, 95
*This One Summer* (Tamaki), 126n3
Thrash, Maggie, 158–61, 160 fig. 4.5. See also *Honor Girl*
Tokyopop, 2
*Tomboy* (Prince), 136
TOON Books, 4, 15
Top Ten Most Challenged Books lists, 126n3

Touchstones of Hope, 89. See also Acknowledging; Indigenous Peoples: and Restoring; Relating; Truth Telling
*Tough Love* (Denson), 128, 140–41
*Toxic Childhood* (Palmer), 11–12
transgender, 5, 125, 126, 129n4, 137n6, 137–38, 156, 162, 164–65
*Transposes* (Edwards), 5
trauma: autobiographies as mediators of, 28; and children's literature, 33–34; and family, 49; and fantasy, 142; and healing (*see* healing); intergenerational, 116 fig. 3.7, 116–17 (*see also* Indian Residential School); in migrant literature, 57; PTSD, 38, 49; transforming, 109–10; through understatement, 42; visibility of, 31
Trites, Roberta Seelinger, 129, 131, 134, 153
*Triumph-Adventure Comics* #1, 85
trope, 9–11, 35n3, 57, 134, 173, 175, 188, 192–94
Trudeau, Justin, 87n3, 108
Trudeau, Pierre Elliott, 87n3, 106n8
Trump, Donald, 61, 80, 84, 137n6
Truth and Reconciliation Commission, 100, 108–9, 124
Truth Telling, 89, 93–94, 108, 124
Tullis, Brittany, 21, 27, 219
Tutsis. See *Deogratias, A Tale of Rwanda*
*Tyranny* (Fairfield), 206–7, 207 fig. 5.6

Uganda. See *War Brothers, The Graphic Novel*
Ukazu, Ngozi. See *Check Please!*
UN Convention on the Rights of Persons with Disabilities, 186
UN Optional Protocol on the Involvement of Children in Armed Conflict, 36n4
*Uncanny X-Men*, 87n3
*Understanding Comics* (McCloud), 5, 30, 168, 208
United Nations Children's Fund (UNICEF), 8
United Nations Convention on the Rights of the Child (UNCRC), 6, 31, 35n3, 36n4, 124, 191

United Nations Declaration on the Rights of Indigenous Peoples, 124
United Nations High Commissioner for Refugees (UNHCR), 8–9, 73–74
United Nations Refugee and Works Agency, 78
Universal Declaration of Human Rights, 74
Urban Outfitters, 86n2
Usdin, Carly. See *Avant-Guards, The*

vaccines, 209, 211–12, 220
Valero-O'Connell, Rosemary, 143, 146 fig. 4.2. See also *Laura Dean Keeps Breaking Up with Me*
Van Camp, Richard, 96, 120n10
Vermette, Katherena, 90n5
victimhood, 9n4, 11, 32, 35n3, 38, 43–44, 47, 54–55, 57, 71, 88, 100, 182–83
victim-perpetrators, 37–38, 42–43, 49. See also *Deogratias, A Tale of Rwanda*
Victoria's Secret, 86n2
visibility, 13, 31, 33–34, 57, 85, 127, 133, 137, 144, 175, 188–89, 194
*The Vitals* (Allegheny Health Network/Marvel), 216
VIZ Media, 2
Vizenor, Gerald, 93
Vowel, Chelsea, 85, 105–7, 109–10, 118

Wall, John, 29, 30, 34–35, 37–38
war, 8, 12, 22, 29, 33–41, 44, 49, 58–61, 67, 73–80, 85–86. See also *Child Soldier*; child soldiers; *Deogratias, A Tale of Rwanda*; displacement; migrant literature; *War Brothers, The Graphic Novel*

*War Brothers, The Graphic Novel* (McKay and Lafrance), 5, 30, 43–47, 46–48 figs. 1.3–1.5, 49, 54–55
Warley, Linda, 87–88
Watters, Shannon. See *Lumberjanes*
*We Are Resilient* (Marvel), 220
Wertham, Fredric, 16–17
White Paper 1969, 106n8
Whitlock, Gillian, 27–28, 57–58
*Will I See?* (Robertson), 92–93, 101–5
witnesses, 7, 8, 9, 33, 76
Wochowski, Lana, 125, 126, 128
Wojnarowicz, David, 169
Wolf, Doris, 92–93, 100–101, 106, 117, 119, 120, 123
Woodhouse, Barbara Bennett, 10, 30–31
Woolcott, Tory. See *Mirror Mind*
wordarrows, 93
wordlessness. See *Arrival, The*
World Health Organization (WHO), 8, 209
World War II, 73, 74, 80, 87
wound culture, 57

Yahgulanaas, Michael Nicoll, 89–90
Yang, Gene Luen, 15
Young Adult Library Services Association (YALSA), 15, 50
Young Adult (YA) literature, 15, 129, 131, 156

Zdarsky, Chip, 87n3
*Zenobia* (Dürr), 5, 22, 31, 57–58, 61–63, 69, 99

# STUDIES IN COMICS AND CARTOONS

Jared Gardner, Charles Hatfield, and Rebecca Wanzo, Series Editors
Lucy Shelton Caswell, Founding Editor Emerita

Books published in Studies in Comics and Cartoons focus exclusively on comics and graphic literature, highlighting their relation to literary studies. The series includes monographs and edited collections that cover the history of comics and cartoons from the editorial cartoon and early sequential comics of the nineteenth century through webcomics of the twenty-first. Studies that focus on international comics are also considered.

*Growing Up Graphic: The Comics of Children in Crisis*
ALISON HALSALL

*Muslim Comics and Warscape Witnessing*
ESRA MIRZE SANTESSO

*Beyond the Icon: Asian American Graphic Narratives*
EDITED BY ELEANOR TY

*Comics and Nation: Power, Pop Culture, and Political Transformation in Poland*
EWA STAŃCZYK

*How Comics Travel: Publication, Translation, Radical Literacies*
KATHERINE KELP-STEBBINS

*Resurrection: Comics in Post-Soviet Russia*
JOSÉ ALANIZ

*Authorizing Superhero Comics: On the Evolution of a Popular Serial Genre*
DANIEL STEIN

*Typical Girls: The Rhetoric of Womanhood in Comic Strips*
SUSAN E. KIRTLEY

*Comics and the Body: Drawing, Reading, and Vulnerability*
ESZTER SZÉP

*Producing Mass Entertainment: The Serial Life of the Yellow Kid*
CHRISTINA MEYER

*The Goat-Getters: Jack Johnson, the Fight of the Century, and How a Bunch of Raucous Cartoonists Reinvented Comics*
EDDIE CAMPBELL

*Between Pen and Pixel: Comics, Materiality, and the Book of the Future*
AARON KASHTAN

*Ethics in the Gutter: Empathy and Historical Fiction in Comics*
KATE POLAK

*Drawing the Line: Comics Studies and INKS, 1994–1997*
EDITED BY LUCY SHELTON CASWELL AND JARED GARDNER

*The Humours of Parliament: Harry Furniss's View of Late-Victorian Political Culture*
    EDITED AND WITH AN INTRODUCTION BY GARETH CORDERY AND JOSEPH S. MEISEL

*Redrawing French Empire in Comics*
    MARK MCKINNEY

www.ingramcontent.com/pod-product-compliance
Lightning Source LLC
Chambersburg PA
CBHW020122240426
43673CB00038B/565